WITHDRAWN

MAKING SPACE FOR THEATRE

D1434811

THE LEARNING CENTRE
HAMMERSMITH AND WEST
LONDON COLLEGE
GLIDDON ROAD
LONDON W14 9BL

HAMMERSMITH WEST LONDON COLLEGE

344856

The publishers acknowledge
the generous sponsorship of
The Building Centre Trust

and the encouragement and support of
The British Council

MAKING SPACE FOR THEATRE

British Architecture and Theatre since 1958

Edited by

Ronnie Mulryne and Margaret Shewring

Consultant Editors

Iain Mackintosh
Michael Reardon

MULRYNE AND SHEWRING LTD
Stratford-upon-Avon

First Published 1995
Mulryne and Shewring Ltd.
30 Avenue Road
Stratford-upon-Avon
Warwickshire CV37 6UN

© Mulryne and Shewring 1995

No part of this publication may be reproduced, stored in a retrieval system, or transmitted in any form or by any means, electronic, mechanical, photocopying, recording or otherwise, without the prior permission of the publisher and copyright owner.

The rights of the authors to be identified as authors of their work has been asserted generally in accordance with the Copyright, Designs and Patents Act 1988.

ISBN 1 900065 00 2

Produced, Designed and Typesetting
A.H. Jolly (Editorial) Ltd.
Yelvertoft Manor
Northamptonshire NN6 7LF

Printed in Belgium by
Snoeck - Ducaju & Zoon, Ghent

Cover Photographs: Edinburgh Festival Theatre
Front: Paul Bock
Back: Alan McCrone

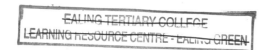

EALING TERTIARY COLLEGE
LEARNING RESOURCE CENTRE - EALING GREEN

EG02468
HAMMERSMITH AND WEST
LONDON COLLEGE
LEARNING CENTRE

1 5 MAY 2006
344856

792.0942 MUL
Media & Performing Arts

CONTENTS

Above: The Mermaid Theatre, Puddledock, London. 1970.
(see also p. 180)
(*Photo courtesy of Strand Lighting Archive*)

Left: The Theatre Royal, Haymarket, London. 1994.
(*Photo: Ian Grundy*)

SPACE IN THE THEATRE
Sir John Gielgud

Space concerns everyone connected with the theatre, from the architects who first design the building to the actors who play in it and the stage designers and directors who labour in it. Also (even if they are quite unaware of it) the audience who, we hope, will fill it.

It has always surprised me that today's audiences have so quickly become reconciled to the astonishing innovations established during the seventy odd years that I have worked in the theatre. At the turn of the century, the designs of Gordon Craig and Adolph Appia strove to banish painted scenery, footlights and overhead borders, and to raise or widen the height and depth of the proscenium arch. Their scenes were to be lit from above or from the front of the house, and relied for their effect on lofty screens, steps and deep engulfing shadows. Although they were to prove an immense influence in years to come, it was to be many years before the work of these men began to appeal to the general public, or to persuade contemporary managers to employ them. Granville-Barker's Shakespearean productions (1912–14) were to arouse great enthusiasm from the cognoscenti, but were generally considered elitist and controversial. Barker presented almost full texts, built apron stages, simplified settings, reduced intervals and insisted on swiftness of speech, but his methods were stubbornly resisted by the Old Guard, loyal disciples of Irving and Tree, who defended their fading splendours to the last gasp.

Barker was something of a genius. Brilliantly talented and progressive, whether as actor, playwright or director, he formed admirable ensemble casts, advocated the National Theatre, and was undoubtedly destined to dominate the British stage but for the disastrous intervention of the 1914 war, when, divorced from his actress first wife, Lillah McCarthy, he broke away from Bernard Shaw, his great men-

Sir John Gielgud, Actor. Born 1904. 1995 still alive and working

tor, and retired altogether from the theatre, a disillusioned guru, never to fulfil his magnificent promise and achievements, but spent the rest of his life with translations and his superb prefaces to Shakespeare.

In 1919, Nigel Playfair, one of Barker's most enthusiastic pupils (who incidentally gave me my first professional engagement as an actor) set up his address at an unfashionable old theatre, the Lyric Hammersmith. Here, with the financial help of Arnold Bennett, and the decorative brilliance of Claud Lovet Fraser, he launched a successful series of productions, including a delightful *As You Like It,* followed by a simple but highly original revival of *The Beggars' Opera,* which soon became an enormous success. About the same time, Basil Dean arrived in

London from Liverpool, and, with a rich business partner, Alec Rea, and a talented designer, George Harris, became an important impressario, staging strong domestic dramas as well as light comedies, ranging from Flecker and Galsworthy to Noel Coward and Frederick Lonsdale, gathering strong casts of players and introducing cycloramas and Schwabe new lighting inventions from Germany.

The next powerful influence was to come from Tyrone Guthrie, a friend and contemporary of mine, whose mercurial energy and Irish quicksilver enthusiasm brought him speedy triumphs. But he soon became impatient of the confining limits of the London West End, and after making his mark both at Stratford and the Old Vic, he directed a famous revival of *The Three Estates* at the Edinburgh Festival (in the Assembly Hall), and then moved to Canada, where he inaugurated a hugely successful Shakespearean Festival at Stratford, Ontario, in a tent theatre which he had designed with the help of his partner Tanya Moiseiwitsch, soon to be enlarged into a fine theatre, and another a few years later, in Minneapolis.

I have only once played on an open stage in England, in a rather indifferent production of *Caesar and Cleopatra* (1971) at Chichester, when I found the width of the auditorium and the closeness of the audience distracting and unhelpful, though I also remember playing Hamlet once in a semi-circular Senate House in Madras in 1945, and finding I could use the audience to great advantage, particularly in delivering the soliloquies more intimately than in a proscenium theatre. I was much impressed by a pre-London performance of Ronald Harwood's play *The Dresser* which I saw at the Royal Exchange Theatre in Manchester, an auditorium with an unorthodox stage-audience relationship. But in an extremely well-acted production of *The Duchess of Malfi* at the

Roundhouse in London I found it impossible to follow the complicated dialogue (though I knew the play extremely well) because the actors had to turn continually in order to present their faces to one another and to the spectators, and the groupings, though ingeniously contrived, seemed to destroy the progressions of the dialogue, and make a restless havoc of the text.

During the middle years of my stage career, there was a great variety of experimental staging, but the directors, both at Stratford and the Old Vic, appeared to demand a fairly strong leaning towards backgrounds of decorative splendour, though the influence of Michel St. Denis and Joan Littlewood seemed to create a challenge to this with more basically simple settings. Anthony Quayle and I, as well as George Devine, failed with an abstract decor and costumes for *King Lear* in 1955, by the Japanese designer Isamu Noguchi, yet Peter Brook declared that this production was an inspiration for his own fine revival of the same play many years later. Designers like Motley, Sophie Fedorovitch, Jocelyn Herbert and John Bury were gradually working towards simplified creations which were to become the typically selective brilliance of Devine's kitchen sink productions at the Royal Court, while John Bury, working at Stratford East, used real materials – railings, pavements, bricks and mortar – and created finally, at Stratford-on-Avon, the splendid metal gates and shutter screens which so grandly featured in *The Wars of the Roses*.

Of course, the arrival of the cinema, and then of television, provided all kinds of fresh problems for actors and directors in the theatre. The long shot, medium shot and close-up were soon to be eagerly accepted by audiences, and these inventions were to change the whole space of the actor's field. He quickly realised that he could easily be magnified, followed, and if necessary, dwarfed by the varying distance of the camera. His voice could be strengthened, his whispers could become audible, his declamatory powers subdued, his facial expression intimately exposed.

The old actors had demanded the best position for themselves in every scene, and woe betide their supporting players who trespassed by getting too close to them. They also expected to be lit to the best advantage. Irving, though he loved dark scenes and mysterious backgrounds, still insisted on a special beam which followed him throughout his performances of Mathias and Mephistopheles. Even in the 1930s, the lights were slowly and subtly raised as Marie Tempest made her first entrance in *Dear Octopus*. Now, with the advent of film and television, these special arrangements could no longer apply, and of course in the cinema, directors and cameramen controlled completely, without the actors knowing what they were doing.

In rehearsal, actors are rightly concerned with the space between them in playing their scenes. I well remember arguing fiercely with Peter Brook, when I entered as Leontes to accuse Hermione, in *The Winter's Tale*. Brook placed me on a balcony, while the Queen and her attendants stood below on the main stage. I felt strongly that I should be on the same floor level as the others, but finally played the scene as Brook desired, though I never felt very happy with the arrangement. Very possibly from the audience's point of view Brook's insistence worked more effectively, and I am an obedient pupil and have always trusted him implicitly.

Obviously, it is difficult to judge how readily a modern audience resents or applauds the dominance of the director during the last fifty years. I am old-fashioned enough to resent the tampering with the great classical plays by putting them into modern dress and filling the stage with contemporary reminders of their basic topicality. Many of these experiments have of course succeeded splendidly, but too often the craving for novelty has led to perversity and confusion.

How firmly must the playwrights and players insist on explicit stage directions being carried out? Presumably the genius of Eleonora Duse must have enabled her to adapt her personal acting style to the abstract setting which Craig devised for her in *Rosmersholm*. But would it have pleased Ibsen himself? Would Shakespeare have recognised his *A Midsummer Night's Dream* in Peter Brook's brilliantly original invention? And would Priestley have applauded his reconstructed *The Inspector Calls* or Tchekhov have approved of picture frame settings for *The Seagull* and the transfer of *Uncle Vanya* into Wales? Why choose the Edwardian Era, when Jews in England were the favourites of the Court, as a background setting for *The Merchant of Venice* as Jonathan Miller conceived it? Yet the actors seem to adapt themselves fairly meekly to these experiments and the audiences accept them greedily, while the critics seem often to fail even to notice them at all. Perhaps they are grateful for an excuse to review classical revivals which they have had to watch too often over many years.

Both in London and New York, the old horseshoe theatres remain the best home for light comedy and domestic drama, and the actors respond immediately to the pleasure of appearing in them, though few audiences perhaps appreciate the tremendous difference of acting at the Phoenix Theatre, for instance, in the 1933 *Love for Love* before moving to the Haymarket, or at Wyndham's in *No Man's Land* after moving from the Lyttleton. The Mermaid is to my mind the best designed of the theatres built recently, while at the Olivier, though magnificently equipped with miracles of scenic and lighting equipment, the stage is too wide and the auditorium too unwieldy, except for spectacle. Drury Lane, Her Majesty's and the Haymarket have the ideal proportions and acoustics to be the actor's dream, partly because they are built of wood and plaster instead of concrete. I have never much liked the abolishing of the curtain, that magical barrier of mystery which anticipates, as well as hinting at, pleasures to come.

The preponderance of big musicals has led to fantastic and complicated devices to enthral the public. Should the machinery go wrong, complete disaster strikes. Microphones abound. Singers cannot be adequately heard without them, and they sprout everywhere, from concealed stands, scenery, and even the bosoms of the actors. Silence, both at home and in the theatre is at a discount nowadays. Perhaps breathing space is what we really need in the theatre as well as in our private lives.

PREFACE AND ACKNOWLEDGMENTS

Making Space for Theatre was conceived as a book and catalogue to complement the British Council exhibition of the same name launched at the Royal National Theatre in London at the beginning of June, 1995, and subsequently seen at the Quadriennale in Prague, before touring in two versions to all five continents. The exhibition, proposed originally to the Drama and Dance Advisory Committee of the Council, was devised, researched and edited by Iain Mackintosh of Theatre Projects Consultants, from whose energy, imagination and knowledge we have benefited at every stage of the enjoyable if arduous process of bringing together and editing this book.

Making Space for Theatre concerns itself with British theatre building of the last forty years. The thirty buildings featured in the exhibition were selected from the many new theatres of the period by a distinguished panel of theatre architects and experts under Professor Derek Sugden of Arup Associates, who has also with some other panel members contributed to this book. A decision was taken to add theatres built abroad with a considerable input from British architects, and these too were selected by the same panel.

The book falls into two related parts. The second of these catalogues and further illustrates the exhibition, giving architectural details of the theatres, supplying plans and providing photographs and drawings. It also includes a statement of intent and a users' verdict for each theatre. The first part draws its boundaries more widely than the exhibition was able to do, by including some additional theatres and found spaces, as well as taking in a wider historical range. In doing so, it offers a series of discussions of theatre space by those concerned with the practical matters of theatre construction, and by those users of theatre buildings, actors, directors, writers, designers and audiences, for whom the decisions of architects and their clients have practical and aesthetic consequences.

In editing the book, we have incurred a great many debts to individuals and companies. It has been a privilege to work with Professor Sugden and his panel, and with John Tod, Director of the Arts Division of the British Council, with Tim Butchard and Simon Gammell of the Drama and Dance Department, and especially with David Elliot and Marsha Lebon of the Exhibitions Department, whose patience, imagination and flair have made the sometimes difficult liaison between book and exhibition far more practical and enjoyable than it might have been. We have also greatly enjoyed and profited from working with Clive Barda, the specialist photographer for the exhibition.

A great many photographers, libraries and architectural practices have been generous in allowing us to call on their expertise and their possessions. We should mention in particular Ian Grundy of Interludes in Scarborough, Richard Kalina of Richard Kalina Photography, Martin Charles of Martin Charles Photography, Bob Wain of the Birmingham Repertory Theatre, Andy Collier of Strand Lighting, Marian Pringle and her staff at the Shakespeare Centre, Stratford-on-Avon, Patrick Spottiswood of the International Shakespeare Globe Centre, Gary Young and Philip Dennis of Terry Farrell and Company, Brenda Frost of Nottingham Playhouse, and Jennie Gardner of the Citizens Theatre, Glasgow. We were very warmly received and assisted by David Cheshire of the Theatres Trust, and by its director, John Earl. Ken Woodward took an immediate interest in our project and forwarded it with helpful suggestions. Sheila Devo of Triumph Productions was very supportive in making important contacts for us. Numerous other people have been immensely patient with our requests, and active in meeting them, including Steven Wood and Sarah Burn of the Royal National Theatre, Derek Nicholls of the Grand Opera House, Belfast, Paul Iles of the Edinburgh Festival Theatre, Wiff Maton of the Birmingham Repertory Theatre, Jodi Myers of the Arts Centre, University of Warwick and John Blackmore of the Leicester Haymarket.

Many of our contributors have given most generously of their time and knowledge, to the extent that they have become as much initiators as contributors. The generosity of the theatre profession as a whole has been demonstrated to us once again in our work on this project. Fittingly, this generosity has been shown most handsomely of all by the profession's most eminent living member, Sir John Gielgud, who at the age of ninety four wrote our Prologue, and revised it, not only uncomplainingly but promptly and with great good humour. The biography prefixed to his contribution is at his own request.

We gratefully acknowledge generous support from the Building Centre Trust towards the production costs of this book.

We owe special thanks to our Consultant Editor, Michael Reardon, for the unfailing courtesy and immense knowledge he has brought to advising us on the architectural aspects of the book, and for enlarging our appreciation of theatre space generally. We thank Eithne and John for understanding and forbearance while the book made heavy demands on our time and energy.

Our greatest debt is again, as in our previous book, to Alec Jolly of A.H. Jolly (Editorial) and Judith Boden-Cummins of Snoeck-Ducaju, Belgium, for being involved so very fully in this project. They have been a constant source of imagination and ideas, as well as being active beyond the call of duty in attending meetings, giving advice and hospitality, and indeed playing an equal part with ours in bringing this book to completion.

Ronnie Mulryne
Margaret Shewring

Above: Interior of the Shakespeare Memorial Theatre, 1879. Engraving of auditorium and stage for opening production, *Much Ado About Nothing.* (*Photo: Shakespeare Centre Library*)

Left: Interior of the Shakespeare Memorial Theatre, by Dodgshun and Unsworth, 1878, *c. 1920.* (*Photo: Shakespeare Centre Library*)

INTRODUCTION

Ronnie Mulryne and Margaret Shewring

Ronnie Mulryne is Professor of English (since 1977) and Director of the Centre for the Study of the Renaissance at the University of Warwick, where he was for five years Pro-Vice-Chancellor. He was previously (1962–77) lecturer and then Reader in English Literature at the University of Edinburgh, and before that (1960–62) Fellow of the Shakespeare Institute of the University of Birmingham. He has been Chairman of the Drama and Theatre Board of the Council for National Academic Awards, Chairman of the Drama Projects Committee of the Arts Council of Great Britain, and is now Chairman of the Drama and Dance Advisory Committee of the British Council. He is a member of the Board of Directors of the Birmingham Repertory Theatre. His publications are on Shakespeare, Elizabethan and Jacobean Drama, and theatre generally.
(*Photo: Michael Gould, University of Warwick*)

It may be too much to claim that over the last forty years a revolution has taken place in our understanding of theatre design and theatre space. Revolutions are, or give the appearance of being, sudden and destructive. They often end up reconfirming the social and political circumstances out of which they arose. The change we are now experiencing in thinking about theatre building is one which, it could be argued, has been centuries in preparation. It is also one which, to take a less ambitious view, has been quite consciously germinating at least over the period since the late Michael Elliott wrote and broadcast the eloquent article *On Not Building for Posterity* which we include in this book. Elliott felt that in 1973 the time had come to take stock of the kinds of theatres we devise for our plays and players. Beginning with a disillusioned sense of the monumentality of the National Theatre and the recently completed civic theatres, he asked questions which his own company at Manchester were already asking as they planned their new playhouse. They are questions we have continued to ask and answer in varying ways ever since, not least through the work of the National, the civic theatres and the Royal Shakespeare Company. Indeed the questions Elliott formulated had been implicitly put ever since the first post-war civic theatre, the Belgrade in Coventry, opened for business in 1958 (p. 118). Perhaps from our current perspective we may think that Elliott's outlook in 1973 was excessively influenced – how could it be otherwise? – by the small-scale experimental companies of the sixties and early seventies. Yet his pivotal essay raises in acute form matters of debate that continue to exercise all of us, and which form the implicit or explicit agenda of contributors to this book. What kinds of theatre space best provide for the realisation of the classical and contemporary writing that forms the pro-gramming of our theatres? What kinds of space complement the social and cultural preoccupations and practices of our society? How do we plan and build theatres that are not only enlivening spaces to work and be entertained in, but also help to provide the experience distinctive to theatre and distinct from film and television? How, practically, do we ensure that audiences hear and see? What are the special needs of dance and music theatre? The forty years of British theatre building which the present book surveys and celebrates have been years, if not of revolution, then certainly of earnest questioning, and at least some answers.

If a theme emerges from these pages it is that of theatre and community. It would be absurd to argue that as a result of these forty years of building and experiment we are returning to a Greek sense of the place of theatre in the community. Manifestly, too much has changed, socially, politically and in our culture at large, for such a regression to make any sense, practically or aesthetically. The allusion to Greek amphitheatres in the design of important theatre buildings in recent decades, even when masquerading under the banner of technology (better acoustics and sightlines), can be read as a wish-fulfilling return to the community-based values for which the Greek theatres are said to stand. (No one, it must be remarked, has had much to say about the position of slaves in Greek society.) The amphitheatre houses, it has turned out, pose considerable problems for theatre professionals, and not only in those very areas of hearing and seeing where their virtues have been most eloquently proclaimed, but also in the representation they offer of a *false* community, or perhaps one should say of a community rarely experienced in performance. The fragmentation of our values, as well as the physical conditions of the amphitheatre houses themselves, and the training and skills of our actors in an age of cinema and television, have ensured that only exceptionally have

Margaret Shewring is lecturer in Theatre Studies at the University of Warwick and course director for the Centre for the Study of the Renaissance. She has been secretary of the Standing Committee of University Drama Departments and has held a number of senior university posts, particularly in the area of Graduate Studies. She is a member of the Artistic Sub-Committee of the Board of the Birmingham Repertory Theatre. Her publications include *This Golden Round: The Royal Shakespeare Company at the Swan,* (with Ronnie Mulryne) *Theatre and Government Under the Early Stuarts, English and Italian Renaissance Theatre, Italian Renaissance Festivals and their European Influence* (all edited with Ronnie Mulryne) and papers on Shakespeare, Elizabethan drama and the modern theatre. Her critical edition of *The Great Favourite* attributed to Sir Robert Howard, based on her doctoral thesis appeared in 1988.
(*Photo: Michael Gould, University of Warwick*)

these amphitheatres, outside opera and musical, achieved a sense of common experience and purpose among audiences. The most distinctive *alternative* form, what has become known as the courtyard theatre, so precisely and vividly described by Iain Mackintosh in an important article and book,[1] has had more success in evoking and confirming a sense of audience engagement or 'community', in the Cottesloe, for example, or the Tricycle, or the new Other Place at Stratford, or the theatre called the Courtyard at Leeds. This has been so at least on a sufficient number of occasions to suggest that the form of the courtyard, discussed in this book by Michael Attenborough, Declan Donnellan and Nick Ormerod, Roger Chapman and Jason Barnes, among others, offers a receptive spatial configuration for our social preoccupations and aesthetic needs. Perhaps the courtyard too derives from an allusive throw-back to a partially-understood historic theatre or theatres, the earliest and maybe the essential form of the Elizabethan playhouse, as well as the Spanish *corrales*. At least this throw-back appears to be justified by the experience of current audiences, even if their social composition, their political outlook and their cultural interests differ markedly from their Elizabethan or Spanish forebears (who in these respects differed markedly from each other). The evolution of theatre space in the last forty years might be understood as a negotiation between these two forms, modified and influenced by the experience of small and large experimental spaces, whether architect designed or 'found'. It has therefore moved on from modifications of the proscenium arch, and thinking about the social and aesthetic implications of these modifications, to a more far-reaching redesign of theatre space, in which the proscenium arch barely figures. 'Found' spaces, as Neil Wallace argues, can provide liberties often denied to more thoroughly designed auditoria. If technological advance has played a part in this redesign, it has done so more as agent and icon of wider changes, rather than as their cause. The development of our theatres over the last decades, perhaps inevitably, perhaps by conscious choice, represents large changes in our understanding of our social and cultural moment, and especially in our thinking about community.

The manifest success of the courtyard theatre does not however preclude a social and aesthetic need for other kinds of space. The successive alterations of the Main House at Stratford for the Royal Shakespeare Company, taking the Elizabeth Scott design as an integral stage in the process, offer a vivid illustration of repeated attempts to adjust existing theatre space to the changing needs and wishes of a national and international audience.[2] Even more significant, perhaps, has been the provision by the Company of two alternative spaces within the same small town. (More significant, since it could be argued, though wrongly, that the adaptations to the Main House were motivated solely by commercial considerations). The Other Place and the Swan chart between them, alongside the Main House alterations, an important sector of theatre redesign over the past several decades. David Edgar's theatrical odyssey, vividly described in this book, brings out the liberties and the restrictions offered by the first Other Place, and by the many tiny and terminally informal spaces of which it was the echo, from the Edinburgh Traverse to the Arts Lab. Begotten virtually by chance, and thus fitting the self-consciously anti-institutional aesthetic of its time, the 'old' Other Place has now been rebuilt as a new and fully designed building, and thus incorporated into the institutional and property structures of the Royal Shakespeare Company – while preserving by allusion and practice something of its aesthetic history. It is apt that Edgar's most recent play, *Pentecost*, has found its home in the restructured Other Place.[3] The nineties of the century, characterised by the detachment of post-modernism, seem to be better served by the structural order of the new rather than the informal disorder of the old Other Place. Thus our theatre spaces define us, even as we design them.

The Swan tells a different but complementary story. In no way a pastiche of Elizabethan theatre spaces, it nevertheless reconstructs the stage-audience relationships characteristic of such spaces, with its thrust stage and overhanging audience galleries. The 'pale golden galleried playhouse', with its 'precision, harmony, versatility, joy', in the words of the *Observer*, brings to performance a strong personality, in contrast to the anonymity of such informal spaces as the first Other Place and its clones.[4] Entering the Swan is quite evidently, in visual and symbolic terms, entering a space set aside for performance, and audience sees audience throughout. A conscious awareness of the theatricality of theatrical space is a characteristic the Swan shares with courtyard theatres generally, and one which plainly differentiates the experience it hosts from analogous performances on film and television. Perhaps this patent difference accounts in part for its success, commending its work as it does to the familiar post-modernist liking for aesthetically self-defining experiences.

However this may be, the conjunction in Stratford of the Other Place, the Swan and the Main House offers a spectrum of theatre experience that embraces much of the diversity of current theatre design. Michael Attenborough argues in these pages that the three spaces interact to provide an aesthetic community that goes well beyond pandering to faddish (post-modern?) culture-sampling. The Main House, in its most recent refurbishment harking back yet more visibly to its art deco origins, serves as representative of another trend in current theatre architecture, the restoration of traditional (mainly nineteenth and early twentieth century) buildings, as at the Prince Edward and the Haymarket in London, the Grand Opera House in Belfast, and the Empire (now the Festival) theatre in Edinburgh. Such restoration stems not only from a sense of the heritage value of these buildings, but from the acknowledgement, as Sir John Gielgud and others say in this book, that they represent sympathetic spaces to play in. The horseshoe auditorium, with its side boxes, especially if the overall dimensions of the house are not excessive, has come to be recognised as supportive of a genuinely communal theatre experience. The new Glyndebourne draws some of its acclaimed inspiration from these traditional sources, and Edinburgh may well prove to be wiser than it knew in flagrantly dithering and delaying before accommodating its Festival opera in the splendidly refurbished Empire. Reconstructed theatres by Frank Matcham, and similar theatres throughout the country, could turn out to be the most successful 'new' theatres of the last forty years. The long history of multiple adjustments to the Main House at Stratford indicates that the building is not in its essential structure adapted to today's theatre performance in the way the Matcham buildings are. It does however provide a stage and auditorium on a scale and with associations appropriate to mainline Shakespeare. Michael Attenborough, Richard Eyre and others argue in these pages that much is lost in presenting Shakespeare and the classics in inappropriately restricted spaces. A second theme running through the volume, notably in contributions by Jude Kelly, Ruth Mackenzie, Roger Chapman and Julian Barnes, as well as the two writers just named, asserts the value for performance of situating a play in a theatre space sympathetic to the implications of its script. Stratford provides a choice of spaces that to some extent at least makes this possible.

A more radical 'refurbishment' than that of the horseshoe and similar auditoria is the current project for the rebuilding of the Elizabethan Globe in Southwark. Andrew Gurr sets out in his contribution to this volume some of the thinking behind this enterprise. It may be an indicator of the renewed, if not revolutionary, interest in the design of theatre space, that initial resistance by the theatre profession to the project has more recently developed into support and participation. The originator of the rebuilding, the late Sam Wanamaker, was himself by experience and conviction a man of the theatre, and the architect, Theo Crosby, who also died recently, understood and loved theatre performance. If the myth attaching to the project has evoked a mix of academic self-importance, museum-curator desiccation, and heritage-industry culture, the reality is more accurately represented by Peter Hall's seemingly impossible wish, expressed in the extract from his *Diaries* prefixed to Gurr's contribution, to be able

Above: Interior of the Shakespeare Memorial Theatre, by Elizabeth Scott, 1932.
(*Photo: Shakespeare Centre Library*)

Right: Interior of the Royal Shakespeare Theatre, with auditorium and stage remodelled by John Napier and Chris Dyer for the 'Wooden O' season, 1976. Dressed for the production of *Much Ado About Nothing*, directed by John Barton and designed by John Napier.
(*Photo: Shakespeare Centre Library*)

to see for himself the space for which the Elizabethan playwrights wrote their work, and thus learn 'something about staging Shakespeare' (see p. 34 below). The interaction of theatrical meaning and stage space, so well understood by Peter Hall in 1975, has now become an accepted truism of academic discourse and theatre design, and as such justifies the Globe project as a practical exploration of Shakespeare's work in an appropriate and influential space.

Part of this book concerns itself with the achievement of community within the theatre auditorium, through the performance of theatre scripts in spaces that respond to their needs and potential. Perhaps a

more characteristic nineties concern lies in the community function of theatre understood in a more sociological perspective. Jude Kelly and Ruth Mackenzie both emphasise the role of their theatres in providing a point of reference for the communities in which they are situated. Marvin Carlson's recent book *Places of Performance: The Semiotics of Theater Architecture* (Cornell University Press, 1989) summarises how 'in every historical period and in every culture the physical matrices of the theatrical event – where it takes place within the community, what sort of structure houses it, and how that structure is organized and decorated – all contribute in impor-

tant ways to the cultural processing of the event' (p. 204). Take away the jargon, and Carlson's historically directed preoccupations emerge as the current interests of some of the most farseeing of today's theatre directors. A sceptical reader will take it that these declared interests merely compensate for the declining cultural influence of theatre, attended by a minority of a minority, and regarded as marginal by politicians and opinion formers. Yet the social role of theatre as imaginative focus of our concerns, a place to meet and know one another, takes on greater reality in playhouses that construe themselves as community- and not, in the narrow sense, culture-houses. It is an apt extension of making space for theatre for architects and designers to concern themselves, as several contributors to this book do, not merely with stages and auditoria, but with the whole complex of the theatre building in its two-way traffic with its community. Theatre is situated in its community, in ways that Carlson outlines, in a fashion that goes well beyond mere physical location.

Robert Hewison describes in these pages some of the sociological changes that have taken place in the composition of theatre audiences this century, and the reflection of these changes in both play writing and theatre space. The cultural forces that have been at work over the period, reinforced by technical developments, have both encouraged new thinking in the design of theatre space and posed some awkward challenges for the use of spaces already in existence. The architectural structures that signal an influential place for theatre in the cultural and political community have seemed ill at ease in a society distrustful of 'high' culture generally, and one that has preferred irony and nuance to grand gesture. The accent recently has been on intimacy and flexibility, with small auditoria given preference in critical regard, even within those national and regional playhouses that have been built with the arguably necessary aim of preserving for theatre an influential place in the nation's cultural life. For the large auditoria, the problems have not been matters of profile and presence alone. Francis Reid's wide-ranging summary of developments in seeing and hearing, and Derek Sugden's historical survey of acoustic science, show that economics as much as cultural politics have played their part in influencing theatre design, whether in the direction of multipurpose auditoria, with all their attendant problems, or towards the possible reinvigoration of end stage and proscenium arch as the most hospitable of the larger formats to varying styles of playwriting. As Sugden observes, we are caught in large theatres, given today's actor training, between sound reinforcement and the provision of an unnaturally reverberant acoustic, a choice that may seem to some of our contributors, unconvinced by the

aesthetics of large auditoria, a modern Hobson's, with neither nag the right one. The problem for dance, customarily the most neglected of the performance arts, is not one of hearing though it is one of seeing, as Frank Woods and the late Peter Brinson remark. More evidently than in any other sector, space serves as the medium of dance, a demanding necessity that figures also as expressive lexicon. Yet the provision of even a neutral ground for dance, the rudimentary space in terms of which it can articulate its visions, has been a matter of neglect in a society where word and visual image are kings, and physical movement a script that has become almost illegible. In the case of opera, according to Tom Sutcliffe, the problem has not been neglect, but a tendency towards a regressive confinement of the art to a self- and financially-selected élite. Opera, he tells us, is not by its nature committed to costly presentation and lavish and expansive auditoria, but in essence is an adaptable art that has thrived in a multitude of spaces, from tiny to gargantuan, and should be encouraged in a spirit of experiment to continue to do so.

There has of recent years been talk, most of it unsympathetic, of Designers' theatre following Directors' theatre as the dominant mode of theatre performance in this country. Such a development must seem almost inevitable, given the aesthetics of post-modernism, with its mistrust of theme and through-line, and its liking for the juxtaposition of images unrelated by logic. In a volume concerned with *Making Space for Theatre*, there must evidently be a place for the theatre professional who more than any other, arguably, conceives and fashions the space within which performances take place. Yet the resistance to stage design as a leading craft of theatre is evidenced by the paucity of published studies, mitigated only recently by John Goodwin's *British Theatre Design: The Modern Age* (Weidenfeld and Nicolson, 1989), by Dennis Kennedy's *Looking at Shakespeare* (Cambridge University Press, 1994) and by Jocelyn Herbert and Cathy Courtney's *Jocelyn Herbert: A Theatre Work Book* (Art Books International, 1993). A Manchester Exhibition, *Make Space: Design for Theatre and Alternative Spaces*, (1994),

under the aegis of Theatre Design Umbrella, has given some belated public recognition to the designer's craft. The lurking puritanism of the English, and even the British, temperament may perhaps account for a disregard that is certainly not shared, for example, by Japanese audiences and their professional theatre, nurtured as it is by the visual luxury of Kabuki and sustained by the work of such directors as Yukio Ninagawa. The Japanese is a theatre where a designer such as Setsu Asakura can have whole and lavishly illustrated volumes devoted to her work. Nor is the continental European theatre, including the German and French, anything like as timid in the presence of spectacle as ours. The tendency towards the intimate and small-scale in British theatre has cloaked the achievement of our designers, since their pervasive contribution to shows in small spaces does not trumpet its presence, and has left their work largely unrecognised. We hope that the contributions of Nick Ormerod and William Dudley to these pages goes a little way towards correcting a failure of recognition that is equally a failure of appreciation.

Making Space for Theatre arose from the initiative of a theatre practitioner and architectural consultant who wished to survey and celebrate the record of British theatre building since its revival after the second world war. This accompanying book, with its catalogue of the British Council exhibition, is intimately bound up with Iain Mackintosh's enterprise. It is our hope that through these pages the reader will gain both an appreciation of the achievements of theatre architects, and a sense of the living organism that is British theatre practice, as it defines itself through the space it inhabits.

1 Iain Mackintosh, 'Rediscovering the Courtyard', *Architectural Review*, 175, (1984), 64–71, and *Architecture, Actor and Audience*, Theatre Concepts Series, Routledge, 1993.

2 See Marian J. Pringle, *The Theatres of Stratford-upon-Avon, 1875–1992: An Architectural History*, Stratford-upon-Avon, 1994.

3 See the discussion by David Edgar, pp. 84–88 below, and by Michael Attenborough, pp. 89–91.

4 See Ronnie Mulryne and Margaret Shewring, *This Golden Round: The Royal Shakespeare Company at the Swan*, Mulryne and Shewring, 1989.

PART ONE

MAKING SPACE
Buildings, Perspectives and Overviews

Making Space for Theatre has since mid-century been a topic of debate, sometimes acrimonious debate.

This first part contributes to the continuing discussion, while placing it in a wider perspective, historically, aesthetically and practically.

Architects, critics, technical experts and practitioners consider drama, dance and opera in relation to a wide range of spaces for performance.

ON NOT BUILDING FOR POSTERITY

Michael Elliott

Michael Elliott was until his early death Resident Artistic Director of the Royal Exchange Theatre Company in Manchester. After leaving university he joined the BBC as a television director. He was an Associate Artistic Director at the Lyric Hammersmith with the 59 Theatre Company, and joined the Royal Shakespeare Company as an Associate Director in 1961. He was the last Artistic Director of the Old Vic (1962–63) before it became the National Theatre. He was responsible for more than fifty productions on BBC and ITV, including *King Lear* with Sir Laurence Olivier (Granada Television) for which he won the International Emmy Award. He was a member of the Arts Council Drama Panel for eight years, and a member of the Council for three years, as well as serving on the Building Committee for the National Theatre.
(Photo: John Vere Brown)

Michael Elliott died in 1984 at the age of fifty-two. He gave this talk on the Third Programme of BBC Radio early in 1973. It was captured for posterity by editor Fred Bentham who reprinted it in TABS in June of that year. The date is important: it was after Michael had taken an active role in the building committee of the National who, with architect Denys Lasdun, gave us the Olivier and Lyttleton theatres and before the Royal Exchange opened three rather than two years later in September 1976, ironically eight days before the Olivier.

The piece set the agenda for the 80s. While a previous generation – his generation – yearned for the production and rehearsal facilities plus modern auditoriums with good sightlines as enjoyed by the envied ensemble companies of Europe, the generation of the 80s was to react as Michael had predicted. They rediscovered that the traditional ad hoc nature of British theatre, with only sparse technical facilities, was possibly an asset rather than a liability, since it emphasized the human scale of the actor and encouraged the imagination of both director and audience.

Now in the 90s the pendulum has swung back to a more theatrical style. Perhaps today Michael might have been revelling in the new theatre technology ('production values' as they are now termed) as indicated in his spectacular production of 'Moby Dick' at the Royal Exchange a few months before his death in 1984. Perhaps he could have been the one to unite the arts of architecture and theatre for the millennium. In any event he would have been clarifying issues with a speaking manner and prose style that was envied by all.

We all thought more clearly when Michael was either passionately advancing his views or courteously listening to those of others.

Iain Mackintosh

The modern theatre building is a hyper-sophisticated and very expensive architectural, mechanical and electronic monument, all designed to conjure up a rainbow. But a rainbow that shifts and fades, and reappears in unexpected places. Sometimes it seems ridiculous to hope that so heavy and inert a piece of real-estate can catch that rainbow as it moves rapidly over the landscape of society's changing dreams.

Visiting the several grand new regional civic theatres, or as one leans on the parapet of Waterloo Bridge pondering the huge mushrooming concrete of the new National Theatre, all one's doubts centre round one question – was this the right theatre to build now? And if often one cannot resist the answer no, it is good to remember the dilemma of those responsible. I served on the Building Committee of the National Theatre and I remember those endless and agonising meetings as though they had taken place in the shadow of the ruins of some newly shattered tower of Babel. Every illustrious and experienced voice spoke in a different language, not only from his fellows, but different from his own the month before or the month after. We could all speak of vivid personal dreams of private theatres that held our fancy that week, but to analyse objectively the purpose of a National Theatre over the next century and design an appropriate house for it – that seemed for a long time almost impossible.

There are two reasons why things have come to such a pass. Theatre, like all the other arts, is in a state of change so rapid and chaotic that there is no tradition for the individual to lean on. Secondly, nearly all the new theatres that have gone up belong to a race never seen in this land until fifteen years ago – the large publicly subsidised civic theatre, serving a new public with new fare. When they were designed we had no experience and little

Opposite:
Manchester Royal Exchange, Levitt Bernstein Associates in collaboration with Richard Negri, 1976.
(Photo: Carlton Studios, courtesy of Levitt Bernstein Associates)

knowledge of what the beast was like, what were its greatest dangers, what its richest advantages. And we have always been reluctant to learn from the continent of Europe, where the animal has been breeding more or less happily for over a century. Clearly it is now urgent that we should collect and make available all the experience gained from these new theatres, to assist anyone contemplating another. Or – and this is the interesting question – as we near the end of the major theatre building boom, with several still in the pipe-line, should there be many more? Isn't it time we stopped lumbering our grandchildren with our mistakes – understandable mistakes, but mistakes nevertheless? Don't we need something different, something less expensive, less daunting, less expressive of civic or national pride, more reflective of changing taste – something perhaps less permanent? In future shouldn't we try to retain a certain lightness and sense of improvisation, and sometimes build in materials that do not require a bomb to move them? In short shouldn't we stop building for posterity?

Let me give you some examples. When the late Sir Tyrone Guthrie undertook the Shakespeare Festival at Stratford Ontario (incredibly already twenty years ago) he started in a tent. He was already deeply committed to the evolution of a better theatre. At the Edinburgh Assembly Hall of the Church of Scotland (p. 20) he had improvised a temporary open stage – with the audience on three sides – which worked so well that the first production became a legend – and now in Canada he created an open stage in a tent with equal success. Then, and only then, when it had proved itself in design and economics, was money raised to transform the tent into a permanent theatre. Even then the change did not stop. He floated his theatre again at Minneapolis in an improved form, which was not too well copied at Chichester (p. 156), and which finally came to shore last year after his death in what is really the Tyrone Guthrie Memorial Theatre – the Sheffield Crucible (p. 158). And even there one asks oneself – is this any longer the theatre we need, that was so great an achievement in its day?

Tricycle Theatre, Kilburn,
London, Tim Foster Architects,
1980 and 1989
(*Photo: Steve Stephens*)

Or again when ten years elapses between the design and the opening, as it did with the new Birmingham Repertory Theatre (p. 81), why does it look so hopelessly old-fashioned? Or why does a visit to the Nottingham Playhouse (p. 130), for so long the blue-eyed child, excite one much less than it did a few years ago? And what will they look like after a hundred? On the other hand, why is the Roundhouse, that poorly situated open space in Chalk Farm, one of the most sought-after theatres in London? Why is the Young Vic (p. 172) so successful a building, when local development limited its projected life to five years? Of the new commercial theatres, why did the Royalty get turned into a cinema so quickly, and what will happen to the New Lon-

don Theatre when it is not so new?

Or a personal example. In Manchester, a new civic theatre is due to open in two years (p. 17). It will cost less than half the price of the Birmingham and Sheffield theatres yet it will do the same job. How?

The 69 Theatre Company is negotiating a twenty-one-year lease of the hall of the old Royal Cotton Exchange – once the temple of Manchester's industrial wealth. It has an uninterrupted space larger than Manchester Cathedral, with sixty foot marble columns, three huge domes, and an acre of parquet floor. Here there really might be theatre, because it isn't one. It had none of the old assumptions – it was just a space. Richard Negri, who is creating the theatre for the Company, has designed an extraor-

dinary structure that will rise under the great dome without touching walls or ceiling. It will be a 700 seat, steel framed auditorium, which will have a wholly flexible ground floor – with movable stage and seating – and the rest of the audience seated on four different levels, giving the most intimate theatre for its capacity anywhere in the world. Most exciting of all perhaps, is the relationship of this small concentrated space with the huge volume in the hall outside it, from which it is only partly separated – almost like an open-air theatre indoors. And the pleasure of being able to use the rest of this old building for the restaurants, bars, box office, dressing rooms, exhibition space – and the delight for the audience of wandering round the largest foyers in the country, of such extraordinary character!

Is using such a building a terrible vote of no confidence in our ability to create good new buildings this half-century, apart from cost? Yes, partly. But also the fun and joy of escaping for once from boarded concrete and modern finishes. Nostalgia it is not, since the theatre itself is so modern. Perhaps more the love of marrying the old and the new, the traditional and the revolutionary, the past and the future.

Be that as it may, if it is not as good as we think, it is not built in concrete. It can be modified after a while if we wish, even radically, and after twenty-odd years, it will not necessarily have to serve any longer. Our children can build what *they* like, and must then have.

Do not mistake me. I know we are lucky to have such a place – that they don't exist everywhere – that it might not suit every theatre company – that we are extremely fortunate to have a City Council and a large group of local citizens enlightened enough to understand and support such a scheme. All that is true. But what example it may have for some other towns is in *not* building immediately a monument of glass and concrete at colossal expense, where an awful and final decision must be taken for the audiences of the twenty-first century. Some such there must be, but the sad fact is that whereas many theatres left by the last century are good theatres of their type, most theatres of any type that we build tend to be second rate. Technically of course they are of unparalleled sophistication and with vastly improved amenities, but as places where human beings communicate with each other, and where they can be consumed by a common theatrical experience, they are usually much inferior to the Bristol Old Vic or Drury Lane. So the planning requirement that forces developers to replace a demolished theatre with a new one gives little comfort, since with the best will in the world, which there isn't, the new theatre will nearly always be worse than the old.

That may seem so provocative and controversial a statement that some further justification is re-

quired for it. Even architects find it difficult to understand why it should be so difficult to design a good theatre. Well then, put it this way. An awful lot of passion, energy, inspiration and judgement is needed to create a successful theatre season. How much more must it need to create successfully the whole context within which one season is only a detail. Above all it needs a consuming sense of purpose (which everything from the lighting to the lavatories must reflect). The economic and political realities of getting any theatre built at all are complex enough, but to maintain within those realities the freedom to build a good theatre is another matter, and it is amazing how many and insistent are the practical pressures to make it a bad one. And then *if* that is done, to be able to know clearly, in the confusion of our time, what kind of theatre will make a strong but true statement, and to pursue that ideal unshaken and undeflected through its creation at second-hand by consultants who have no personal experience of your vision, through the nightmare of cutting back on costs and the labyrinth of building and fire regulations, and then at the end to be able to demonstrate visibly the purpose that underlay it all in the work of a new company! No-one can be much more than inadequate for such a task.

I have noticed, recently, that two artistic directors of new regional theatres have said that they are more interested in the possibilities of the studio theatre included in the complex than in the main auditorium. Leaving aside the trendy irresponsibility of such remarks, nothing could show more clearly our dilemma. We are creating in such theatres, unless we are careful, a polarisation between the large, expensive, grand, square and boring on the one hand, and the intimate, cheap, informal, exciting, left-wing on the other. My view is that such polarisation is a disaster. It is integration of culture we need, not more disintegration; apart from the death-knell it must be for the whole company. At Manchester, for instance, there will be no studio theatre – the work that would be done there will be fed into the main auditorium – hopefully renewing what is old, and integrating what is new. But where the main

auditorium is too big, too grand, and lacks intimacy, it is impossible for a repertory company to do its best work in it. In any case excessive size is suicide from a management point of view. It forces the management to pursue what it believes to be a popular policy in the desperate effort to fill all those seats. On Saturday nights they may be very nice – but what about all the other performances? Very soon instead of the management running the theatre, it runs them.

And what about the management? Even the organisational structure of British theatre has changed more in the last two decades than at any time since the sixteenth century. The pattern of what used to be an entirely commercial theatre has dissolved into the split European tradition of the serious subsidised theatre and the boulevard commercial. Regional civic theatre is playing a much larger part than ever before in the national scene. So used are we now to this state of flux with a National theatre, a London branch of the Royal Shakespeare, the Royal Court, and no less significantly a Nottingham, a Birmingham and a Sheffield appearing almost overnight, that we assume it is a normal situation. It is not. The crust, and the arteries, are already hardening in front of our eyes. The great danger of subsidised theatre is institutionalisation which can lead directly to fossilisation. We are not only building huge, inflexible, hard-to-demolish buildings, but huge, inflexible, hard-to-demolish institutions. The new National Theatre on the South Bank, for instance, which will run three auditoria, pull a Government grant in the same category as Covent Garden, and pay enough employees to make the Festival Hall look like a flea-pit, reminds one organisationally more of a battleship than a theatre. We need a securely-based major company that can embody the best of established British theatre. We *need* the big regional theatres, preferably well designed, as the cornerstones of a national pattern. But the more heavy and permanent the theatres and the companies we create, the more our cultural life depends on our realising the equal importance of flexibility, both in bricks and mortar, and in people – the importance of more tran-

Left: The Young Vic Theatre, London, Howell, Killick, Partridge and Amis, 1970. (*Photo: Courtesy of the Strand Lighting Archive*)

Left: Assembly Hall of the Church of Scotland, Edinburgh. Set for *Edward II* and *Richard II*, Prospect Theatre Company, 1969. (*Photo: Courtesy of Rank Strand Electric*)

sitory operations and of less permanent buildings. From a palace you can build an empire, but you will not often find a manger anywhere but in a stable.

But there is yet another danger in building for posterity. Theatre is a public art. It is useless except in so far as there is an audience to receive it at the very moment of its creation – tonight. Tomorrow it has vanished for ever – only tattered scripts and fading memories are left. Our audience will probably be drawn from a minority of the population, but at the moment it is a smaller minority than it should be. When the theatre is good there are many hundreds of thousands, probably millions, who would find it an astonishing experience to be there but would never think of going. Publicity does not touch them, reviews are not read, and the small amount on their rates that keeps the theatre alive is considered an imposition. Some of them may simply be past playgoers long since disillusioned by their experiences, but the vast majority have hardly ever been to a theatre in their lives. The barrier to overcome is not just one of habit, though that is bad enough, but of anti-intellectual and anti-snob prejudice. And if that prejudice has some justification in theatre history, we shall overcome it not only by the shows we put on (because in my experience it is not by plays aspiring too high that they are alienated) but by the way we contact them as potential customers, and by the kind of place to which we invite them. It is not just a question of avoiding nineteenth-century social barriers embalmed in theatre design tradition, but of trying to imagine to what kind of place we would all most be drawn for an evening – what kind of building and atmosphere has the most life, warmth and immediacy. Despite the trade union booking tradition in Germany, I wonder if the German type of civic theatre is what is most attractive in all towns in this country. Does the imposing monument encourage the timid playgoer? Or have the Roundhouse and the Young Vic found another secret of success and not just for the young? There has been much talk of fun palaces, and perhaps there is a quarter truth in the idea. The small minority loves going to Covent Garden or the National, for social and nostalgic reasons, as well as theatrical, but perhaps many of us would find more interest and excitement in less conventional surroundings. Tents, halls, gardens, rooms, warehouses – why have so many of one's most vital experiences been in them, again on both sides of the absent foot-lights. And I am not actually advocating fringe and basement theatre, which is often very boring, but trying to find how their informality can be applied to more major activities. Maybe our new civic theatres need to retain some of the joy and freedom, some of the sense of a direct experience built on few assumptions, that those earlier experiences taught us. The designer said of the new Royal Exchange scheme that it should be 'almost a theatre'. Perhaps we need more buildings that are 'almost' theatres. There is one sense, however, in which we must and do build for posterity, but that is not in brick.

Above all we must try to give to the young vivid memories of a vital experience in the theatre, that after our day will influence them and their work, not in form but in spirit. What else is education? And that applies on both sides of the vanishing curtain. Young audiences, and young professionals, and young trainees. No monuments in posterity are worth having, except a contribution to that invisible and living body of human wisdom which will itself shape the future. The only link between all man's history and all his future is ourselves. There is our long-term responsibility. Build there my heart, and let posterity build its own theatres.

And so, looking round at the buildings we have already left for our great-grandchildren these last years, we may well ask what they will say of them, and of us. If we are not very careful, I think they will stand in the sunlight of other days, shrug tolerantly and say, 'They were good men according to their lights, but the men were dull, and the lights dim.'

Reprinted by permission from TABS, June 1973, vol. 31 no. 2.

WHO DECIDES THE SORT OF THEATRES WE GET?

Iain Mackintosh

The building boom, which is the focus of this book and of the exhibition which inspired it, is Britain's fourth.

First were the open air Elizabethan theatres in Shoreditch and Bankside, all built within forty years from 1576 to 1614. These theatres included the recently rediscovered Rose and the Bankside Globe, currently under reconstruction. Second were the Georgian playhouses, rapidly built in a century of growing prosperity for England, Scotland and Ireland – from one legitimate theatre in all Britain in 1714 to over three hundred a century later. The third boom in theatre building was to accommodate the biggest increase in theatregoing in history, in the forty years from 1870 to 1910. Theatres were built for all classes of the nation: grand theatres and opera houses for the gentry and 'penny gaffs' for the working classes. The fourth, the present, started nearly forty years ago with the opening of Britain's first post-war professional theatre, the Belgrade, Coventry in 1958 (p. 118).

Between these booms society either became hostile to the theatre or was more interested in other amusements. Between 1614 and 1714 came the closure of the theatres in 1642 for the duration of the Commonwealth, after which the restoration theatre of the late 17th century was confined largely to the court and to London. The aftermath of the Napoleonic wars from 1815 saw first agricultural depression and then the rise of Methodism, under which the old circuit companies of the country towns declined until new urban wealth and the railway system encouraged a vital new late Victorian theatre. At these decorated temples of delight the whole population enjoyed spectacles, magic and, in a few theatres, the art of acting itself. Few works of lasting theatrical or literary merit were produced. It is a sobering thought that, with the exception of Shake-

Iain Mackintosh is executive co-director of Theatre Projects Consultants Ltd. After graduating from Worcester College, Oxford, he co-founded Prospect Productions Ltd. (subsequently the Prospect Theatre Company) in 1961. In 1973 he joined Richard Pilbrow as a director of Theatre Projects Consultants. New theatres in the design of which he has taken part include in London the Cottesloe, the Tricycle and the Orange Tree, in the rest of Britain Eden Court, Inverness, the Wilde, Bracknell, the new Glyndebourne and the Lawrence Batley, Huddersfield, and in Europe De Maagd, Bergen-op-Zoom, while reorderings and remodellings have included the Theatre Royal, Nottingham, the Festival Theatre Edinburgh and the Dunfermline Opera House transported to Sarasota, Florida. He was responsible for the 1975 Hayward Exhibition, *The Georgian Playhouse 1730-1830* and the 1982 Royal Academy *Royal Opera House Retrospective 1732-1982,* and is the author of *Architecture, Actor and Audience* (Routledge, 1993) and more than thirty articles for journals and newspapers. In 1995 he was chosen to be a member of the jury for the Prague Quadrennial, the world's foremost exhibition of stage and theatre design.
(*Photo: Clive Barda*)

speare's day, theatre building booms rarely coincide with the production of great theatrical literature.

During the gaps between the booms theatres were built only when they had to be. This was generally after fires, such as when the Covent Garden of Benedict Albano burnt in 1856 and the first theatre at Stratford-upon-Avon in 1926.

In the last hiatus, between 1910 and 1958, there were four causes for the decline of theatre building in Britain: the two world wars, the rise of cinema, the rise of television and the greed of the inner city developer (more theatres were lost in the 50s and 60s to office blocks or supermarkets than in the 40s by bomb or doodle bug). But these causes mask a deeper reason. Theatres were no longer commercially viable. A few variety palaces were built in the provinces such as the Edinburgh Empire of 1928

(p.152), and a few new theatres added to the stock of West End theatres such as the Prince Edward, formerly the Casino, of 1930 (pp. 31, 150) but, unlike the boom of 1870 to 1910, there was no longer a real possibility of recovering the capital cost of new theatres through their operation. When the theatre was commercial there was little discussion of the aesthetics of architecture between owner and designer except possibly on the colour (generally red, cream and gold) and the style (generally 'Louis XVI'). Theatre design was simply the technical skill of getting the maximum number of audience on to a given site (generally small), with a cost-effective façade as functional as the petals of a flower which attracts life-giving insects. And yet these tried and tested theatres work now as well as they did then, with the intrinsic business of theatre design being a given, a source of agreement not a matter for discussion.

In 1928 the first major confrontation between theatre and architecture took place. In America continuity in theatre architecture had not been broken, the country had grown richer as the result of the war and hundreds of theatres were built right up to the double whammy of talking pictures and the great crash at the end of the 20s. In Britain theatre building was all but dead when the Governors of the Memorial Theatre at Stratford-upon-Avon took two fateful steps after the fire of 6 March 1926: they formed committees and decided to hold an open competition.

The farce that followed has not yet been equalled. It certainly set back the cause of Shakespeare and of the creation of a national theatre for a generation. There was a committee of the good and the great. There were technical advisers including manager Sir Barry Jackson and designer Norman Wilkinson. There was the Royal Institute of British Architects to set the rules and choose the jury who, they insisted, were mostly architects. From a short list of six they chose a winner the Governors did not want. The winner, Elizabeth Scott, was well connected but had not designed a theatre before.

At the opening in April 1932 the new Memorial Theatre (p. 13), which has since been modified at least half a dozen times in order to approach theatrical effectiveness, was almost universally praised by architects, and almost universally condemned by the theatre. *The Architectural Review* enthused throughout a whole issue (something repeated only once for a single building, the National Theatre, in 1976). Their critics loved the 'amusing' foyer, the 'beautiful' staircase and everything about the restaurant: 'the chairs and tables, cutlery, curtains, and handrails like forked lightning are worthy of Stockholm Town Hall'. The auditorium they praised for its seating, sightlines, acoustics and the absence of ornament.

Director William Bridges-Adams assisted by Harley Granville Barker had called for a two-tier horseshoe-shaped auditorium with removable forestage. The architectural jury thought these demands over-specific and that they would interfere with the imagination of an architect. Once the winner was selected, theatre people found they had to modify their requirements to safeguard the integrity of Elizabeth Scott's design. 'What we eventually got,' Bridges-Adams wrote later, 'when the architects, pressure-groups, quacks and empirics had finished with us, was the theatre, of all theatres in England, in which it is hardest to make an audience laugh or cry'.

Actor manager Baliol Holloway said of the stage after his first show there, 'it is like acting to Calais from the Cliffs of Dover'. Later he defined more precisely the problem of 'the acreage of blank walls between the proscenium arch and the ends of the circle which completely destroy all contact between actors and audience. It is doubly hard on the actor that the audience does not realise this and is aware only of the actor's comparative ineffectiveness'.

Norman Marshall, who was to chair the building committee for the National in the 60s, wrote in *The Other Theatre,* published in 1947, 'It would be unfair to attribute the drawbacks of this singularly inconvenient building to its architect, engineer and technicians who were continually harassed and bewildered by conflicting opinions and instructions and who worked from start to finish in an atmosphere of perpetual argument.' This was written before 1951 when Anthony Quayle commissioned Brian O'Rorke to start the modifications which would eventually render the Stratford-upon-Avon auditorium tolerable.

Of course it was nobody's fault. The architects blamed the theatre's brief, the theatre blamed the architects. The architects were and still are adamant that a good architect can design the tools of another profession providing somebody has written on a piece of paper how big the tool is and how it is handled. This is called 'the brief'. Note carefully that in the dialogue between the professions the rules, of which the first is the primacy of the written brief, have been determined by the architectural profession not the theatre.

It is no wonder that not one of the thirty theatres chosen to represent nearly forty years of British theatre architecture is the result of a competition, open or closed. Indeed, other than the botched affair of the High Wycombe centre where the winning design of Derek Walker, John Bury and Ted Happold was binned in favour of a routinely dull theatre called The Swan, there has been only one competition of note since 1928 and that was for the West Yorkshire Playhouse, held in 1984. Here the costs soared from £5.8m to £10.7m in less than three years and, though resulting in a cheerful and well used building, gave Leeds a large auditorium, the Quarry, which many find intractable and vertiginous because of its steep stadium character, and a small auditorium, the Courtyard, which is popular but is not perhaps as favoured as others of a genus well represented in this book and the exhibition (see p. 75).

For sixty years the British theatre has with these exceptions avoided competitions and remembered the very different ways in which theatres had been designed in previous booms. The Elizabethan carpenters reported straight to Burbage, Alleyn and Henslowe. Few Georgian playhouses had their architect's name recorded: generally the builder set them out by simple *ad quadratum* geometry and decorated them to resemble as closely as possible the revered Theatres Royal of Drury Lane and Covent Garden.

True, there was a brief period between 1775 and 1812 when distinguished generalist architects such as Robert Adam, Henry Holland, Benjamin Wyatt and Robert Smirke tried their hands at theatre architecture, with different degrees of success (the best of their theatres burnt down with monotonous regularity). There was even a competition in 1809 for Drury Lane which was won by Benjamin Wyatt. His theatre exterior and magnificent foyers survive to this day with only minor improvements, but it is interesting to note that his auditorium was quickly judged to be too wide and lacking in focus. In 1822 theatre architect Samuel Beazley replaced it with an auditorium which worked successfully for nearly a century. A brass plaque in the Garrick Club collection commemorates that 'the interior of this national theatre was entirely pulled down and rebuilt in the space of fifty eight days and reopened on 12 October 1822'. The theatre profession will finally get its way, but at a cost which escalates as building materials become ever more durable and hence radical rebuildings of auditoriums more expensive.

The third building boom of the end of the nineteenth century saw the rise of the specialist theatre architect. Four leading specialists C.J. Phipps (1835–97), Frank Matcham (1854–1920), W.G.R. Sprague (1865–1933) and Bertie Crewe (d. 1935) plus seven lesser firms of J.T. Robinson, Walter Emden, John Briggs, Hope and Maxwell, Owen and Ward, Wylson and Long and Edmund Runtz built almost all of 300 theatres. The leading firms did hardly anything but theatres and while admired by the building trade they were scarcely considered serious architects by other, grander, architects. Indeed Phipps, who also managed some town halls, clubs and hotels, was the only one to make the *Dictionary of National Biography* – until 1993, when I had the honour of making the case to the Oxford University Press for Matcham's inclusion in their special volume of the DNB, *Missing Persons*.

Clearly we cannot return to an age of either carpenters or specialist architects and designers. There is not enough work for more than a few specialist theatre designers or architects in Britain. But now that theatre is for the most part non-commercial, and also considers itself closer to the centre of society, we have to face the fact that theatres and opera houses are regarded as 'great secular cathedrals' or 'society's affirmation of confidence in the city' or whatever the cant phrase of the day is. Being the centre of attention carries responsibilities and obligations which include opening a dialogue with architects. Indeed it is essential if the theatre user is not to be suffocated by the fashionable clothes of couturier architects chosen by the good and the great, or by fellow architects.

But need this be by architectural competition? Competitions have an inglorious record in Europe too. The Bastille Opera House jury rejected all those who did not fulfil the ludicrously over-complex technical brief, and chose a building by Carlos Otts which looks like an architectural model of itself. The Amsterdam Musiektheater, as long awaited as an Edinburgh opera house, is a muddled fusion in 1986 of an interesting exterior by an Austrian architect, William Holzbauer, and a superannuated auditorium design by a Dutchman, B Bijvoet, made in 1956. The Essen Opera House of 1988 is an exercise in that most distracting of architectural conceits, the asymmetric auditorium, and was built precisely to the design of Alvar Aalto long after his death, and even longer after he had won the competition thirty years previously. (Aalto would surely have altered things as the design developed; his widow allowed nothing to change.) All the evidence points to the disastrous consequences of adopting the belief that competitions improve theatre design – and yet the case still has to be answered because the British Lottery agencies of the Arts Councils of England, Scotland, Wales and Northern Ireland have nailed 'competition' to their mastheads.

The case against competitions other than experience includes some fundamental reasons:

Competitions do not allow designer and user to collaborate, which is all the more important if neither of the principals, user or architect, has experience of building theatres

Competition briefs eschew the qualitative in favour of the quantitative (many architects are not great readers, their skills being visual and plastic, hence the need for theatre people and architects to talk, talk, talk and share experience not just for the theatre consultant to deliver a list of areas and seat numbers)

Entrants to competitions and the juries are pre-occupied by the exterior – what it looks like in the city landscape – because these competitions are rarely judged by the interior which many believe can be 'fixed by experts'. Theatres designed from the outside in always fail

Juries generally have a majority of architect members (European regulations insist on this) who tend to look over their shoulders not at the theatrical users but at their architectural peers – hence they want to appear to be 'up to the minute'

The briefs are rarely written by artists but by those who know the height of a grid rather than the purpose of an auditorium and, as a consequence of this and the tight time scale, entrants gain no insight into the essentials of theatre architecture. Hence not enough attention is devoted to the bit that matters most, the auditorium

The difference in architect selection for the new Glyndebourne and Cardiff opera houses could not have been more marked. At Glyndebourne designer John Bury undertook a planning exercise to demonstrate the scale of the new auditorium, which had to hold 50% more than the old. Sir George Christie took good advice to draw up a list of twelve architects to interview. This was reduced to nine, who received not a brief the size of the Cardiff telephone directory but Sir George's 'thoughts'. Example: 'the feel of the auditorium – what it is going to be dressed in. It's got to be hugely welcoming. Timber-clad not plush gilt or velvet. It has to be both functional and friendly'.

Nine came down to two. More talk. Then one. Michael Hopkins and Partners were appointed, soon to be joined by consultants chosen jointly by the client and architect. Then an open dialogue when all could contribute and everything was possible followed by Decisions and, when a realistic budget had been set, albeit larger than that originally proposed, rigid cost control by a good project manager and a fine builder.

In Cardiff, the brief was all numbers except for an interesting appendix on acoustics. The client was a new *ad hoc* body who did not even own the site. The Welsh National Opera, who were to occupy the theatre for just under half the year, were side-lined, literally, with a connecting door which could be opened or shut. Nobody bothered to detail the artistic policy for the larger part of the year or discuss just how a theatre can be half an opera house and half a variety house for musicals, pantomimes, cabaret and dance (the shape of an opera house is fundamentally different from that of a house for musicals and variety). The jury excluded any actor, singer, dancer, director, musician, stage designer or theatre manager. The architect members persuaded the innocent client to hold a two-stage competition with four seeded to the second round (two world-famous architects refused to be so seeded). Interviews and public consultation took place after the winner had been chosen by majority vote of the architects and the good and the great. The land owner was not given a vote.

Stratford all over again? No, there is time to put things right if the auditorium has design priority. Some will say there were mistakes en route (one of the most incredible being that the telephone directory sized brief got its sums wrong in the all-important ratio of net usable space to gross building – the difference is corridors, stairs, walls and ducts – which made a nonsense of the budget). Despite all this, and while the competition was being judged, a prominent arts management consultant, who had been involved in setting up the whole thing, wrote an article in a national newspaper in praise of open competitions if the organisers had got themselves the right jury and the right brief. He is now said to be less keen on competitions. But around the same time Lottery agencies reaffirmed the belief that all arts buildings in receipt of more than £1m ought to hold a competition. Why?

The architects themselves are moving against competitions. The Cardiff competition engendered £3m worth of un-paid design work – more than the total fee of the winning architect. But the theatre profession is strangely silent.

What is needed is a careful statement by the theatre profession, who are after all the sole users of these new buildings, on how architects and their design teams should be selected. While a case can and perhaps should be made for keeping this complex matter in the hands of specialists, as in the 19th century, new problems and new challenges need new solutions that can best be provided by a new generation of architects and engineers. There are ways of finding these new engineers, designers and architects other than through open competitions. For example, allow everybody to apply, spend a great deal of time reading their proposals (not designs) and narrow down the list for interview. Take trouble with the interviews (it can't cost more than the deliberations and study trips of the Cardiff jury). Narrow the list again. Invite the few to a series of working 'charettes' with the users and the owners of the new building. Send them away to do a little work on the bits that matter, not set out the whole building in detail. Display the results to the public. Talk again. Share visits to comparable buildings. Let users not architects select the final winner. A steady love affair that grows is generally preferable to a blind date.

Perhaps the theatre's most important contribution to the debate will be to suggest that the new theatres and opera houses should not be great public buildings, however much a Godless people wants secular cathedrals. Should we, as Michael Elliott asks elsewhere in this book, 'stop building for posterity'?

Michael Elliott, who led the creative team for the Royal Exchange Theatre and Company, died at the age of 52 in 1984. His piece in this book was written in 1973 after he had served on the National Theatre building committee and while the consequence was being constructed. He thought he was writing at the end of a building boom. At first sight he was not. Of the thirty theatres detailed in this book and in the exhibition sixteen had not been started in 1973.

But look more closely at the sixteen. Five are restorations or remodelling of existing theatres. Six are conversions of found space. Only five are theatres on a 'green field' site, those of Ipswich, Pitlochry, Plymouth, Northampton and Glyndebourne. The first two are medium scale conventional playhouses, built on tight budgets and lacking flytowers, which could have been designed five years earlier. This leaves three larger theatres: the Theatre Royal Plymouth (p. 124), the Derngate Northampton (p. 126) and Glyndebourne Festival Opera (pp. 55, 128). The third of these is a single purpose building. The first two, however, are interesting and innovative and neither could have been conceived before its time.

Plymouth and Northampton use new technology to confront the new requirement for a building serving a wider range of theatrical, musical and non-theatrical activities than had been demanded in the past. Plymouth does it with a single moving ceiling. Northampton does it with six audience towers on air castors and large elevators on which seats move. Northampton has engendered a second even more successful theatre in Cerritos, California (p. 56). It really does suggest that new approaches for the twenty first century are possible. And they are all three of manageable theatrical proportions.

To achieve such successful multi-purpose theatres a well-informed building committee is needed, which is prepared to travel together with architects and consultants and to study comparable solutions to comparable problems. This can't be done in a competition.

Meanwhile the producing drama, dance and musical theatre companies seeking their own creative stages and auditoriums for their original work are advised to avoid both competitions and committees. But there is a price. Directors, designers, managers, actors and musicians must give up time to discuss designs which from concept to completion may take up to five years. They must find words to explain what they want. They must not be put off by those who say one can't design for a particular director or house style, because the director will have moved or the style changed by the time the theatre is complete. Purposeful directors like Elliott of Manchester or Frank Dunlop at the Young Vic created idiosyncratic buildings to their own taste and that of their immediate associates. Nearly twenty years later the same ephemeral theatres are loved as much by other directors, even if they may be using them slightly differently. The spirit lives and the flame burns more strongly in these relatively low cost simple theatres than in the temples devised by high-priest architects advised by committees and consultants with their briefs and specifications full of statistics.

Thus in the case of playhouses which are primarily to be stages for resident companies the answer would seem to be to rally behind either the rare theatre director of vision or the architect of experience and conviction such as Peter Moro at Nottingham (pp. 71–74, 130). At the large-scale Plymouth and Northampton indicate innovative possibilities for the multi-purpose touring theatre. Glyndebourne shows the way for a single-purpose new medium-scale theatre. What is much more uncertain is how the theatre acquits itself if told that with unlimited Lottery money, it has to inhabit 'a major public building'. I suspect that such casting of theatres as secular cathedrals is portentous and is to expect too much of an ephemeral art.

This is not to say that great new theatres will not be built in the future. But something suggests that now is not the moment. Compare Charles Garnier's enduring Paris Opera of 1876 with Carlos Ott's infuriating Bastille Opera House of 1989. What British theatre architecture does offer both its own theatre users and a world elsewhere is a talent for modest buildings economically planned and attuned to the needs of its users. Britain never had a tradition of princely patronage or monument building in the theatre and is unlikely to excel at grandeur and showiness. But what it has been good at, and will continue to be good at, is creating imaginatively-conceived theatres that serve the true purpose of theatre architecture: the channelling of energy from actor to audience and back again.

SACRED SPACE AND SECULAR SPACE

Michael Reardon

Based on a conversation with Ronnie Mulryne and Margaret Shewring.

In a recent interview with Peter Holland,[1] Tim Furby and I made some points about theatre space which I would like to develop here.

I recalled that before the Swan Theatre was designed, I had tried to interest Trevor Nunn in doing some of his work not in theatres but in galleried churches, because it seemed to me that the architecture of such buildings had the power to draw the audience together in a way that modern theatres do not. I suspect that the commission to design a galleried space for the Swan was the eventual result of that exchange.

For a long time I have been interested in the relationship between theatre and architecture in general and in the relationship between religious and social rituals in the Renaissance period; for example between the ceremonies of the princely household and the Book of Common Prayer.

People who study Renaissance plays have always been aware of the spaces for which they were written but one sees a growing interest in the social context of theatre. Anne Barton's brilliant lectures on 'Parks and Ardens' is an example of this, but a similar process can be seen in other areas of scholarship. Architectural historians, once largely concerned with things like attributions and style, have become interested in what went on inside the buildings. Eamon Duffy in his book *The Stripping of the Altars* gives us an insight into how medieval churches were used and demonstrates just how theatrical medieval religion was in practice.

Unfortunately, architectural historians are rarely interested in theatre and tend to underrate its influence on architecture. In fact they are embarrassed by it. I once heard a speaker at a seminar on English classical architecture dismiss Inigo Jones' designs for the Masques as 'mere ephemera'. 'Real architecture', she added,' must be solid'.

In designing the Swan, we set out to create a very strong architectonic form – a framework within which the actor and audience would exist on equal terms and interact. This was of course what Trevor wanted, and I suppose it is the exact opposite of the 'black box' approach that had prevailed at Stratford. I have noticed that designers have abandoned the ideal of 'invisibility' and are restoring historic theatres, which of course were never intended to be 'invisible'.

There has been a similar reaction in the design of churches, where the concept of neutral space, in which the liturgy itself will create order, has been succeeded by a wish for more structured buildings which make a statement of purpose even when not in use. For some years the design of religious buildings has been over-influenced by St Paul's condemnation of earthly temples, resulting in a reductionist view of the church as merely a shelter for the people of God. This may be valid theologically but, in cultural terms, there is more to Christianity than the Pauline view and, for sixteen hundred years at least, the church has seen its buildings as bearers of meaning.

In the Renaissance period, when Society was structured in a hierarchical way, it was easier to relate the design of space to the social structure. In our very fragmented and individualist society, this is much more difficult, but the best theatre, like the best religious worship, can still create a sense of community. This is difficult in neutral space but it does happen in theatres like the Swan and the Manchester Royal Exchange which have a ship-like feel to them and a sense of sharing a common voyage.

Again, there are parallels with religious worship. Protestantism and particularly the Evangelical tradition lay stress upon the individual 'my relationship with God' whereas the older Catholic tradition was rooted in the idea of a worshipping commu-

Michael Reardon is a practising conservation architect who has also designed a number of theatres, including the conversion of the former Conference Hall into the outstandingly successful Swan theatre, and the new Other Place (both for the Royal Shakespeare Company at Stratford-upon-Avon), as well as the Riverside Arts Centre at Hammersmith. He has also refurbished the Memorial Theatre at Stratford, the Oxford Playhouse and the Watermill Theatre at Newbury. His degree in Architecture at Cambridge and diploma from the Birmingham School of Architecture were followed by work for the City of Birmingham Housing Department and the New Towns Commission at Redditch, where his first scheme gained a National Housing Award. He has a strong interest in the relationship between drama and liturgy, and between Church and theatre space. He was appointed (in 1975) Surveyor of the Fabric to the church that is now Birmingham Cathedral, has been since 1984 Surveyor of the Fabric to Hereford Cathedral, and is advisor on liturgical planning and design to the Dean and Chapter of Norwich Cathedral. He is a member of the English Heritage Churches and Cathedrals Committee.

The Interior of Birmingham Cathedral after if had been re-ordered and redecorated by Michael Reardon, based on the concept of the Eucharist as a Masque of Transfiguration. (*Photo: F.R. Logan Ltd., Birmingham*)

Interior of the Swan Theatre, Stratford-upon-Avon, Michael Reardon and Associates, 1986. The Opening Production, *The Two Noble Kinsmen,* by Shakespeare and Fletcher. (*Photo: Martin Charles*)

nity, in which the division between sacred and secular is blurred.

Gothic cathedrals were certainly not conceived as spaces for congregational worship, even though they were sometimes large enough to contain the entire population of the city. They were images of the Heavenly City, in which liturgical action and architecture were inextricably bound together in total theatre. At Wells on Palm Sunday, as the procession representing the entry of Christ into Jerusalem approached the west front – whose form is probably derived from the *frons scenae* of the Roman theatre – singers concealed behind the statues burst into '*Hosanna filio David…*' and, as the great doors swung open, '*Attollite, portae…*'

Of course, this is not a world that we can recreate, but an understanding of it might help us to recover the dynamic relationship between theatre and architecture, between the actor and the building and between the church and the liturgy. Alas, few clergy have any sense of theatre and as the dynamics of space, movement and gesture do not form part of their training the potential for liturgical drama is often unrealised.

The theatrical parallel is the Masque in which the scenery was not simply a 'setting' for the action, but an integral part of it. For this to work there had to be a language of visual and verbal symbols which were supplied by the classical world, with which the educated spectators were familiar.

The division of theatre and architecture, of 'scenery' and 'real buildings' is a modern phenomenon. The first appearance of the Renaissance style may well have been in the scenery designed for princely entries and festivals. A researcher once told me that the royal expenditure on 'scenery' during Henry VIII's reign was equal to that on permanent buildings. I am fascinated by the light this throws on both the priorities of state and the relationship between theatre and architecture. Much of what we regard as 'architectural' development probably took place in the context of these very 'ephemera'.

Nor should we forget that buildings were constantly altered in appearance. Churches changed

Interior of the new Other Place, Stratford-upon-Avon, Michael Reardon and Associates, 1991 (*Photo: John Saint Laurent*)

with the season as altarpieces were opened and closed. Many devotional objects like the famous Annunciation of Nuremberg were only unveiled at certain times of the year. The Lenten veil in the chancel was raised and lowered like a theatrical tab. For a royal entry, the city would assume a different appearance.

Perhaps we are obsessed with the permanent and unchanging – as in our timidity in adapting and using historic buildings. The word 'building' itself signifies a continuing process and it is perhaps not without significance that Cathedrals are now referred to in conservation circles as 'monuments'.

One of the most gratifying things about the Swan is the way in which a dynamic has developed and the diverse ways in which Directors have learned to use the space. While some Designers have complained that the Swan is constraining, it seems on the contrary to have had a liberating effect on the style of Direction.

We have to recover the importance of movement, not only of the actor but of the audience. In Renais-

sance court theatre the entry of the Prince must itself have been a significant part of the action. Prior to the Reformation, congregations rarely sat down and ritual involved movement around the building. Although the Other Place has been used as a promenade theatre I do not think this has yet been tried at the Swan, at least by the RSC.

Perhaps an understanding of ritual movement is something that we have lost in England though in Italy, even now, the ability to 'make an entrance' remains a crucial skill.

If I were asked to name the theatres I like, they would all possess a strong architectural character and a feeling of envelopment. The Royal Exchange would certainly be amongst them and probably the Tricycle, and of course The Swan, and then smaller eighteenth century theatres, the Renaissance survivals like the Teatro Farnese and the odd curiosity like the Teatro Bibbiena at Mantova – which was not designed for drama at all.

1 'Stratford Stages: Two Reviews', *Shakespeare Survey* 47, Cambridge, 1994

SEEING, HEARING & CONTACT

Francis Reid

Francis Reid has worked for over forty years as a backstage jack-of-all-trades in professional theatre. His primary field is lighting. He was lighting designer for Glyndebourne Festival Opera throughout the sixties, and has subsequently been responsible for the lighting design of at least 300 productions, including over 30 in London's West End. He has, in addition, been involved in most aspects of theatre production. From 1979 to 1981, he was Director of the Theatre Royal, Bury St Edmunds, and from 1982 until 1987 was Head of the Department of Theatre Design at London's Central School of Art and Design. He has written seven books on theatre design, lighting, technology and administration, including *The Stage Lighting Handbook*, now in its fourth edition, and translated into Spanish and Swedish. He has led seminars and workshops across the world, from Adelaide to Wolfenbüttel, and Bangalore to Taipei.

Until the early years of this century, the word 'theatre' carried clear images of a standard form. Although theatre building had been in continuous evolution since the Renaissance, the pace of change was so gradual that there had been apparent stability from one generation to the next. But, throughout the twentieth century, change has accelerated to such an extent that performances now take place in such a wide array of co-existing formats that virtually any space has theatre potential, provided that an audience is able to see and hear the actors. In addition, for successful theatre, the space needs to catalyse the elusive contact that not only binds actor and audience but individual members within that audience.

During the nineteenth century the single room concept of such earlier theatres as the Richmond (Yorkshire) Georgian Theatre thrust the action into the auditorium, enhancing both visibility and audibility (pp. 37, 142). Actors were content to play in front of, and divorced from, a scenic background. Candle and oil generate a low light level and the actor whose face cannot be clearly seen is an actor who is difficult to hear. By sharing the audience space, actors could be both seen and heard. Contact was very close. But nineteenth century audiences showed increasing preference for such pictorial theatres as the Sheffield Lyceum with actors and scenic environment integrated within a frame (p. 148). This conflict between visual spectacle and textual nuance has been with us since the earliest theatres and it continues unresolved.

So, as the twentieth century began, 'theatre' had become synonymous with a proscenium framed stage offering, to an audience stacked on every available wall surface of the auditorium, a window into a world of illusion. Despite hints of new technologies, the visual environment of most productions involved painted canvas, either as flown cloths or manhandled flat frames. The painted perspective may only have worked from the centre seats, but the audience at the sides were prepared to let imagination aid their perception.

Unlike much of central Europe, where a tradition of court and civic subsidy allowed the retention of eighteenth-century style shallow seating tiers offering good contact with the stage, Britain's commercial approach necessitated the development of deep galleries to maximise seating capacity and revenue. Many of these theatres, such as the Belfast Grand (p. 146) were built by Frank Matcham on restricted sites and displayed tremendous ingenuity in exploiting small, often irregularly shaped, plots of land.

Inevitably, there were reactions to the standard proscenium theatre with its circles and boxes. A particularly influential reaction was that of Wagner who, seeking a more integrated fusion of text, music, acting and scenic environment, looked afresh at the auditorium of the classic theatre of the Greeks and Romans. Boxes and balconies were discarded in favour of a single rising fan-shaped tier offering all members of the audience a clear sight line to a picture stage. The proscenium was still present but less positively defined as a frame. However, the scenery remained in the old tradition, although such visionaries as Adolphe Appia and Edward Gordon Craig were publishing designs ahead of audience taste and technical feasibility. The format of Wagner's Bayreuth Festspielhaus of 1876, while sympathetic to the broad spectacle of music theatre on an epic scale, was less satisfactory for spoken drama's more intimate rapport between actor and audience. Consequently, until after the advent of the cinema, the rising fan-shaped tier did not replace balconies and boxed horseshoes in the majority of theatres.

Conservation is a recent trend. In the years in which twentieth century theatre building got underway, the existing theatres were seen as something to be reacted against in a search for the new. The preferred options were to gut the shell and provide a new interior, or to demolish and start again. There was a pressing need for theatres to respond to the challenge of the cinema which, inevitably, became the major influence. It was virtually impossible to compete with the glamour and excitement of the new medium's stars and exotic locations, but new theatres could at least copy the cinema's improved standards of audience comfort. While the old theatres certainly had some comfortable seats, there was a rigid hierarchy extending from luxury through to acute discomfort, with seeing, hearing and contact all directly related to seat cost. Stemming from the technical requirements of viewing two-dimensional projected images on a screen, clear straight-ahead sightlines to the screen from all seats in the house became the prime architectural virtue. Moreover, turning theatre on its head, the worst and therefore cheapest seats were now those nearest to the screen (stage). Apart from developments arising from technical requirements, the 1914–18 war had triggered a rapidly changing social climate to which the cinema responded by aiming for equal standards of comfort in all parts of a house approached by a single entrance. Theatre, its survival threatened by the new medium, had no option but to follow.

There was also considerable new thinking about the whole nature of theatre and the relationship between actor and audience. There was an increasingly perceptible shift away from the standard turn-of-the-century view of theatre as a place of entertainment to something which was not only for entertainment. There was nothing particularly original in this concept, just more emphasis placed upon it. In Britain, the stimulus for drama came from the embryonic repertory movement with perhaps Terence Gray's Cambridge Festival Theatre as the prime catalyst. In music theatre, the major influence was such refugees from Hitler's Germany as Carl Ebert.

Outside Italy, the late nineteenth century had seen boxes decrease in number. Balconies which had once been partitioned into small individual boxes now had long rows of seating, and the few remaining boxes now became much larger and were concentrated around the proscenium as a positive feature of the grand frame. From the 1920s they became residual as in the Edinburgh Empire now refurbished as the Festival Theatre (pp. 96, 152), often to the point of being purely decorative rather than seriously intended for occupation. Whereas at least three audience tiers had been common, a desire to reduce extreme vertical sightlines made a single balcony normal. With boxes removed and balconies no longer curving around the sides of the auditorium, the walls became decorative surfaces rather than a place to hang people.

Providing every member of the audience with a clear sight line resulted in the furthest seats being more distant from the stage than in a traditional theatre with similar proscenium opening and seating capacity. Any house from about 700 seats upwards had problems of viewing distance from its back rows, a problem increased at ground level by the tunnelling effect of balcony overhang. The large screen images of cinema gave the view from the distant rows an acceptable scale, but with live theatre the effect was that of looking through a reversed telescope.

The walls where the audience had once hung were now influenced by Art Deco. At the turn of the century Matcham had used exotic fibrous plaster impressions of Arabia, India and the Orient to offer exotic fantasies on a suburban night out. This became one of the styles of cinema interior decoration, although theatres tended to follow the alternative cinema style of clean lines, soft curves and concealed cove lighting.

The influence of the cinema had enhanced the sense of occasion inherent in any visit to a theatre by extending comfortable seating to all parts of a house which was structured and decorated in accord with the clean lines of an era which was particularly intent on looking forward rather than back. The shape of the new theatres improved sightlines but tended to reduce sound levels and to erode the degree of contact between audience and actor.

In the 1960s and 70s, Britain built a network of regional playhouses such as the Leatherhead Thorndike (p. 134). Most of these new theatres were proudly functional. Decorative elements were an unacceptable frivolity. This was not just a matter of modernist building style, it was a manifestation of serious purpose. The 1956 and 1965 visits to London of Brecht's Berliner Ensemble had rallied the protagonists of theatre as a serious political and social force dealing with mankind's agonies rather than with the potential civilising influences of beautiful sights, sounds and thoughts. Concrete was the medium, fair faced or shuttered. Paint was shunned unless it was black. In a move to maximise contact, the proscenium arch was abandoned in several new theatres. The major catalyst for this was the simple end-stage of the original London Mermaid (p. 6), converted from a riverside warehouse but now sadly replaced in the course of site development. Some other new theatres allowed the stage to thrust into the audience as at the Chichester Festival (p. 156) and the Sheffield Crucible (p. 158) or be surrounded by audience as at the Manchester Royal Exchange (p. 17).

By the late 1960s a series of standard forms of postwar theatre seemed to be emerging, although many of the 1960s designs were not completed until well into the 1970s and even 80s. This was a period when there was almost an international consensus as to what was meant by a new theatre. Its concrete exterior was uncompromisingly functional. Geometric modules were a favourite starting point with curves quite rare. The proscenium, unstressed to minimise any framing effect, was formed by the simple termination of side walls and a sloping ceiling. It was very convenient that this configuration was particularly good for incorporating the ceiling bridges and wall slots required by the growth in lighting ambitions and technology that were a feature of the period. People no longer papered side walls, except in a few opera houses which continued the tradition of shallow boxes and circles but angled the seating to face the stage to improve sightlines.

The Royal National Theatre on London's South Bank summarised many of the trends of this period. The Lyttleton (p. 93) remains firmly a proscenium house despite elaborate arrangements for limited flexibility in the proscenium zone. The Olivier (pp. 95, 120) represents the open stage single room philosophy with its stage thrusting into a sharply rising arc of seating and, by making the entire acting area into a deep drum revolve, incorporating elevators for changing whole scenes, seeks to bring the scenic versatility of the proscenium stage to the thrust. For budgeting politics, the smaller Cottesloe theatre (p. 166) was disguised as a void during much of the design and building periods. This allowed its detailed design to incorporate more up-to-date thinking than was possible within the extended concept-to-opening time scale of the main houses. It was also subject to less committee compromise. Thus, while firmly in the black box studio tradition, the Cottesloe incorporates the side wall audience galleries that were central to a major rethink in theatre philosophy which was already underway at the Billingham Forum (p. 132) and the Inverness Eden Court (p. 136) and would soon accelerate.

With considerable expansion in the scale of theatre buildings to incorporate improved audience circulation areas, restaurants, bookshops, exhibition spaces, high technology stages and extensive workshops, it was inevitable that a reaction would be provoked. 'Let's get back to basics.' 'A few planks and a lot of passion are all that is needed to stage a dramatic event.' 'Theatre cannot thrive in monumental buildings with hierarchical organisations.' Perhaps the words most associated with the movement which became particularly strong during the 1970s are 'fringe' and 'alternative'. While much of it did make political or social comment, the new artistic anarchy was more particularly a response to the structured formalities – even solemnities – of mainstream theatre. It set out to be cheap and cheerful, utilising available space, improvising a performance environment without the aid of any but the most simple technologies. Its performances mixed words, music and dance with a disregard for what was seen as the ponderous logic of the established playhouses. It was all about contact – actors were so close to the audience and involved with them, that seeing and hearing could not fail to be good. The result has been that many spaces such as the London Almeida (p. 178) and the Glasgow Tramway (p. 57), not originally thought of as theatres, have acquired simple staging facilities – particularly scaffolding grids to hang lights. Indeed, there is now virtually no space which cannot be considered for performance.

In Britain the fringe was, and is, a mainly touring operation with productions kept small for mounting in a wide range of simple spaces. However, although a street corner or a couple of planks may be a fine place to project a passion, if that passion is projected with any success it will soon attract an audience who will require seating arranged so that they can see the actors. It will be necessary to devise a means of getting them to their seats, not forgetting taking their money. Success will require raising the planks so that more people can see. As the audiences increase can they still hear? Can they still see? Will they lose contact with the actors? Where will the actors dress? In no time at all we have re-invented a theatre building. Yesterday's anarchy feeds tomorrow's orthodoxy.

During the 1970s, there was a gradual realisation that something of the excitement of the old theatres had been lost. There was now so much emphasis upon the actor to audience relationship that the other fundamental relationship of performance had been overlooked – the interaction between members of an audience that makes them more than just an assembly of individuals. This was largely the result of rigorously pursuing the ideal of perfect sightlines. The removal of sight obstructing pillars with the advent of cantilevered balconies was very welcome, but the relentless pursuit of a totally pure sightline, often to the exclusion of other considerations, tends to erode contact. Excessive raking of auditorium floors and spacing of seats tends to provide pure sight at the expense of seating each viewer in isolation. They are less aware of their fellow audience and they are farther away from the actor.

So once again audiences began to be hung on the walls. Initially the smaller houses tended towards rectangular formats rather than traditionally curved horseshoes or bells. The wrap around galleries on at least two levels were shallow and tended to have a single row of seats. Even the centre sections remained relatively shallow and free from any deep cantilevered overhang in the Victorian tradition. The entire auditorium tended, once again, to be contained within a room in the Georgian manner.

In their smaller versions, these new theatres lend themselves very well to a promenade style of production, developed particularly in the Cottesloe, where the action moves around the auditorium with the audience making way as the acting area ebbs and flows. The rectangular linearity of the first courtyards (as they became called) was partly a consequence of the geometric functionalism of the postwar era and partly of the spaces (often found spaces within existing buildings) in which such theatres as the London Tricycle Theatre (pp. 18, 174) and the Winchester College Theatre (p. 176) were constructed. But more looking backward to find a way forward soon produced increasing curves as at the Glynde-bourne Opera House (pp. 55, 128) and even the addition of nonfunctional decorative elements. The 'bells' and 'horseshoes' of the earlier theatres are being rediscovered and developed in such theatres as the Basildon Towngate to improve sight lines. These formats also find considerable advocacy among practitioners of the mystical art of acoustics.

Hanging people on walls is not an ideal situation. Sightlines get progessively worse as seats are placed higher and closer to the stage. In the old theatres many people sat in boxes for social reasons and seats could be highly priced accordingly. Today such seats are the cheapest in the house. Indeed it is in the in-

The Prince Edward Theatre,
London.
(*Photo: Ian Grundy*)

terest of a good performance to sell them cheaply enough to ensure that they will be filled and help the audience to gel. People-papered walls get more people closer to the stage so, for the poorer seats in any theatre, the basic alternatives are pure sightline and a long-distance lack of contact with the stage, or impaired sightline and a close contact.

The rediscovery of the advantages of papering the walls with people has perhaps been the major influence during the final decades of the century. Most new theatres, whether or not built in this format, show increasing concern with minimising isolation and emphasising contact between individual audience members. Theatre complexes with more than one auditorium increasingly include a 'courtyard'. For example, the West Yorkshire Playhouse (p. 75) has both thrust and courtyard auditoria which enable productions to be mounted in a wide range of styles. Theatres of the cinema age, on being refurbished, have had additional seating added to their side walls to enhance their contact, notably the London Prince Edward (pp. 31 and 150). There is, inevitably, a downside to all this: the recapture of wall surfaces by audience has made some problems for lighting. People now sit in what would otherwise be ideal lighting positions with the result that much ingenuity is required to incorporate discreet mountings for spotlights.

Over the past half century there has been much talk of an adaptable theatre. Many solutions have been proposed and some have been tried. The most successful attempts at adaptability have been in small studios where the seats can be moved around between end-stage, traverse and in-the-round formations. However, mostly as a consequence of the time and labour involved, the tendency has been to settle down into the most successful format – which is usually end-stage. In the larger theatres, there have been many complex versions of the proscenium zone, but essentially these have just been minor variations involving an elevator which can alternate between additional seating, orchestra pit and small forestage, in some cases in conjunction with adjustable framing from a movable proscenium arch. Such arrangements have little significance for the actor/ audience relationship beyond the first few rows.

The adaptability problem is not just one of being able to change form between today's different production styles. Performance ideals and staging methods develop over the life of a theatre building and modern construction materials are particularly intransigent when it comes to future structural modifications. Pouring concrete imposes current thinking upon future generations. This was not a problem for earlier theatres: there was a permanent shell of stone and brick but it was fitted out internally as a theatre with a timber structure which was virtually free standing. During the seventeenth, eighteenth and early nineteenth centuries in particular, developments in auditorium form were carried out by the carpenters and painters responsible for the stage scenery. (Discovering the original form of the Bury St Edmunds Theatre Royal in preparation for a proposed restoration by its owners, The National Trust, has taken intensive detective work involving detailed on-site debate, reference to contemporary practice and the application of Ad Quadratum geometry.)

However a return to this adaptability now seems possible. The breakthrough came with the Northampton Derngate (p. 126) using new technology, in the form of the air castor, to permit large sections of stage and auditorium to be moved around on the hovercraft principle. Heavy sections can be floated and moved with very little physical effort, but once the air cushion has been removed they sit on the floor as solidly as if they were permanent.

At the beginning of the twentieth century, theatre architects and their clients tended to react against the past, rejecting the good equally with the bad. During the final decades, rediscovery has been the predominant influence. But the results are far from pastiche. Reassessment of fundamentals has led to redeployment of solutions which had been slowly evolved but hastily discarded. Paused on the threshold of a new century, there is an opportunity to exercise history's most fundamental benefit: to move forward, first look back. The danger is that in rediscovering the past we may reject what is good in the present. How will theatre buildings evolve in the next century? Can we resolve the conflicts between the requirements of a wide diversity of types of performance and modes of operation?

The Future
Drama requires close contact between actor and audience, with subtleties of facial movement visible and an acoustic favourable to speech clarity. For *Music Theatre* the required contact is more in the nature of a rapport than physical proximity, so that the unnatural facial expressions involved in singing sustained notes do not intrude, and the full breadth of choreographic images can be encompassed within the field of vision. This visual width needs to be matched by an acoustic which encompasses a wide dynamic range and provides an appropriate degree of reverberation to enhance the timbre of vocal and instrumental sounds. *Spectacles*, whether high technology musicals or solo appearances of recording stars, place an emphasis on broad visual effect and on electronically processed sound which aspires to the quality of the best compact disc player and personal stereo.

Although some musicals are small and intimate, and some plays may be staged with a broad epic sweep, the requirements for spoken drama and musical theatre are virtually incompatible. In terms of intimacy and acoustic, a good lyric theatre is a poor house for drama. Conversely, unless a musical work is quite small, the auditorium volume of a theatre of playhouse scale is insufficient to contain the sound. While many contemporary dance works are choreographed for an intimate theatre, the great classical ballets not only need big stages but can have their overall impact lessened by being viewed too closely. Differences between musicals and spectaculars are less distinct. The spectacle house will be bigger, its stage to hold the technology of performance and its auditorium to hold the necessary box office. There is no clear dividing line as to when a lyric theatre becomes a house for spectaculars. The division is not so much a matter of size but of acoustic. A

Lyric Theatre will be able to perform the large works of the musical repertoire with natural sound, whereas a spectacle house is likely to be dependent not just upon amplifying the natural sound but subjecting each individual voice and instrument to a mixing process involving considerable electronic enhancement.

The heart of a theatre's format is the relationship between stage and auditorium. Although the range of variation approaches the infinite, there are four key formats.

The most common remains *proscenium* where the interface between auditorium and stage is clearly defined by a traditional proscenium arch varying from an unstressed termination of walls and ceiling to a formalised frame. In many respects the proscenium stage is the most flexible form because the alternatives tend to be so individual that they can only accept productions which have been specifically planned for them. This makes the proscenium stage the most suitable one for touring. Although only the smaller proscenium theatres are really suitable for drama, this format is the one that can most readily handle musical theatre.

The point where the proscenium theatre becomes *endstage*, with the stage sharing the same room as the auditorium, is not sharply defined. Essentially it is a proscenium theatre without a proscenium and so in most cases will accept the same style of productions as a proscenium theatre. However, in larger theatres some form of proscenium arch, however unstressed, makes the complexities of technology easier to hide and to handle. Without a proscenium, some method has to be devised of focusing audience attention towards the acting area and away from lights, machinery, crew and waiting actors.

A stage may *thrust* partially into an auditorium so that the audience are seated within an arc of about 90 to 120 degrees or more deeply so that the seating is grouped on three sides, i.e. within an arc of 180 degrees. The more its stage thrusts into the auditorium, the more that theatre tends to have an individuality to which any touring company has to adapt. The production style of many smaller fringe companies makes it possible for them to make rapid adjustments to accommodate to a wide range of formats but, as the size and formality of a company increases, particularly the complexity of its scenery, such adaptations become difficult.

Ultimately the thrust is so deep that the stage is *surrounded* by audience. This is often called theatre-in-the-round, although it may be of any geometric shape. Such a stage is really rather individual and requires quite a lot of respacing of touring productions, even for the most flexibly minded fringe companies.

All these options can seat the audience in courtyard formation, including deep thrust as at the Stratford-upon-Avon Swan (p. 168) and surrounded as at the Richmond (Surrey) Orange Tree (p. 162).

A large population centre may have the resources to support, and the audience to fill, several theatres, each dedicated to the needs of specific areas of the performing arts. But how can a wide range of performance types be housed in communities which because of low population density or other resource restrictions are unable, or perhaps unwilling, to build on such a scale? Should we build positively in one format, with flexibility very limited so that there will be negligible compromise of that format? Or should we accept some limited compromise in order to provide limited flexibility? New technology has increased the possibility of the long desired multiform theatre. But is the capital cost justified? Or the running costs of maintaining the technological equipment and staffing the changeovers? Is the future a mix of alternative forms with very limited variations? Or total multiform flexibility? Only one thing seems reasonably certain: it is unlikely that theatre will ever again have such a standardised format as it had at the beginning of the twentieth century.

SHAKESPEARE'S GLOBE

A Reconstruction

Andrew Gurr

Monday 19 May [1975].
My first introduction to the great theatre at Epidaurus. I was overwhelmed by it. The whole day was unforgettable. It's exactly as if someone had said to me, 'The Globe has after all been preserved on the South Bank, come over and have a look at it, then you might understand something about staging Shakespeare'.

From John Goodwin ed., *Peter Hall's Diaries* (Hamish Hamilton, 1983)

The Growth of the Idea

The idea of reconstructing Shakespeare's own playhouse is not new. It began in the nineteenth century as scholars learned more about the original staging and as the reader's interest in Shakespeare on the page began to mingle with the theatregoer's interest in Shakespeare on the stage. Plans to rebuild the Globe on Bankside emerged with strong support in the 1890s. In 1900 William Poel proposed to petition the London County Council for a site on which a replica of the Globe might be constructed. After the Boer War ended in April 1902 a specific proposal was put to them. This imaginative scheme, developed out of Poel's experiments with staging Shakespeare in the 1890s, was first shipwrecked by building regulations and then became hopelessly entangled in the arguments over a national theatre, which some advocates wanted to be based on Shakespeare's original playhouse. There was still a lot of doubt about the shape of the building, and even more uncertainty about the precise location of the site (not properly determined until W. W. Braines fixed it in 1924), but enthusiasm was mounting.

The desire to build a replica of the Globe partly grew out of dissatisfaction over the limitations of the traditional nineteenth century theatre, with its fixed sets and proscenium arch. Traditional theatres and opera houses set plays in a 'picture frame' more suited to the eye than the ear, and took so long over scene-changing that much of the text had to be cut.

The 1930s was a vigorous decade for theatre scholars, when rebuilding the Globe at last began to seem an entirely practical possibility. John Cranford Adams, basing his calculations on evidence now discredited but which at the time seemed thoroughly plausible, stirred imaginations both in London and the USA. The Chicago World Fair of 1933–34 displayed a large model of the Globe at the centre of its promenade area, where it stirred the imagination of the young Sam Wanamaker. Replicas were actually built at San Diego; in Odessa, Texas; for Iden Payne's Festival in Ashland, Oregon; in Cleveland, Ohio; in Cedar City, Utah; and at the Folger Shakespeare Library in Washington DC. The number of playhouses is a measure of the mounting enthusiasm. They had varying pretensions to accuracy as reconstructions of Shakespeare's original playhouse, of course. None of them had the peculiar geographical advantage of Southwark. That lay with the plans of the Globe-Mermaid Association of England and America, which was formed in London in 1935.

In its way the Globe-Mermaid Association was a close precursor of the International Shakespeare Globe Centre. Its plan was to build a theatre, library and pub on the Bankside, on the site now occupied by Bankside Power Station. The complex was to comprise a replica of the Globe, a tavern to be called the Mermaid, designed with Tudor half-timbering, to recall the old legend of Jonson and the other poets drinking at the original Mermaid celebrated by Francis Beaumont in his famous poem, and a museum and library for Shakespeare studies.

There was much talk in 1951 before the Festival of Britain. That scheme came to nothing, partly because recent scholarly work had cast doubt on the Cranford Adams models and the scholars needed time to find a new consensus about the original shape. Not until 1970 under the energetic stimulus of Sam Wanamaker, who had been resident in Southwark since the 1950s, did the present scheme begin to seem feasible. In 1971 the first World Shakespeare Congress in Vancouver approved a proposal put by Glynne Wickham to support the project, and the work of gathering a scholarly consensus about the

Andrew Gurr is Professor of English at the University of Reading, and Director of the English Department's Renaissance Texts Research Centre. His publications include *The Shakespearean Stage, 1574–1642*, now in its third edition, *Playgoing in Shakespeare's London*, and editions of plays by Beaumont and Fletcher and by Shakespeare. He is on the Board of Directors of the International Shakespeare Globe Centre, and for the last fourteen years has served as principal scholarly adviser and chairman of the Academic Advisory Committee to the Shakespeare's Globe rebuilding project.

exact shape of a possible reconstruction began again.

The Globe Rebuilt

Given the fragile and fragmentary nature of much of the evidence about the Globe's original design, the reconstruction described here must necessarily be regarded as conjectural. Any reconstruction involves some elements of guesswork, and this scheme necessarily depends on quite a few guesses to fill gaps in our knowledge. It is an experiment. Without having tried to reconstruct the original shape we should know far less than we do at the present time about Shakespeare's Globe. The huge labour of turning the fragments of evidence into a full-scale, practical piece of architectural design has already revealed far more about the original design than any study of the fragments alone could have done. The final experiments can only begin once the Globe is available for staging plays in front of an audience willing to endure the Elizabethan audiences' discomforts.

The Globe reconstruction itself is first and foremost the centrepiece of a display of theatre history. Visitors to the complex will be able to follow three stories, each converging on the Globe playhouse from a different direction. The life of the city, the life of the player and the evolution of the playhouse in which the city enjoyed his plays are the three stories of the exhibition. Their meeting point is the reconstruction of the Globe itself.

Centrepiece though it is, the playhouse on its own is just a shell. It was built for playing, and to see the building without a play being performed in it is to have only a part of the full experience. The standard time for an Elizabethan performance to begin was about 2 p.m. by the sun and by Greenwich Mean Time. Under British Summer Time (from March to October) in London, through the season when the weather is most likely to make outdoor playgoing a pleasure, this means 3 p.m. A complete experience

Above: Model of the proposed development at Bankside, London, showing the Globe and Inigo Jones theatres and associated commercial properties. (*Photo: Andrew Fulgoni*)

Right: The Globe Theatre Under Construction (*Photos: Richard Kalina Photography*)

Left: View of the Globe development looking North East across the Thames, 1995.
(*Photo: Richard Kalina Photography*)

productions such as Jonson's 'Humours' plays, and performed kingly roles – including, so legend declares, the ghost in *Hamlet* – in his own plays. Shakespeare wrote, therefore, for a highly specific stage, a purpose-built machine, not for any theatre in the abstract nor for the printed page. Half of his plays never reached print until seven years after his death, and he never encouraged any of them into print in his lifetime, since printing the texts meant that other acting companies could make use of them. The Globe's stage was the sole means of publication he expected.

A play in performance is a dynamic event, the product of a huge complex of details, from the penetrating quality of an actor's voice to the hardness of the bench a spectator may be sitting on or the state of the weather. We need to know these details, the precise shape of the stage and the auditorium, the quality of the light, the effects on sound and vision of an open-air arena and a crowded auditorium, the interplay between actors performing on a platform in an open yard and the packed mass of thousands of spectators, many of them standing, all in broad daylight. None of these effects, each of which influences the others, can be gauged without a full-scale reconstruction.

The design for the rebuilt Globe is the product of many years of research, debate and calculation by hundreds of scholars. So far as we can tell, the Bankside reconstruction makes the best use of all the available evidence. It applies all the information we have about Tudor techniques of building design and timber work, the history of playhouse design as it evolved through the sixteenth century, as well as the hints in the plays themselves about the conditions they were written for.

The geographical location in Southwark of a rebuilt Globe is important in ways which became disconcertingly clear to its designers only when the design itself was under detailed consideration. That the Globe amphitheatre was open to the sky had

of the exhibition must conclude with a late afternoon performance at the Globe, where one must hope that British Summer Time lives up to its name. The plays staged there will mostly be Shakespeare's own, and they must be performed by actors who have themselves experimented with the alien conditions the Globe imposes on modern actors. They will offer continuous staging (no pause for act or scene breaks or interval), acting at high speed to an audience either sitting or standing in full view; and 'strong' acting to cope with the demands of open-air acoustics and an audience concentrating exclusively on the actors and their words, listening on their feet.

A new tradition of ensemble playing will have to develop to cope with the complex, novel and probably unforeseeable demands on acting in the Globe repertory. Much more will depend on the actors than on the staging or on any elaborately predetermined features of 'production'. It will certainly not be the now-standard 'director's theatre'.

Why Rebuild the Globe?

No playwright has ever had more intimate knowledge than Shakespeare of the playhouse for which he wrote his greatest plays. He helped to finance it and every working day he acted on its stage. As a 'sharer' in the company he performed in early Globe

Right:
The Georgian Theatre
Richmond, N. Yorkshire, 1788,
restored for the Georgian
Theatre (Richmond) Trust,
1963.
(Photo: Clive Barda)

Overleaf:
Interior of the Theater De
Maagd, Bergen-op-Zoom,
Netherlands, 1991.
Architects Onno Greiner
Martien van Goor.
For description see Catalogue
Part Three.
(Photo: Sybott Voeten, Breda)

been known for centuries, but the precise effect of sunlight on the performances only became an important question recently. The natural assumption for anyone to make, and especially for playgoers used to artificial light shining on the actors, was that London's reluctant and all-too-often invisible sun would have shone benignly down on the stage of the original Globe to light up its players through the daily performances between two and five in the afternoon. Only in 1979 was it realized that in fact the Elizabethan designers were careful to make sure the opposite happened. The original builders fixed the stage at a point inside the circle of the galleries so that it had its back, not its face, to the afternoon sun. The 'shadow' or 'heavens' over the stage which kept the rain off the players also protected them from direct sunlight. The Globe's stage was aligned precisely with its back to the midsummer solstice, so that only a diffuse and shadowed daylight could fill the stage. The gallery roof was high enough to keep the sun out of everyone's eyes, players and audience alike, except for the few unfortunates sitting in the topmost gallery opposite the stage in midwinter, when the low sun might reach them from behind the stage superstructure as the performance drew towards its close. Elizabethans did not like the sun. It gave pale London complexions a country look and it faded the bright colours on expensive clothes. The players evidently disliked sunlight as well for its effect on their complexions and their costumes. Probably too – one of the questions the reconstructed Globe will test – the plays needed indirect daylight as a uniform background in the absence of any mechanism for lighting effects, except at the few points where night scenes were signalled by bringing on burning torches or candles.

The physical location of the rebuilt Globe as close as possible to the original site is necessary to provide the original light and sound, vital elements in a daylight performance at an outdoor venue. But there are other elements nearly as vital and even less tangible which have to be considered. All the accuracy of a reconstruction of the physical environment for Shakespeare's plays is of little use without a reason-

ably accurate reconstruction of the conditions of performance, the complex interplay between what happens on the stage and the response in the auditorium. If this radical experiment of reconstructing Shakespearean performances of Shakespeare's plays is to work it needs actors who can abandon what they have been taught. They must learn from scratch the distinctive demands the Globe's peculiar construction lays on them. And, as much as actors, it needs audiences who can respond equally freshly to this strange way of experiencing the plays.

The educational and experimental roles of the project are dependent on the Globe itself, and involve both of the chief components in a Shakespearean performance: actors and audience. The rebuilt playhouse will be a laboratory for actors to rediscover the art of acting in front of large crowds crammed into a small space, many of them watching and listening while on their feet, unable to ignore the people around them. Hamlet's soliloquies, these days usually spoken into the darkness by a solitary figure lit by a single spotlight, emphatically alone, must sound different when spoken in broad daylight on a high platform surrounded by hundreds of entirely visible listeners, some of whose ears are only inches from Hamlet's feet. Modern audiences, too, accustomed to relaxing in soft armchairs in the dark where no twitch or grimace of reaction to what happens on stage can be seen, will need to learn new attitudes. The old music-hall tradition of comedians talking directly to the audience, and possibly even of audiences answering back and exchanging back-chat with the performer, would put modern playgoers much more into the old frame of mind if it was revived at the rebuilt Globe. For all that Hamlet objected to the clown speaking more than was set down for him, Elizabethan clowns were expected to engage in what a contemporary called 'interloquutions with the audients'. Modern playgoers can only adjust to daylight performances and the vigorous high-speed delivery of Elizabethan players by divorcing themselves from the traditional expectations we take with us to our 'sacred' Shakespeare, where the audience sits in reverent silence and dark-

ness, passive and withdrawn from the real activity of the interplay between the stage action and the responses required from the auditorium.

Modern re-creations of the Shakespearean kind of performance cannot be expected to replace or even seriously to alter the kind of performance offered by the Royal Shakespeare Company or the National Theatre, the new Globe's near neighbours. That tradition is too strong, too skilled and too distinctive to be directly affected by whatever these experiments in rediscovering Shakespeare may turn up. The effect on modern stagings of Shakespeare will be even more indirect. Modern audiences, like modern actors, are limited by a lifetime of training in a different kind of experience.

The modern audience cannot be expected to hear Shakespeare, his language altered almost out of recognition by four hundred years of word-shifts, with the same ease an Elizabethan audience enjoyed. That fact, along with the introduction of fixed scenery after 1660 and the growth in the eighteenth century of the custom of providing intervals for refreshments, explains why we take Shakespeare so much more slowly now. But Shakespeare and Shakespeare's language are now the most widely shared element in school courses in every country where English is used. Shakespeare, it can be argued, is as familiar in the world today as he was in London in 1600. Audiences who go to the rebuilt Globe on Bankside in the 1990s will go because they know Shakespeare, and want to know more. Knowing more, by recreating as much as we can of the conditions of the original staging, is the essential objective of the Globe project.

Adapted from Rebuilding Shakespeare's Globe *by Andrew Gurr with John Orrell, foreword by Sam Wanamaker* (Weidenfeld and Nicolson, 1989)

The foregoing chapter was written before the excavation, beginning in 1989, of the Rose playhouse (1587–1603). The Rose, situated close to the Globe, was a smaller house than the theatre used by Shakespeare's company, and somewhat unrepresentative of Elizabethan theatres generally. Conclusions drawn from the Rose excavation have nevertheless been incorporated where relevant into the re-building of the Globe. For a full discussion of the archaeological evidence, and conclusions to be drawn from it, see the third edition of Andrew Gurr's The Shakespearean Stage, 1574–1642 (Cambridge University Press, 1992), especially pp. 123–131. Recent archaeological work on the Globe itself has not substantially altered the views expressed in Gurr's chapter above. The rebuilt Globe is expected to host its first season of performances in 1996.

HEARING & SEEING OR VICE VERSA

Derek Sugden

Derek Sugden joined Ove Arup and Partners in 1953, after working for a contractor and consultant as a civil and structural engineer. He was made an Associate in 1956, a founder partner of Arup Associates in 1963, and chairman of the practice from 1984–87. He was founder principal of Arup Acoustics, to whom he became consultant on his retirement from Arup Associates in 1987. With Arup Associates he was partner responsible for a number of auditoria and buildings for music, including Snape Concert Hall, the Theatre Royal, Glasgow, and Buxton Opera House. His most recent work for Arup Associates was the new Glyndebourne Opera House. He is a visiting Professor at University College, London and the Bartlett School of Architecture and Planning, and a Visiting Critic at the University of Pennsylvania, School of Fine Arts, Department of Architecture. He is Chairman of the Building Centre Trust.

Theatre Acoustics

A theatre, as opposed to a concert hall, must be concerned with clarity of speech – 'intelligibility' as the acousticians erroneously call it, because we are talking about something which is first apprehended by the senses and not the intellect. The Greek and Roman amphitheatres are a good starting point. It was these auditoria that Vitruvius referred to in the first known written work concerning architectural acoustics. His description of the 'voice' in Chapter III (6–8) Book V of *The Ten Books on Architecture* (Dover, 1960) has not been surpassed:

> Voice is a flowing breath of air, perceptible to the hearing by contact. It moves in an endless number of circular rounds, like the innumerable increasing circular waves which appear when a stone is thrown into smooth water, and which keep on spreading indefinitely from the centre unless interrupted by narrow limits, or by some obstruction which prevents such waves from reaching their end in due formation. When they are interrupted by obstructions the first waves, flowing back, break up the formation of those which follow.
>
> In the same manner the voice executes its movements in concentric circles; but while in the case of water the circles move horizontally on a plane surface, the voice not only proceeds horizontally but also ascends vertically by regular stages. Therefore as in the case of the waves formed in water, so it is in the case of the voice: the first wave when there is no obstruction to interrupt it does not break up the second or the following waves, but they all reach the ears of the lowest and highest spectators without an echo.
>
> Hence the ancient architects, following in the footsteps of nature, perfected the ascending rows of seats in theatres from their investigations of the ascending voice, and by means of the canonical theory of the mathematicians and that of the musicians endeavoured to make every voice uttered on the stage come with greater cleanness and sweetness to the ears of the audience. For just as musical instruments are brought to perfection of cleanness in the sound of their strings by means of bronze plates or horn echeia, so the ancients devised methods of increasing the power of the voice in theatres through the application of harmonics.

We must, however, be aware of the seductive prose of Professor Hickey Morgan's translation. It has been responsible for many acoustic myths about 'the perfect acoustics' of the classical amphitheatre. Voices and sound waves descend as well as ascend, and there is no evidence whatsoever of the 'canonical theories of the mathematicians' or of the ancients devising 'methods of increasing the power of the voice in theatres through the application of harmonics'.

Following Vitruvius, scientific interest in acoustics revived only with the Renaissance. In 1650, Athanasius Kircher, better known as the inventor of the magic lantern, discussed the problem of the sound mirror and the associated problem of the whispering gallery. The speed of sound was measured by Martin Mersenne in the early seventeenth century with only a 2.7 per cent error. Galileo mentions the laws of vibrations in his 'Discourse' and Otto von Guericke demonstrated in 1672 that sound, unlike light, cannot travel in a vacuum. After the relation between pitch and frequency had been established – and here again the first work was by Galileo and Mersenne – many people, beginning with F. Savant (1791–1841), were concerned with establishing the frequency of audibility. George Ohm, the author of the famous law of electric currents, put forward a law of audition, according to which all musical tones arise from simple harmonic vibrations of definite frequency and the particular quality of musical sounds is due to combinations of simpler tones of commensurable frequencies. He held, moreover, that the ear is able to analyse any complex note into the set of simple tones, in terms of which it may be expanded mathematically by means of Fourier's theorem. This discovery, or proposition, stimulated a host of researches in physiological acoustics.

The greatest of these was the work of Hermann Helmholz (1821–94), whose treatise *Sensations of Tone* (*Die Lehre von den Tonempfindungen als Physiologische Grundlage für die Theorie der Musik*), published in 1862 (Dover, 1954), ranks as one of the greatest masterpieces of acoustics. Here he gave the first elaborate theory of the mechanism of the ear, the so-called resonance theory, and was able to justify theoretically the law of Ohm. In the course of his investigations he invented the resonator, now so well known by his name and employed in modern acoustics for many applications. It was the work of Helmholz which stimulated Lord Rayleigh's first work in acoustics, which was a paper concerned with the pitch of resonators and finally led to the classic two volume work *The Theory of Sound* (Dover, 1954) published 1877.

From the eighteenth century onwards, in addition to the work of the scientists, many composers, musicians and architects became interested in the subject. The violinist Tartini and the composer Rameau were both interested in harmonics and the reason for the frequency interval between them. Since the reception of sound by the ear in enclosed spaces like rooms and auditoria is a common experience, it was natural that some attention should be paid to harmonics in the design of these spaces. The first discussion of improving hearing in rooms was limited to purely geometrical considerations such as the installation of sounding boards and reflectors.

In 1858, a Boston physician, J.B. Upham, wrote several papers indicating a much clearer grasp of the more important matter involved, namely the reverberation or multiple reflection of the sound from all the surfaces of the room. In 1856, Joseph Henry, the celebrated American physicist, who became the first secretary of the Smithsonian Institution, made a study of auditorium acoustics. In spite of this work, the subject was generally neglected by architects. There were and still are gross misunderstandings of the nature of the problem, and attempts were often made to correct acute acoustical defects by such inadequate if not absurd devices as stringing wires across the offending space.

In 1895 Wallace Clement Sabine, an assistant professor at Harvard University, was instructed by President Eliot to propose changes for remedying the acoustical difficulties in the lecture room of the Fogg Art Museum, a building which had just been completed in Cambridge Massachusetts. It is now known as Hunt Hall. His colleagues looked upon his new assignment as a grim joke and his senior professor warned him that he was 'undertaking a problem that fairly bristles with difficulties, the extreme complexity of which seems to indicate that a complete solution is hopeless'. About two years were spent in experimenting on this room, and after a further three years of research Sabine gave acoustics the classical reverberation equation.

Room Acoustics

The history of the application of mathematics to the analysis of a sound field in an enclosed room is less than 100 years old. It is only 95 years since the building of the present Boston Symphony Hall, the first auditorium to have the benefit of acoustic guidance and analysis by Wallace Clement Sabine himself. It is still rated amongst the few great concert halls in the world (*see* illustration below).

Since Sabine's work at the turn of the century, the learned papers and books have come thick and fast, but where room acoustics are concerned most acousticians have become either famous or notorious because of their work in the concert hall rather than the theatre. The first paper I know of concerning itself exclusively with theatre acoustics is again by Sabine, Chapter 7 in his *Collected Papers on Acoustics* (Cambridge [USA] and London, 1922). The paper is introduced by a quotation from Vitruvius and quite rightly gives more precise modern definitions than the normal translations from the Latin. Later in the paper his explanation of the limited range of the spoken voice compared with music explains why acousticians have not had as much concern for the theatre as for the concert hall. He even draws comparison, when considering the spoken voice, with the 'highly developed science of telephony', where at that time it was apparently sufficient for much of the work to adapt the theory and design to the single frequency of 800Hz, approximately A in the second octave above middle C. He did add, however, that for some problems investigation must be carried out over a considerable range of pitch and that it was 'therefore necessary to determine the reverberation even for the speaking voice, not for a single pitch, but for a considerable range, and the quality of a theatre with respect to reverberation will be represented by a curve in which the reverberation is plotted against pitch'.

The open amphitheatres of the classical world have long fascinated the architect and acoustician and are brilliantly analysed and described in Lothar Cremer's paper 'Different Distributions of the Audience' (Applied Science Publishers, 1975), which also deals with the European Baroque Theatre and Op-

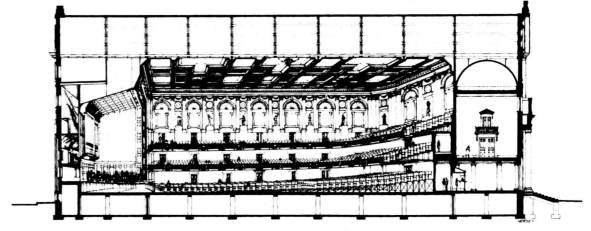

Drawing of the Boston Symphony Hall, USA. (*International Federation for Theatre Research*)

era House and the seating pattern of the 'shoe-box' concert hall of the nineteenth century. Following this important paper, given in 1974, the Institute of Acoustics held a one-day symposium on Theatre Acoustics in February 1978 (contributed papers, meeting no. 14). Papers were given by many acousticians on both general principles and particular auditoria. Richard Cowell in his opening paper quite rightly called for low background noise levels particularly from mechanical plant (and may I add lighting?); for methods of dealing with thrust and open stages, for further study of the role of electro-acoustics in theatre design; for the setting of acoustic parameters for multi-purpose halls; and, most important, for the development of ways of providing effective advice to architects and design teams by the use of models and feedback from existing theatres. Apart from papers on the acoustic design of specific auditoria, (and here I would particularly mention Dr Fahy's paper on Eden Court, one of our most interesting post-war theatres), there were four papers concerned with speech 'intelligibility' and research into theatre acoustics (Papers by N. Bowman, H.G. Latham, G. Andreas, and M. Barron). A paper by the late Geoff Berry on the Alfred Beck Centre described the performance of an 'assisted resonance' system in a multi-purpose auditorium.

One of the more recent books which does include a chapter on theatres is the late Vilhelm Lassen Jordan's *Acoustical Design of Concert Halls and Theatres* (Applied Science Publishers, 1980). Chapter 5 describes Jordan's design and analytical work on the New York State Theatre, the Metropolitan Opera House of New York, the Ruhen Dario Theatre of Nicaragua and the National Theatre of Guatemala. He begins by stating that it has often been proclaimed that the classical horseshoe theatre shape has specific acoustical virtues, although there are quite a few examples of classical theatre auditoria which have been criticised for built-in acoustical defects. He also warns about the question of size. A horseshoe theatre seating 1,500 is quite different from a theatre with 2,800 seats. The time delay of the first ceiling reflections alone can increase from 50–70

milliseconds to 100–120 milliseconds, which will affect articulation considerably. He also considers the use of models as a design check and the measurement of EDT (early decay time) and 'steepness'. This book, one of the few on acoustic design of auditoria by a practising acoustician, is eminently readable by architects and those concerned with the technical aspects of theatre design.

In the last ten to fifteen years the use of computer programs based on ray analysis, and on the use of 1:50 scale models which are excited by a spark, have developed to a very sophisticated degree. Computer model analysis based on acoustic ray programs is particularly effective for middle and high frequencies in auditoria where the geometry is generated with straight lines. Real model analysis is essential for auditoria based on curved geometry, and is to be recommended for all important large auditoria which rely for their success on excellent natural acoustics.

The Major Use for an auditorium
Since Sabine developed his equation for the calculation of reverberation time published in *The American Architect* (vol. xiv) in 1990, there have been enormous developments, and complexities abound in the study of room acoustics. The myths are still with us and in some places are probably reinforced by the professional acousticians. Acoustics is still considered a pseudo-science in many circles and is still a happy hunting ground for charlatans, but probably no more so than many more highly organised professions. Despite the current complexities, it is still important to define the major use for an auditorium and to be very discriminating in our choice and calculation of reverberation time for particular uses, *pace* Sabine, Parkin and Jordan.

The domination of virtually every aspect of our society by the 'commissars', however, has turned every new theatre into a 'multi-purpose auditorium', which has to deal with everything from wrestling and mayoral banquets to string quartets and heavy rock. These new auditoria, designed by accountants rather than by architects, tend to be large, especially

those in North America, the birthplace of the multi-purpose auditorium. They rely on sound reinforcement systems for practically all forms of entertainment, although in opera and drama their promoters are careful to use the euphemism 'enhancement' to ease their Protestant conscience. The use of electronic hardware by the pop and rock world has given the whole sound reinforcement industry regular shots in the arm, so that even an after dinner speech in a small room requires the use of some appallingly designed sound reinforcement system, obligatory to ensure that the speech is loud enough, but mercifully unintelligible.

Back in the 1960s, Professor Peter Parkin, who had been designing sound reinforcement systems and column speakers in some of our cathedrals in such a way as to ensure that the Word of God could be heard and not just made louder, turned his attention to the problem of raising reverberation time in the Royal Festival Hall. His invention, assisted resonance, was finally installed and commissioned under his personal supervision in 1964, and has been accepted by audience and musicians alike as a practical improvement and also acceptable at an artistic and aesthetic level. (*See*, for example, P.H. Parkin ‘"Assisted Resonance" in the Royal Festival Hall, London: 1965–69', BRS Current Papers, 17/71.)

Although the professional actor will quite rightly insist first on the right sort of auditorium – which also means the right size of auditorium, where he can speak with no further aid than a geometry and construction which ensures excellent and natural acoustics – the large auditorium is probably here to stay. If it is, can we now look forward to subtly designed systems which enhance the voice and increase articulation, and at the same time have sufficient potential to create a good acoustic for the lyric theatre? We may on the other hand eschew all electronic devices and pursue an acoustic somewhat more reverberant than the usual drama theatre, but with the geometry and materials so carefully chosen that the spoken voice is heard as Vitruvius describes it in the amphitheatres of the classical world.

OPERA – NOT OPERA-HOUSES
In the Theatrical Vanguard
Tom Sutcliffe

The most basic account of theatre applies equally to opera. Theatre is a meant and revealing event targeted on the attention and understanding of an audience. It can only have consequence through the involvement of its audience in what is being done by the artists (including actors, designers, musicians, dancers, singers) who are its agents. So the assisting presence of those audience members is essential. Their interpretative reaction to what they take the event to mean, the pleasure they have in it, the stretching imaginative discoveries it provides, are the whole point. Live performances always vary. What a member of the audience misses is gone for ever.

Yet this phenomenon – no less elusive and ephemeral than a change in the weather – provides a potential conversion experience that can be permanently transforming and memorable for audience members. And, because of the way music argues among the very roots of emotion and belief – underpinning the dramatic, politically fraught, narrative context common to all music-theatre – the powerful kind of reaction that the theatrical experience invites is at its most acute in opera.

Historically, the concept of opera-house as distinct from theatre reflects practical considerations. Because opera requires a larger army of performers and auxiliaries than any other kind of theatre with a wider range of specialisations, because it is therefore the costliest performing art, because great singers can, unamplified, affect an audience of thousands, opera promoters have always tended to maximise their scale of operations. Opera-houses are mammoth for the same reason as airport terminals. It is no accident that New York's Metropolitan is the largest purpose-built opera-house in the world. Its size enables it to be popular and democratic, and thereby attractive to sponsors and efficient at raising money from ticket-sales.

The main shared characteristic of specialist opera-houses in Europe and America has been an acoustic moist enough to suit orchestral music and singing, and foyers and seating arrangements sufficiently comfortable to satisfy patrons of various socio-economic levels. Germany has many purpose-built opera-houses because its 18th and 19th century political structure – as a patchwork of kingdoms, princedoms, duchies and Hanseatic or episcopal territories – provided a heritage of cultural plant. Italy is similarly blessed, though many of its old (and often small) opera-houses no longer function. In Britain the post-war novelty of an acquired national taste for opera (and a developing tradition of new operas especially by Benjamin Britten and, in due course, truly distinctive interpretative skills to go with them) has had to adapt to a context of sufficiently large theatres which had not been designed expressly for opera but were adequately suited to it – acoustically and in terms of the tightly focused relationship between the listening, looking audience and a comparatively intimate and proximate stage.

Neither a huge audience nor complicated stage machinery is an essential element of the operatic art. In recent years in Britain opera has been staged successfully on the largest and on the smallest scale. There has been *Carmen* in the round at Earls Court for an audience of up to 8000, directed by Steven Pimlott and designed by Stefanos Lazaridis – with hundreds of extras, horses, dogs, musical interpolations, and special Spanish dancers as well as a smugglers' procession descending from the roof on a rope walkway like an element in the Royal Tournament military displays that annually occupy this exhibition hall. At the Almeida Theatre (p. 178) with capacity for 350 there have been Gerald Barry's *The Intelligence Park* directed by David Fielding, designed

Tom Sutcliffe was a professional countertenor and early music specialist after graduating from Oxford in 1963. He made his opera debut in Darmstadt as Ottone in Monteverdi's *L'incoronazione di Poppea* in 1970, and worked with Nikolaus Harnoncourt. He edited *Music and Musicians* magazine before joining The Guardian newspaper where he has become widely known as opera critic. He is a columnist for *Opera News* in New York, a regular broadcaster on radio and television, a contributor to *Classic CD, Opern Welt* etc. His monumental description and explanation of recent controversies about the theatrical interpretation of opera, *The Staging of Opera, is* complete and should be published in London in early 1996.

by Bettina Munzer, and Stephen Oliver's *Mario and the Magician* directed by Tim Hopkins, designed by Nigel Lowery (to name but two novelties there) – both with chamber orchestras and moderate-sized companies and sets that 'interpreted' the new operas they were accompanying, rather than simply providing a 'realistic' context for their narratives.

Opera has been performed in various public halls and sports centres – such as the Stockland Green and Cocks Moor Wood leisure centres in Birmingham, and the International Racquet Centre in Telford – by the City of Birmingham Touring Opera (Director: Graham Vick) setting up special ramps of temporary seating for audiences and using small-scale stage sets that needed none of the normal stage machinery, but containing in themselves whatever mechanical gadgets for scene changes they required. CBTO performed a version of *The Ring* abridged to two evenings with barely 20 instruments using an adapted and reorchestrated accompaniment. Other works in the CBTO repertoire staged by Graham Vick and designed by Paul Brown have included *Falstaff, The Magic Flute,* Rameau's *Les Boréades* and Ravi Shankar's *Ghanashyam.* The last work was specifically intended to cross the divide between the conventional 'opera' audience (predominantly white and middle class) and the large Asian population where CBTO has its home base. Opera has also been performed (by Opera Factory) in concert halls like the Queen Elizabeth Hall with the orchestra on stage to the left or right of the performers. A superlative interpretation of *Cosi fan tutte* (in English) was directed by Opera Factory's founder David Freeman and designed by David Roger, as a modern-dress alfresco seaside tale – as it were Alan Ayckbourn on Bondi beach, Sydney, Australia where Freeman himself originated. And opera has been done in so-called semi-staged versions at the BBC's Albert Hall summer promenade concerts with action and acting, but almost no setting or costumes: Glyndebourne productions and casts being adapted to Spartan circumstance with almost no loss of dramatic intensity and meaning. At full capacity Albert Hall audiences can be as large as 8000.

Meanwhile in Britain opera has continued to be experienced by substantial audiences at lyric theatres adapted for touring in the main provincial centres – in Glasgow at the Theatre Royal, in Sheffield at the Lyceum, in Belfast at Frank Matcham's delightful and perfect small Opera House, at the Theatre Royal, Plymouth (pp. 144, 148, 146, 124), and at Southampton, Bristol, Liverpool, Nottingham, Newcastle, Oxford, Birmingham, and Manchester. These theatres were originally (in most cases) built to receive tours of revue and musical comedy, seating from 1100 to 2000. The new Festival Theatre in Edinburgh is one of the best adapted of all such theatres, providing for thrilling focus in acoustically grand circumstances with comfortable accessible modern, purpose-built glass foyers (pp. 96, 152). Used for opera by Britain's touring provincial companies, any lack of star vocal quality has often been answered by a focused theatrical excitement in the style and excellence of production. No British opera company has had a monopoly of experiment: all have drawn on youthful modern adventurous talents without fear of controversy, so that opera has been in the vanguard of theatrical discovery, benefiting from the path beaten by Felsenstein in East Berlin, Strehler in Milan, and Peter Brook at Covent Garden in 1948 and 1949 and years later (1981) in Paris. British directors like Tim Albery, Richard Jones, Nicholas Hytner, Graham Vick, Steven Pimlott, David Pountney, are becoming famous world-wide – in company with American directors David Alden and Peter Sellars who have found second homes in Britain. A whole new generation of designers exploiting the insularity and independence of Britain to create a different autonomous tradition have grown up to accompany the new opportunities: names like Stefanos Lazaridis, David Fielding, Nigel Lowery, Richard Hudson, Tom Cairns, Antony McDonald.

Opera has also been done in new smallscale theatres accommodating up to 500 seats by Opera 80 (now renamed English Touring Opera) with a chamber-scale orchestra of around 24 players. This company was fostered scrupulously by the British Arts Council through thick and thin, and takes opera on the widest circuit to venues previously served if at all only by piano-accompanied tours. Not that there has been anything lacking in piano accompanied work by Scottish Opera-Go-Round, for example, which presented a remarkable *Macbeth* staged by Richard Jones with Nigel Lowery's designs, and an equally powerful *Jenufa* by Matthew Richardson designed by Ashley Martin-Davies on even more economical operatic terms. In fact Opera 80 presented one of the most memorable and controversial opera productions of the 1980s, *Don Giovanni* staged by Steven Pimlott with designs by Tom Cairns, which led to the ousting of the company's visionary young music director, David Parry. Most of these smaller-scale theatres (like the Sherman in Cardiff and the Octagon in Yeovil) have their audience seating arranged on a straight ramp, on what was considered the democratic principle where every audience member had 'perfect sightlines'. The small scale of these often feeble theatres allows everybody in the audience to be reasonably near the performance. But the most recently built operahouse in Britain – at Glyndebourne (p. 128) – adopted a traditional horse-shoe-shaped auditorium with many seats near the proscenium on three tiers giving an extremely limited view of the stage. The success of the new Glyndebourne lies in its intimacy, the fact that a horse-shoe shape can accommodate a 50 per cent increase in audience capacity and a huge increase in the volume of the auditorium while bringing the cheapest seats a lot nearer the stage than they had been in the former barn-like acoustically dry and disappointing Glyndebourne operahouse. It was typically ironical that Glyndebourne should have built a ducal style of theatre, to bring a modestly substantial audience together in a pleasing social environment, most of them with excellent sightlines, and all experiencing superb acoustics in which small-voiced singers need have nothing to fear. Glyndebourne's teething problems, compared with the Bastille Opera's, are minor. Glyndebourne is a perfect solution to the question its owner and its patrons asked about the nature of the occasion and the nature of the art – unlike the

Sydney Opera House, where the opera theatre has completely inadequate wingspace and many seats at such distance from the stage with such poor acoustics for voices that audiences can only divine what's happening by reading the surtitles (even in English-language operas). The town with the most famous and archi-tecturally memorable 'opera house' in the world actually now needs to build a proper opera theatre.

Historically speaking, the 'perfect' opera-house is generally accepted as being Wagner's predominantly wooden 1800-seat construction at Bayreuth, half as large again in capacity as Glyndebourne with the seating ranged on a single quasi-amphitheatrical tier of slightly bowed lines. Yet most of the recently-built new opera-houses have taken a different line and misunderstood the virtues of Bayreuth. They have provided neither ideal acoustics nor desirable proximity to the performers (though Bayreuth's house is admittedly on an epic scale). Backstage facilities such as the vast revolve stage of the Frankfurt Opera, with its diameter three times as wide as the proscenium opening – so that transformations using the revolve pass across the proscenium rather than pirouetting on it – have enabled some directors and designers to realise extraordinary concepts, significant and telling in interpretative terms. There was a whole Carthage cityscape in Ruth Berghaus's famous staging of *The Trojans* for instance. Yet the theatrical imagination is never constrained by facilities. It must always aim to expand the audience's mind rather than the mere physical walls of the theatre. What matters about interpretation in the theatre is, finally, always being realised in the mind of the audience.

Inevitably opera with its necessary extravagance of resources and objectives is fraught with contradictions. Its Florentine pioneers at the turn of the 17th century were thinking of a neoclassical revival of classical Greek theatre, which had used vast amphitheatres and engaged entire societies. Yet they proceeded to operate on an intimate scale in princely courts. The ancient Greek stage had been as little concerned with illusion and spectacle as Shakespeare's theatre was. But spectacular opera became,

very early in the history of the operatic art, a subject of raging controversy. An art committed to the artificiality of sung conversation (and the even greater artificiality of castrated men adopting heroic roles) soon found itself awash with debate about the need for realism in the representation of, for instance, sea battles.

After a long period with comparatively few new sources of operatic masterpieces, the critical issue in opera at the dawn of the 21st century has become how to release the submerged meaning and present day relevance of the classic repertoire. In opera what is in effect an international pantheon of operatic masterworks has grown up in a comparatively short time, since the founding aristocratic Florentine experiments contemporaneous with Shakespeare. The histories of opera and modern theatre are in fact coterminous. How far is it necessary for performance to be dominated by the needs of simple narrative realism? How far should operatic interpretation, freed to experiment above all by its nature as a kind of musical debate, benefit from a theatrical equivalent of the cinematic editing and montage readily accepted and understood by television and film audiences – in other words with eclectic associative stimuli to the imagination. How much should *Gesamtkunstwerk* (Wagner's total art work, his concept of the operatic art) insist on technical resources, complicated stage machinery for elaborate realisations of a designer's dreams which often are based in the folk memory of 20th-century surrealist painting, to create its morally provocative world? What is the ideal way of presenting opera's combination of visual, dramatic, musical and metaphysical elements to audiences?

Since the theatrical experiments of Godwin and Herkomer in the late 19th century, and the theoretical debate led off by Edward Gordon Craig and Adolphe Appia, the nature of theatrical and operatic interpretation and its purpose have been in question. Ironically opera – being the most socially and politically reactionary of the theatre arts – has invited the most radical revolution during the last 20 years. What has been happening to opera on stage,

and to the idea of what kind of audience and what kind of event it should stimulate, has owed little to the varied theatre spaces in which opera has been performed. Simply, the demands of opera on its audience's commitment and imaginative attention are greater than ever. It has something to offer everybody (as cinema has) and is not just elitist – however complex. There is now an awareness that an ideal opera stage, once the needs of accompanying instruments are met, needs only a slightly different acoustic from, but very similar intimacy to, an ordinary 'spoken theatre' stage. In the work of designer Axel Manthey and director Ruth Berghaus (formerly of the Berliner Ensemble), in the very occasional operatic outings of Patrice Chéreau and his designer Richard Peduzzi since their revolutionary 1976 centenary *Ring* at Bayreuth, just as in the work of the British young operatic turks at the English National Opera and elsewhere, the possibilities of opera have been explored in a revelatory fashion. Of course such superbly competent and fascinating artists can be equally at home on an epic scale. But this new kind of theatrically attentive operatic work demands a degree of intimacy – physical, mental and emotional.

Glyndebourne is, by international standards, an extremely small opera-house. But if opera is properly to mobilise orchestras, fine acting, free-throated and technically adept singing, and really profound and visually imaginative productions in front of a properly versed and engaged audience (which must to an extent, no doubt, be a self-selecting and elitist phenomenon) it needs to operate on a modest scale and be wary of attractive short-cuts like surtitles – however instantly gratifying those new aids may be for a certain kind of literary understanding by audiences of the operatic text they are encountering (so rarely their own vernacular in Britain, America, Belgium and Holland).

Opera is a shared yet elusive and mysterious narrative form, a kind of neoreligious humane propaganda medium. Its shrines, a myriad of theatrical spaces of different shapes and priorities, need to guard their subtlety and their miraculous imaginative worlds.

THEATRES FOR DANCERS AND THEIR AUDIENCES

Peter Brinson and Frank Woods

Peter Brinson who died in 1995 was founder/director of the Royal Ballet's *Ballet for All* company before becoming director of the Gulbenkian Foundation's UK branch. This brought many innovations to British dance in the 1970's and 1980's. The recipient of honorary degrees and two national awards for services to dance, he was the author of many books and influential dance studies. In the years before his death he was helping to establish a national service for dancers' health and injuries.

Now is a hopeful moment for Britain's dance theatres. In the golden autumn of 1994 the Arts Council of England published Mark Foley's *Dance Spaces*. Edited by Fiona Dick, it hit the target of dance needs. The National Lottery's Millennium Fund, with other lotteries money, is dedicated likewise to spaces for the arts. Of all the arts, dance needs space.

'Space', argues Lord Gowrie in his introduction to Foley's book, 'is the fundamental requirement for all dance. Yet our dancers frequently have to make do with spaces which are cramped, stages which are too hard and conditions which fall far short of the best … To be unable to see the dancers' feet or patterns created on the floor is like seeing only half the picture. Artists and audiences alike deserve the best possible spaces for the creation, rehearsal and performance of dance'.

These comments by the chairman of the Arts Council of England reflect the low status of dance in British history. Through literature, drama, music, architecture and the fine arts, rather than dance, the British have expressed their history and their feelings about the world. Very few theatres, therefore, have been designed in Britain specifically with dance in mind.

In France, the Paris Opera and Lyons Opera, in Holland the Netherlands Dance Theatre, in Russia the Bolshoi and Mariinski Theatres, in Italy La Scala Milan, in Sweden the Drottningholm Court Theatre near Stockholm, in Denmark The Royal Theatre were designed with dance in mind. True, the buildings are for lyric theatre not for dance alone. Almost always dance has had to share its space with opera. But the space for dance is there in the lyric theatres of Europe.

In London only the Royal Ballet at Covent Garden has a stage purpose-suited to dance. Drury Lane Theatre seems promised for ever to music theatre. And why not? On a smaller scale the Place Theatre near Euston Station in central London was created for dance, as was the Bonnie Bird Theatre across the Thames in south-east London. Other similar stages throughout Britain can present small dance companies. For major dance productions outside London, the Birmingham Hippodrome is now home to Birmingham Royal Ballet and there are similar large dance spaces in half a dozen other cities. This is not enough to allow most British citizens to see the dance their taxes have subsidised. In London itself no nationalised Dance House yet exists. It is a disgrace that the capital city of the United Kingdom cannot present major dance companies from Britain and abroad for lack of appropriate dance theatres. This is why today's opportunities are uniquely important.

Two examples illustrate the opportunities. One is new, the other a conversion of what already exists. Chester in Concert, now being created, counts on Millennium funds from the National Lottery. Sadler's Wells counts on the Millennium Fund and other money. Chester, an administrative centre for England's northwest, is a social mixture of garrison town, bishopric, local government centre and communications hub for Britain's northwestern region. Roman, Medieval, Tudor, Georgian and Victorian architecture reflect this history. Yet it has never possessed a significant theatre nor artistic tradition to nourish the people of its predominantly rural area.

Chester in Concert attempts to end this isolation. It is a visionary scheme to apply today's philosophy that the arts are the focus of any large community. Therefore, it proposes a 1600 seat auditorium with surrounding smaller arts venues to bring all the arts, not just some of them, to enrich the quality of life,

Frank Woods is an architect with experience and continuing interest in the design of performance spaces. Architect to Sadlers Wells Theatre from 1982 until November 1991 for the Lilian Baylis Community Theatre, he also produced the feasibility plans for the renovation and stage improvements to the main house. He has written and broadcast on the subjects of dance and theatre. He worked on the original designs for the Barbican Arts and Conference Centre and for the Music Hall at the Guildhall School of Music and Drama.

Drottningholm Court Theatre, Denmark.

economy and artistic opportunities of the people in and around Chester. Motivating this conception, and giving it a uniqueness rare in large-scale ventures, is the notion that an educational role should be as important as the performing and creative roles. This education in every kind of art will not be confined to the building. It will reach out into the villages and towns of Cheshire to enrich leisure and win families and individuals to enjoy the arts.

The centrepiece is a glass-roofed revolving auditorium designed by the architect Terry Farrell (*see below, right*). This can be turned in 20 minutes to face a stage at one end or a concert platform at the other end. The stage can accommodate the largest dance productions. The complex as a whole includes also a 300 seat studio theatre, and a 600–700 seat auditorium for Chester's existing Gateway Theatre, a film theatre and rehearsal, production, dressing room, education and conference space.

Older by two and a half centuries is Sadler's Wells Theatre in the London borough of Islington, north of the Thames. It was used first as a theatre in 1753, becoming a fashionable resort for the waters of its wells and the quality of its entertainment. Over the years its stage was made famous by the actors Edmund Kean and Samuel Phelps with their productions, the great clown Grimaldi and, towards the end of the nineteenth century, many music hall artists.

Reopened by Lilian Baylis in 1931, the theatre be-

came an early home of what are now the Royal Ballet and English National Opera. Today it is the only theatre in London to present annual seasons of opera, ballet and drama. Always, though, its 19th century stage has proved too small for major presentations of lyric theatre. If the theatre is to survive for the twenty-first century it must enlarge its dancing space.

Designed by Matcham & Co and re-built in the early 30's to a utility budget, the resultant theatre is little more than a basic cinema design. Gielgud admirably summed it up when he commented at the time, 'How we all detested Sadler's Wells when it opened first. The auditorium looked like a denuded wedding-cake, and the acoustics were dreadful'. *Plus ça change…* ! It says much for the theatre managements' dogged perseverance over the years that it has survived for so long. This is almost wholly due to their policy of acting as a receiving house for visiting ballet companies, as well as being the original home of the Sadler's Wells Royal Ballet. It has played an illustrious role in the history of ballet and dance in the UK but it has to be seriously questioned as to how long it can continue unless something radical happens. Given that it cannot be moved lock, stock and barrel to a more central West-end site (which is the ideal strategy) then it must, with great urgency, attend to its inadequate stage and back stage facilities and to improving front of house for its devoted and long suffering audiences.

During most of the eighties, one of the authors of this article spent over eight years developing proposals not only for such radical improvements to the main house (p. 48) but also to the design and development of the community theatre in Arlington Way, now known as the Lilian Baylis Theatre. This had to be shoe horned into the site behind a collapsing Georgian façade, which had to be replicated or echoed in the new design for Town Planning reasons. The budget for such an exercise was inevitably restricted – so much so that the work on the rehearsal space above has never been completed. This space was carefully developed and related to the size of the main house stage, assuming that this

was to be enlarged as had been already planned. The accompanying illustration shows the relationship between the two spaces.

The recent publication of the latest proposals – by a newly appointed architect – replicate the eighties design proposals and all ballet and dance lovers can only fervently hope that this old theatre can be revitalised (p. 49).

The urgent need for London and the Nation to have its own, well endowed, Dance House is recognised worldwide by all those involved in dance. What is less easy to resolve is what is actually needed and where it should be sited. The proposed complex in Chester, described earlier in this article, has to be recognised as the right solution. Just as the Royal National Theatre is not one theatre but three, so the Dance House needs to have facilities to cater for the myriad forms of dance and audience. A large company on the wrong sized stage will not work, as Sadler's Wells has shown so often, any more than it makes any kind of sense to put a small group on an overlarge stage with a sparsely populated audience in a vast auditorium. There is need for both the chamber ensemble and the symphony orchestra.

Whilst it is true that a major 1500 seat dance house with an appropriate stage is urgently needed in the

Chester in Concert: A 1600 seat theatre and concert venue planned for the year 2000. The complex will incorporate Chester Gateway Theatre. Terry Farrell's design incorporates a circular revolving auditorium which will change in under 30 minutes, allowing rapid turn round of facilities and simultaneous performances and conferences. (*Photo: Nigel Young*)

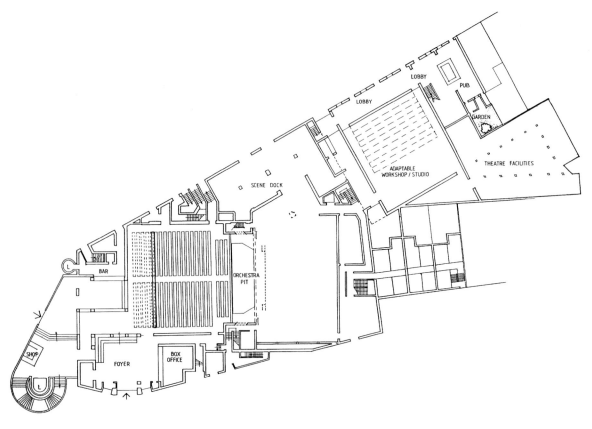

south east of the UK, it is also true that it needs the support of smaller spaces as well. What would make the best sense would be to develop a complex of say three spaces, (as at the National Theatre) linked to a national network of other dance spaces around the country. After all, the Royal Shakespeare Company works well in its several theatres in various locations. To concentrate all the resources and facilities in one location would be to rob so many of the nation's dance audiences of the opportunity to see world class companies perform. If such a network could be developed, then the existing important dance spaces in London such as The Space, the Riverside, the Bonnie Bird Theatre and Sadler's Wells would all fit into the total dance fabric of the nation. This fully developed network of venues would offer companies who tour, particularly those from other countries, the comfort of knowing that a certain standard of performance space would be guaranteed.

Many fear that the Millennium Fund prospects carry with them the risk of developing a series of white elephants with inadequate funding in place to run them. There needs to be dialogue and discussion between all those truly caring about the provisions for dance in this country, in order that some cohesion and good sense can be brought to bear; an overall strategy could then make proper use of these exciting possibilities.

The first ballets in Italian and French courts 500 years ago were created to tell stories explained in poetry, displayed in costumes and made wonderful by elaborate scenery. The space was so arranged that its perspective benefited especially the principal spectator, usually a king or royal guest for whose pleasure the ballet was created. This can be seen still at Drottningholm Court Theatre beside the summer palace of the Swedish Kings near Stockholm (p. 47).

Opened in 1700, the theatre was abandoned after the assassination in 1792 of its principal benefactor, the founder of Sweden's Royal Dramatic Theatre and Opera, King Gustaf III. Opera then included ballet, so the stage at 19 metres deep, still one of the deepest in Sweden and proportionally wide, was an ideal dance space for its time.

Above: Illustration from feasibility studies for the enlargement of stage and improvements to front of house facilities at Sadler's Wells Theatre, London (*Frank Woods of Chamberlin, Powell and Bon, architects*)

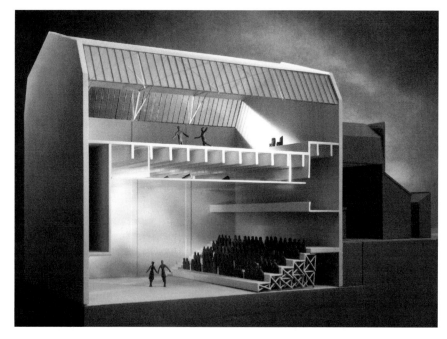

Right: Photograph of study model of the Lilian Baylis Community Theatre with full size rehearsal space above (*Frank Woods of Chamberlin, Powell and Bon, architects*)

Like the sleeping beauty the court slept for 100 years. Rediscovered in 1921 with all its ingenious stage machinery still intact, the theatre needed only a clean-up and new ropes before its magic again could fascinate an audience. Today, scenery can be changed once more in audience view quicker than in many modern opera houses. Cloud chariots, rolling waves with sailing ships, trap doors, wind and thunder machinery help to create the illusion of classical heroes, gods and goddesses who were the theatrical symbols of the *ancién regime*. An unique asset is the thirty or more stage settings and costumes by leading designers of the late 18th century. Because of them and because of the theatre, retained as it looked at the time, we can see how operas by Gluck and others must have appeared when first presented.

Drottningholm Court Theatre is, therefore, not only a monument of theatrical history but also of the attributes which make dance space suitable for dance. The first essential is space clear of all obstruction and of a size appropriate to the number of dancers. The second is clear sight lines for the audience. At Drottningholm the audience observes from tiered seating with nothing to divert the eye. At the front, perspective is precise for those at the centre. Other

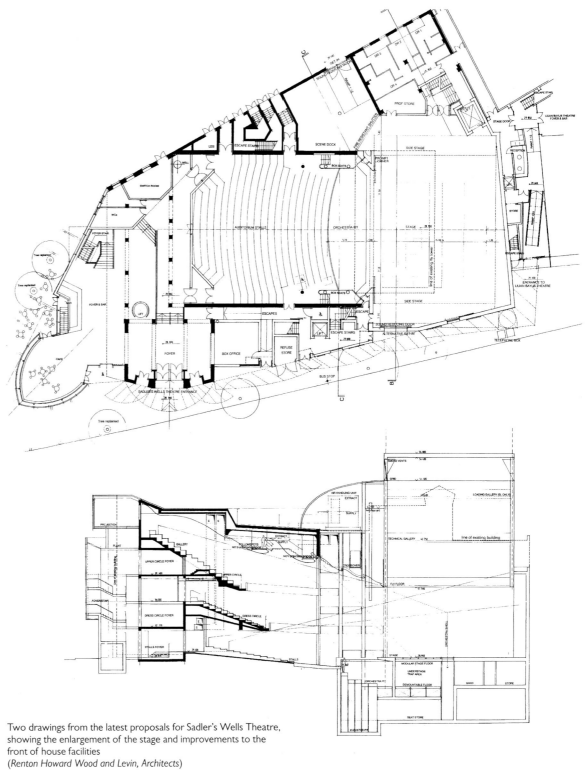

It is important that the sight lines for the audience when viewing dance are elevated more than for other performance arts so that it is possible to appreciate the floor pattern and spatial depth of the choreography
(*Drawing from* Dance Spaces *by Mark Foley, Arts Council 1994*)

Two drawings from the latest proposals for Sadler's Wells Theatre, showing the enlargement of the stage and improvements to the front of house facilities
(*Renton Howard Wood and Levin, Architects*)

seats behind are marked still with the ranks of nobility and royal servants to whom they were allotted.

Today the necessities of space for dance remain the same. However elaborate the scenery, that empty space of which Peter Brook spoke must remain empty, neither too large nor too small for the number of dancers taking part. In Britain, because of the dominant demands of drama and music hall inherited from the 19th century, dance companies often appear on unsuitable stages. The audience impact is reduced. *Ballet for All*, the Royal Ballet's smallest group of six dancers and two actors, need a space at least 25 ft x 25 ft clear of wing space. The largest companies are listed today by Foley as needing 50 ft x 50 ft, medium companies 40 ft x 40 ft and small companies 30 ft x 30 ft.

This is not all. British theatre dance embraces many dance cultures which over the years have become part of British dance culture. Therefore stage spaces must accommodate the needs of dancers from India, the Caribbean, China, Spain and South America as well as north America and Europe. We have to understand and address these needs.

As has been quoted at the beginning and stressed throughout this article, space is a fundamental requirement of dance. Not only is it a prerequisite but it is true to say that those embarking on new dance facilities must never forget that space is also the greatest of luxuries. To cut down the space required in favour of other apparent essentials, such as a sprung floor, is short sighted indeed. Of course, in an ideal world, dancers need sprung floors just as they need adequate heating and ventilation, but generally speaking space can rarely be added. One can always add a sprung floor, or air conditioning, better audience seating, or more 'state of the art' lighting rigs, as and when budgets allow, but without that precious commodity space, little can be changed. As dance specialist and architect, we would urge everyone already involved in or contemplating Dance House provision, to examine carefully this most basic luxury, and ensure that they do not underprovide the initial space; if they do they could, in years to come,

end up with another Sadlers Wells problem.

Undoubtedly a sprung floor is not a luxury; it is desperately important to the wellbeing of the dancer's health. However, how many dancers who tour can honestly say that they cannot dance on an unsprung, or inadequately sprung, floor? The advent of cushion floors, however inadequate they are, does make dance possible on surfaces which otherwise would be deemed to be undanceable – not ideal, but is it better than no dance at all?

It is not appropriate for this article to go into detail about all the technical requirements for dance, but it is perhaps pertinent to summarise certain key points.

Dance needs both performers and audiences and each have their own special technical requirements to enable a performance to be successful.

As has already been emphasised, dancers need space in which to perform and space at the sides and rear of the performance stage to cater for stopping and starting before and after they enter or exit. Exits at speed require ample space for deceleration if dancers are to avoid injury. Of course, the actual areas both on and off stage vary according to the size and nature of the ballet company. They also need space for rehearsal. It is very important that the rehearsal spaces are correctly sized so that the stage space can, within reason, be replicated. It can be extremely frustrating for both choreographer and dancers if the practice space is smaller than the stage itself.

Dancers, being subject to the severe law of gravity, need a surface which absorbs some of their body weight energy and a resilience which softens their impact on the actual surface of the floor itself. There are many ways in which that can be achieved – ranging from a flexible plastic dance floor which can be rolled out on most surfaces to a fully sprung floor on flexible mountings. One of the inevitable problems of stage floorings in a house shared by dance and opera is that its surface is frequently damaged by devices fixed to the floor to secure scenery; this presents a real danger and risk of injury to the dancers.

Equally demanding are the requirements for the

lighting rigs. The three dimensional nature of dance and movement frequently requires strong side lighting from vertical batteries of lights called lighting booms. These booms are large units and they present formidable obstacles to dancers as they exit into the wings, particularly if wing space is limited.

But what of the needs of the audience? Not all theatres serve their audiences well, initially cramming them into inadequate foyer spaces which seriously lack any real sense of drama and excitement and then ushering them into auditoria designed and built with insufficient understanding of sight lines. Frequently, theatres designed for the lyric theatre and drama have little reference to the needs of a dance audience where there is a very real need to see the dancers' feet as well as the body and facial language (p. 49). It seems almost too obvious to point this out as a reason why Dance Houses have special design needs and why drama theatres are, so often, unsatisfactory for the performance of dance. Whilst it may be acceptable to see the play *Romeo and Juliet* performed from the knee up, it robs the ballet of the same name of its *raison d'être*. Equally, restricted sight lines for *La Bohème* in the Royal Opera House in London or at L'Opera in Paris may be acceptable – at the right price – but totally hopeless for *Sleeping Beauty*.

Space for dance therefore requires much more than sprung floors and flat emptiness. There is a need for fire and safety regulations to serve audiences and artists, for spaces around and above the performing area where music can be played, where lights can illuminate, dancers can enter, exit and change costumes, scenery can be stored and designers can enrich a performance visually. Above all, the space must be a place for seeing dance, its steps and movements, its patterns on the ground and its groupings of dancers bodies. The dance world deserves a Lilac Fairy of the Millennium to provide, not only the spaces, but also the financial resources to make ballet and dance accessible to a wider public – through reasonable and subsidised seat prices for one thing. In that way the Sleeping Beauty could awaken to a much better world.

PART TWO

SOCIAL SPACE
Audiences and Communities

Theatre creates social space, as a shared experience and as the imaginative focus of a wider community.

The physical arrangements of the theatre building reflect the structure of society, promote or fail to promote imaginative participation, and engage or fail to engage with a local and in some cases a more extended community.

In Part Two, critics, consultants and theatre directors debate the achievements and frustrations of theatres from experimental studios and found spaces to Arts Centres, Regional Repertory and National Theatres.

THE EMPTY SPACE AND THE SOCIAL SPACE

A View from the Stalls

Robert Hewison

Robert Hewison is a broad-caster and critic who has written on theatre and the arts for *The Sunday Times* since 1981. He has also published more than a dozen studies on aspects of British Cultural History, and has recently been appointed Professor in Literary and Cultural Studies at Lancaster University. His latest book, *Culture and Consensus: England, Art and Politics since 1940* is published by Methuen in 1995.
(*Photo: Roderick Field*)

'I can take an empty space and call it a bare stage. A man walks across this empty space while someone else is watching him, and this is all that is needed for an act of theatre to be engaged.' With typical acuity, Peter Brook, Britain's most distinguished living theatre director, opens a masterly collection of essays on post-war drama by defining the fundamental architectural requirement for theatre: an empty space.

Brook's essays, *The Empty Space*, were first published in 1968, a pivotal date for British drama – for theatre censorship was abolished that year – and for post-war culture in general. The image he evokes has the clarity, power and resonance characteristic of the theatrical images that Brook is celebrated for creating on many different types of stage. Yet although the idea is fundamental, it does not in itself complete the 'engagement' of the act of theatre. A bare stage can be gravid in its emptiness, even before an actor walks across it, but it must be observed. The empty space must be delineated by another, social space. The act of theatre is futile without a witness, the business of theatre could not survive without the social space being filled.

As someone who has spent some fifteen years occupying a part of that social space as a professional critic, I want to devote this essay to a consideration, not of the stage, but of the auditorium.

It is probably the sheer technical difficulty of photographing a brightly lit stage and a darkened auditorium – together with the general inconvenience it causes – that accounts for the comparative rarity of photographic records of a performance taking place before a paying audience. Pictures of productions abound, but they are usually posed for publicity purposes; architectural photographs show the layout of an auditorium, but without people in the seats they look sterile, even dead.

Exceptionally, however, in the early nineteen hundreds, someone had the bright idea of photographing the audience at the New Theatre, Cambridge, as they appeared from across the footlights. The photograph has a historical value in itself, but it also reveals how the social structure of late Victorian Britain was inscribed in the architecture of its theatres (p. 53).

The New Theatre, Cambridge, which opened in January 1896, was a typical provincial version of the West End theatres that had sprung up during the London theatre building boom of the last quarter of the nineteenth century. Many of these still house London's commercial theatre today. The auditorium has a raked ground floor, and two galleries above, the lower of which curves towards stage boxes on either side. The particular value of this photograph is that it shows that the ground floor is divided towards the back by a wooden wall. This wall represents one of the last links with the theatre of Shakespeare's day. In an Elizabethan playhouse the whole of the ground floor would have been given over to people standing in what was graphically known as the 'Pit', democratically sharing this common space

while wealthier people occupied the galleries and even the sides of the stage. By the end of the nineteenth century however, the Pit had been pushed back by a barrier in order to make way for seats in front of the stage, which became known as the Orchestra Stalls. By the early twentieth century the Pit had disappeared altogether, replaced by the Rear Stalls that you find in a West End theatre today, and the cheapest seats were at the top of the theatre, in the gallery colloquially known as 'the Gods'.

The social significance of these divisions is clear from the clothes worn by the New Theatre's audience. While those in the Orchestra Stalls (price five shillings) and the Dress Circle (four shillings) are in full evening clothes (which is why the Dress Circle has that name, for one was expected to wear evening dress to sit there), those behind the wooden barrier in the Pit Stalls (two shillings) and in the Gallery (sixpence) are ordinarily dressed. Those in the Gallery are noticeably seated closer together, on benches, in contrast to the more comfortably disposed persons below them.

The New Theatre is thus both an economic and an architectural model of the contemporary class structure, although ironically the upper, middle and lower classes are reversed in their dispositions within the house. In grander establishments this social separation would have been continued outside the auditorium, with separate entrances, stairways and bars to keep the various classes of customer apart. (To this day, the discovery that the cheaper seats in many West End theatres cannot be reached via the foyer, but only through side entrances, can confuse foreign visitors.)

In one essential aspect the New Theatre's audience was united, in that they had all come to see the same show, but their relationship to the stage created divisions that can still be felt in a theatre of that design, even when pricing policy and the suppression of the Pit and the old form of Gallery – now renamed the Upper Circle – have created a more homogeneous, and necessarily more affluent, audience. But one wonders what any member of that New Theatre audience, from the Gallery to the Orchestra Stalls, would have made of a performance of *Vagina Rex and the Gas Oven* at the Arts Lab in Drury Lane in 1969.

Sadly, there is no photograph to record this event, but it made such an impression on me as a young theatre-goer that I wrote an account of it at the time. The Arts Lab had been opened in 1967 by the American emigré and pioneer of the underground, Jim Haynes, who had helped to found the Traverse Theatre in Edinburgh in 1963. It occupied a small warehouse, roughly converted into a ground floor gallery, below which was a small basement cinema whose only seating was tiers of carpeted foam rubber. In another building at the back was the 'theatre', a black painted space with rostra that could be quickly arranged into any configuration that was wanted.

It was into this black hole that I squeezed on a Friday evening in February 1969. Jane Arden's play, which carried a powerful and – in those days – novel message about the abused place of women in a world dominated by men, had acquired considerable reputation during its short run, partly because the chief performers, Sheila Allen and Victor Spinetti, were well known from the 'legitimate' theatre. All the seats had been taken, so along with many others I squatted on the floor, at the front. There was no stage as such, and there was so little empty space that at one point Spinetti asked me to hold the microphone used during the songs.

Stage censorship having been abolished only months before, writer and actors were free to express themselves as they wished, and stage nudity still carried a political as well as an erotic charge. After a parody of a strip-tease the naked Sheila Allen, together with a supporting chorus of equally nude young people, went through an enactment of child-

A Footlights Audience at the New Theatre, Cambridge, in the early 1900s.
(*Photo: courtesy of the Cambridge University Footlights Club Archive*)

birth. I noted at the time: 'A photograph is projected over the stage, a view looking up a naked woman's thighs. The torso, breasts and head fall on the wall, but the thighs and groin fall onto a sheet held by two naked players. Behind the sheet the Woman [Allen] and the cast moan and groan. Suddenly the sheet tears, and a head pops out, followed by the rest of a naked man. The rest of the cast follows, and the room is filled with naked babies .... I was so close to the action, the absence of any clear separation audience/players (who at one point crawl nude over the front ranks) made me feel completely part of the ritual that took place.'

Vagina Rex and the Gas Oven closed soon afterwards, and the Arts Lab not long after that, but that night remains one of my most powerful theatrical memories. I quote it here, because it represents one of the extremes of the theatrical revolution that post-war theatre makers and theatre architects have been engaged in. The revolution is both cultural and architectural, and the two elements are not easy to separate out. Rightly so, for they have been trying to achieve the same thing: a reconnection between the stage and its audience, and a reintegration of the audience as a social unit This has been done intellectually and emotionally through what has been said and done on the stage, physically through changing the audience's relationship with each other and with the 'empty space' designated for performance.

That the post-war revolution was launched from a theatre eight years older than the New at Cambridge, and with much the same arrangement of its auditorium, suggests that scale, rather than plan, is the key to successful communication between stage and audience. It is the intimacy of the Royal Court in Sloane Square, with its 395 seats, that has kept it a bubbling crucible of new writing ever since George Devine launched the English Stage Company there in 1956. The Theatre Royal, Stratford East (1884) and the Citizens' in Glasgow (1878) are other examples of theatres that have transcended their Victorian origins. (In both cases, a committed management and being located in working-class districts has had a lot to do with it.) The first new theatre to be built

since the Second World War, the Belgrade in Coventry, played a part in the Royal Court revolution, for by an arrangement with the Court, Arnold Wesker's *Chicken Soup With Barley* was premiered there in 1958.

While the revolution launched by the Royal Court was driven by what was said and done, attempts to change the physical relationship between audience and stage had begun a few years earlier. While the fan shaped cinema auditoria of the 1920s and 1930s had already suggested a more democratically uniform arrangement of seating on two levels (an unsuccessful theatrical version of this being the original design of the Shakespeare Memorial Theatre in Stratford-upon-Avon in 1932), it was the director Tyrone Guthrie's efforts to recover an old relationship between audience and stage, rather than invent a new one, that had a significant impact.

In Elizabethan theatres the groundlings in the Pit had stood on three sides of a stage pushed forward towards the facing galleries. Guthrie, a theatrical democrat through his long association with Lilian Baylis's Old Vic Company, saw the advantages of this so-called thrust stage in uniting actors and audience, and in 1948 he began to put this into practice, with the temporary stage and seating installed in the Assembly Hall, Edinburgh for his annual Festival productions (p. 20).

A significant line of new theatre buildings has sprung from this idea. The hexagonal Chichester Festival Theatre (1962) (p. 156) has been a particularly successful example, where a spacious auditorium, tiered like an ancient Greek theatre, but angled rather than fan shaped, manages to hold the audience together as a unit while creating a stage large enough for spectacle. Though actually holding fewer people than Chichester (1,022 rather than 1,394) the Crucible in Sheffield (1971) (p. 158), where the audience are very clearly on three sides of a long tongue of stage, has never felt to me so warm and enclosing. Again, scale as well as plan is important. The 'temporary' building erected in Waterloo in 1970, which has now become a permanent fixture, the Young Vic, has tiered benches for 450 on three

sides of the stage, with a single gallery above, creating a genuine sense of theatre – as – forum (and Shakespeare has usually done well here) (p. 172).

Quite the most successful of the Royal Shakespeare Company's five theatres is the Swan at Stratford (1986), which combines rows of benches around a low thrust stage with wooden galleries above, holding 458 people in a space that nonetheless feels like a room. While being in no sense a slavish recreation of an Elizabethan or Jacobean playhouse (in a sense it is a synthesis of the 'summer' and 'winter' types of pre-Restoration theatre layout) the Swan has proved remarkably successful for modern productions of the repertoire of that period (p. 168).

Tyrone Guthrie had noticed that one of the advantages of a thrust stage was that while the audience focused its attention on the stage, it was nonetheless aware of the spectators around it, thus emphasising the collective nature of the event. A logical extension of this process is to surround the playing area entirely, leaving gaps only for exits and entrances. The pioneer of theatre-in-the-round in Britain was Stephen Joseph, who founded The Studio Theatre in 1955. This was a touring theatre travelling from hall to hall, carrying its seating in a lorry, but it led directly to the foundation of two permanent theatres-in-the-round, the Library Theatre in Scarborough, and the Victoria Stoke-on-Trent (p. 59).

Both theatres have been notable for creating a particular sense of local identity. The Scarborough theatre changed location, and under the management of the writer and director Alan Ayckbourn became the Stephen Joseph Theatre, following Joseph's death in 1967. The Stephen Joseph is about to move again, to a new, purpose built setting within a disused Scarborough cinema (p. 101). It is to be hoped that the lessons have been learnt from the experience of Peter Cheeseman at Stoke-on-Trent, who took over the running of the theatre there. The Victoria moved from its original converted cinema into a brand new building in 1986, but the new building, while having much better facilities overall, has an auditorium that is too wide to create a strong feeling of contact across the central playing area.

Glyndebourne Festival Opera,
Michael Hopkins and Partners,
1994.
(*Photo: Richard Davies*)

Cerritos Center for Performing
Arts, California, USA, 1992
Architects, Barton Myers of
Los Angeles.
(For description see Catalogue
Part Three)
(*Photo: Tim Street-Porter*)

The Tramway Theatre,
Glasgow. Stages in the
construction process. For
details see pp. 61–63.
(*Photos: Alan Crumlish*)

Above: The Martha Cohen Theatre,
Calgary Centre for Performing Arts,
Alberta, Canada 1985.
Set out for *Candide*,
dir. Michael Dobbin, 1990.
Architects Raines, Finlayson, Barrett and
Partners, 1985.
For description see Catalogue Part
Three.
(*Photo: Courtesy of Alberta Theatre Project*)

Opposite:
The Auditorium of the
New Victoria Theatre,
Newcastle-under-Lyme, 1986
(*Photo: Courtesy of the Theatres
Trust Archive*)

When the director Sam Walters moved the theatre-in-the-square that he had founded in a room above a pub in Richmond, Surrey in 1971 to a converted school hall across the road in 1991, he managed to double the number of seats, from 80 to 160, without losing any of the intimacy and immediacy of the space.

The most successful theatre-in-the-round, however, is the Royal Exchange in Manchester. Sitting as it does like some spacecraft within the vastness of the city's former cotton exchange, the surrounding void generates a distinctive echo, but within the three-level structure itself there is an absolute concentration on the playing area that draws all 750 seats into the orbit of the stage (p. 17, 160). Since it opened in 1976, designers have discovered all sorts of ingenious ways of introducing scenery up through the floor or down from the cupola. From time to time the Royal Exchange Theatre Company has reverted to Stephen Joseph's original practice by taking its shows on the road, and presenting them in the round in sports halls and other non-theatrical venues.

One of the impulses to experiment with both architectural form and dramatic content, which grew ever stronger during the 1960s, was the conviction that conventional theatres were in themselves an inhibition to communication and expression. The original Traverse Theatre in Edinburgh was no more than a few rows of old cinema seats arranged on either side of a room. The People Show, founded in 1966 and presenting their 100th show in 1995, began their long life as an experimental troupe literally underground, with performances in the basement of a bookshop in the Charing Cross Road. Welfare State International, another heroic survivor from that period, began life as a pop group performing theatre in dance halls, and have made parades, rituals, ceremonies, circuses and all the devices of street theatre their speciality. In 1973 they temporarily took up residence on a scrap-heap in Burnley, Yorkshire, converting it into an 'environment' where performance and everyday life became virtually indistinguishable.

Much of the activity of 'the fringe', whose eruption in the late 1960s gave fresh energy and impetus to the whole of British theatre, was outside normal

theatrical spaces for practical as well as ideological reasons, for the economics of theatre made such places unavailable to then. Converted warehouses, like the Arts Lab, or adapted rooms in pubs, like the King's Head Theatre in Islington (1970, and very little changed) were far more suitable. But they undoubtedly had a direct effect on the mainstream, by questioning the need for what the fringe saw as expensive and grandiose mausoleums.

In 1970 the Royal Court acknowledged the arrival of this new wave by temporarily taking all the seats out of its auditorium in order to accommodate a two week festival presenting the work of twenty fringe troupes in all their richness and diversity. The lasting effect of the fringe on theatre architecture has been the expectation that all new buildings will have, in addition to a main auditorium, a flexible studio space where experiment can take place. (Hence the addition of The Pit to the Royal Shakespeare Company's facilities in the Barbican, and the addition of the Cottesloe to the design of the National Theatre.) This has served to contain, as well as encourage, experiment. New work tends to be confined to the studio, and limited to its scale, while studio programmes are regularly sacrificed in order to keep a main house open.

When it came to designing the auditorium of the main house itself, there is no doubt that architects sought to erase the social divisions built into Victorian theatres by lowering the stage, sometimes to floor level, and steeply raking the auditorium in a single sweep that echoed the stepped seating of ancient Greek theatres. This was both a practical way to create a single room, and a nod to the supposedly democratic tradition of Athenian theatre. The Mermaid, converted from an old City of London warehouse in 1959, is an early successful example (p. 6, 180), but in later versions of this design – Birmingham Rep (1971), Leicester Haymarket (1973), – the raking of the seats has become steeper and steeper, until in the Quarry Theatre of the West Yorkshire Playhouse (1990) the pitch is positively vertiginous (pp. 70, 75, 81).

Since a 'national' theatre can be expected to embody in its architecture the theatrical traditions and current practices that it presents on its stages, it is worth asking what morals can be drawn from the three auditoria under the roof of Denys Lasdun's South Bank design. The first is that however ingenious, no single space can do justice to every kind of play, and no play entirely depends on an appropriate architectural setting for its success. At least three different theatre types are a necessity, and the flexibility of the Cottelsoe provides for many more. At first glance, the proscenium arch – although technically there is no arch, merely an opening – of the Lyttelton marks it out as a traditional theatre form, but it is noticeable that the democratising impulse of the post-war period has led to the elimination of boxes and a second gallery (p. 93). The loss from this frontal, squareish layout, which actually makes the stalls and balcony audiences unaware of each other, and gives the actor two different eye-lines to accommodate – is the lack of a sense of physical connection between auditorium and stage, such as was formerly created by the curving arms of galleries and boxes in Victorian theatres.

The Olivier is plainly an attempt to exploit the democratic tradition of an Athenian stepped theatre, with an open stage suitable for spectacular and large events (p. 95). The balcony is set back, above and behind the last row of the stalls, so that it makes a more continuous sweep than if cantilevered out, while the raised side sections of the stalls appear to reach out towards the stage. Yet the notion that the stage itself is 'in the corner of a room' (the corner being formed by an imaginary right angle created by extending the side lines of the auditorium until they meet towards the back of the circle formed by the stage) suggests that a certain intimacy is also being aimed for. The sheer volume of the 1,160 seat auditorium makes this hard to achieve, though it can be done by actors of the calibre of Ian McKellen and Anthony Hopkins. (A genuine example of a theatre in the corner of a room is the 60-seater Old Red Lion, above a pub in Islington.) What the Olivier has encouraged is a grander style of design and production, and in the recent trilogy of plays by David Hare examining the state of the nation, *Racing Demon, Murmuring Judges* and *The Absence of War*, directed by Richard Eyre, the theatre has proved a suitably epic setting.

Yet there is no doubt that it is the Cottesloe, holding between 200 and 400 people, depending on its layout, that has proved the most consistently successful National Theatre space (pp. 105 and 166). At one stage in the planning it was not intended for public use at all, and then was eliminated altogether, but this chequered history seems to have given it the accidental quality that often turns out to be the virtue of a theatre that has been converted from other purposes, such as the Almeida in Islington (p. 178), or the Tramway in Glasgow (pp. 57, 63). I have experienced the Cottesloe in all sorts of configurations, from promenade performances to central, 'landing-strip' layouts to conventional end-on productions, and I can only conclude that it is its scale and proportion that sakes it successful. That, and the fact that it harks back to the oldest English form of theatre, the courtyard theatre, with its three tiers of side galleries, while the raked central seating (when it is in an end-on configuration) reinforces the impression that the audience is a single witness to the play.

In the best theatre, the audience is more than Brook's detached observer of an empty space. It is a temporary community, reaching out to embrace the community of the artists on the stage. That sense of community can be created in many ways: shivering in the rain at a performance of *A Midsummer Night's Dream* at the Open Air Theatre in Regent's Park, roaring out the responses at a Christmas pantomime, mingling with the actors in a promenade performance, sitting in judgement on the characters of Priestley's *An Inspector Calls*. The theatre in Britain still serves as an informal forum in which society meets to amuse itself, and to argue with itself. That is why the social space created for the audience is as important as the empty space offered to the actors. Indeed, the magic of the empty space can only be created, if it is happily surrounded by a full one.

PETER BROOK, THEATRE SPACE AND THE TRAMWAY

Neil Wallace

When the history of theatrical space in Europe this century is written, it will be dominated by the philosophy, work, and legacy of Peter Brook. This may seem an extravagant claim: how could the thinking or achievements of a single director – even this one – outweigh the influence of Matcham, Crewe, or Sprague? Of Craig or Guthrie? Of Europe's leading contemporary designers, engineers and architects? The answer is simple, and lies in the word 'space'. It is Brook who has shown us that architecture for the theatre and space for the theatre are, unfortunately, two very different ideas which sometimes conflict; it is Brook who has never separated considerations of space from what an audience experiences in the theatre; and it is Brook who has, uncompromisingly, insisted on unconventional performance conditions in pursuit of the best possible relationship between actor, space and spectator. For these reasons, the anecdote (*see* below, right) – with which he opens his latest book *There are No Secrets* – is not really anecdotal at all, but a foreshadow of everything he's said and done on the subject of theatre space in the last twenty-six years. (Nor, for that matter, is it an isolated incident: Brook's instinctual dislike of insensitively designed, 'given' space for public assembly has sent organisers the world over looking for better alternatives, or required an ad hoc rearrangement of furniture until the optimum conditions for contact have been achieved.) And seminal though the four essays which comprise *The Empty Space* were, and continue to be for countless theatre practitioners all over the world, the book is a paradoxical kind of credo. A credo certainly, because Brook clearly described some simple ideas and principles which would either guide theatre makers towards, or away form, the immediate or living theatre. Paradoxical for the reason that he's never wavered from the same ideas and principles whilst simultaneously disavowing anything constant, fixed, or final in the work of the Centre International de Recherche Théâtrale,

Neil Wallace lives and works in Amsterdam, where he runs his own production company, Offshore Cultural Projects. He has had wide experience of the arts world in England, Scotland and Wales, having worked for the RAA for Lincolnshire and Humberside (1980–83), as Chief Executive and Director of Chapter, Cardiff, and from 1987–94 as Deputy Director of Glasgow's 1990 Cultural Capital of Europe programme, and Programme Director of the Tramway. He is currently working with Jean Guy Lecat on the book *Making Space: The Theatre Environments of Peter Brook* to be published by Methuen in 1996. (*Photo: Glasgow City Council, Wylie*)

*O*ne day, in an English university, while giving the lectures that were the bases for my book **The Empty Space**, I found myself up on a platform in front of a big black hole, and right at the back of that hole I vaguely distinguished some people sitting in the darkness. As I began to speak, I felt that everything I said was quite pointless. I became more and more depressed, for I couldn't find a natural way of getting through to them ... Luckily I had the courage to stop and suggest we look for another space. The organisers went off, searched throughout the university and finally came up with a small room which was too narrow and very uncomfortable but where we found it possible to have a natural and more intense relationship ... From that point on I was able to talk freely and the audience was liberated in the same way ... The strong lesson concerning space that I received that day became the basis of the experiments that we undertook many years later in Paris, in our International Centre of Theatre Research.

Peter Brook, *There are No Secrets: Thoughts on Acting and Theatre*, Methuen, 1993, page 3

later the Centre International de Créations Theatrales. So the core, the one consistent quality of his work, has been discovery, research and renewal.

Nowhere is this more evident, or his legacy more tangible, than in the domain of theatrical space. From the point at which Brook 'left' the RSC and the UK, his need to experiment with space and environment as an integral part of all his theatrical research was clear in all of the workshop and preparatory work of the late sixties, leading to the creation of CIRT in 1970. There was the LAMDA *Theatre of Cruelty* season; the move to Paris and the experiments and workshops held in the vast Mobilier National (a Government warehouse for the storage of valuable carpets and tapestries in state ownership); the improvised plays and stories which the company gave there for children, some of them with special needs; the experimental *Tempest*, seen briefly at the Roundhouse; the extraordinary masked version of *Kaspar Hauser*, performed all over the suburbs of Paris in supermarket malls, offices and other open spaces; and of course the preparation for Ted Hughes' *Orghast*, eventually staged at Persepolis, Iran, in the colossal Valley of the Kings (probably one of the most ambitious and large-scale site-specific performances ever mounted anywhere). And, in 1974 after the desert and American expeditions of 1971 and 1972, the re-opening of the Bouffes du Nord with *Timon d'Athènes* – 'a lost theatre for a lost play' as one French critic described it.

From the moment that the Bouffes readmitted a public for the first time in over a generation, a public astonished by this space 'marked by life'(actually by untreated fire and water damage), theatrical history was made. The fascination, the innate theatricality of the Bouffes was not only to do with the near perfection of its proportions – altered crucially by the installation of a new floor placing actor and first row on the same level – but because this was, essentially, 'found space'. For over twenty years,

Brook and his collaborators have tried to recreate, as faithfully as possible, the playing dimensions and the fundamental aesthetic of the Bouffes du Nord in dozens of spaces over the world. This has been a prerequisite of the international tours, co-productions and stagings of every production mounted since *The IK* – a body of work encompassing the French and English language versions of *The Conference of the Birds, Timon d'Athènes, Ubu, La Tragédie de Carmen, The Mahabharata, La Tempête, Impressions de Pelléas,* and *L'Homme Qui.* During this period, CICT have performed in old factories, abandoned tram or locomotive depots, in a disused barracks, gas works and flower market, in quarries, and have reopened or adapted two film studios and several theatres to meet their needs. In so doing, Brook's performance demands have created some of the most exciting and dynamic performance spaces and locations ever seen.

The story of The Tramway in Glasgow is typical of these spaces (p. 57). Following an invitation to present the English language version of *The Mahabharata* in Glasgow, the search for a location began immediately. After an exhaustive search of the city – which, taking a cue from the enclosed boatyard used for the production in Zurich, naturally concentrated on the River Clyde and what remained of Glasgow's global ship building industry – seven options were identified. Of these, the last and least likely was the building which had housed the city's Museum of Transport up until 1987. The collection had been moved to new premises and the building now awaited demolition. The site itself was of significant interest in Glasgow's industrial history: about 100 years old, it had begun life as the factory in which the city's huge fleet of trams were actually built, becoming a maintenance depot for the southside until its reincarnation as a Museum in 1962. As theatrical 'found space' it fitted the bill: a period industrial building, aged but without excessive dilapidation, historical but without a dominant or confused architectural character, a choice of spaces which might be converted for theatrical use, and available through the will of the City Council. But because the complex was constructed using a ubiquitous eight metre square grid of cast iron pillars, and the interior of the most obviously suitable space was encumbered with partition walls – some load-bearing and in all the wrong places – it was difficult to see how an epic, open space could be forged for a nine hour production for at least six hundred spectators. For this reason, the Museum of Transport building was at the bottom of the potential site list.

When Jean Guy Lecat, Brook's technical director, arrived for a site visit, the order of preference was instantly reversed. Lecat showed the unique combination of instinct and practicality which has informed the choice and conversion of every space used by Brook anywhere in the world since 1977. In minutes, he demonstrated how a cluttered, pillar-ridden hall could be quickly and cost-effectively turned into a space for *The Mahabharata.* All existing connecting doors, windows and openings would be bricked up; internal wall partitions would be demolished; two huge proscenium walls and, further upstage, a third rear wall would be built to define a huge performance area to be completed by the setting lines of the thrust seating banks which would occupy the rest of the space. The visual problem of the four on-stage pillars was brilliantly solved by both Lecat and Chloe Obolensky, Brook's constant designer and collaborator since *The Cherry Orchard.* The two proscenium walls would bear the load of the pillars, which were removed and the second pair were buried inside the rear wall forever, with the remaining four forming part of the seating bank and conveniently out of view for the bulk of the audience. What might have proved a technical and visual encumbrance on-stage had disappeared without expensive rebuilding or engineering. The entire space was converted in just over three months. In the last weeks before the production opened, Obolensky made two other key decisions contributing to the overall result. The entire space was sandblasted to reveal the warmth of Victorian brick as well as other features which a century of patina had concealed, and the cyclorama wall – originally intended to span the width of the whole space – was instead built as a self-standing, monolithic wall about 12 metres across and leaving void, darkened space on either side of it. When Obolensky and her scene-painter Ulysses Ketsileidis had completed their meticulous plaster and paintwork, a wall constructed some weeks previously looked centuries old, and their work was complete.

Unique as it was, the temporary auditorium of what was to become Tramway met four absolute conditions found in any space used by Brook. First, the audience and actor were in the same space, not segregated, artificially and damagingly, by the stage, auditorium and an interposing wall between. Second, the floor of the performing area was on the same level as the first row of seats occupied by the audience, removing any sense of visual hierarchy or order and helping bind actor and audience. Third, large and voluminous as it was, the design and layout of space was essentially *intimate*: miraculously, Brook and Lecat have achieved this in the most colossal outdoor spaces such as Avignon's Boulbon Quarry, first used for the premiere of *Le Mahabharat* in 1985. (The performing area was little bigger than the Bouffes du Nord.) Fourth, the innate character, history – one might even call it *drama* of the environment – contributed in some magical way to the theatrical experience of which the audience was a part. It is rare to visit or approach any one of these spaces or sites without feeling this. Whether through anticipation, or the thrill of unknowing, or a measured sense of ritual (especially in the outdoor spaces), the pre-performance sensation suggests that, before a single actor has appeared, or a note of music been sounded, or a house light dimmed, the theatrical adventure, the story, has already begun.

This body of experience in transforming found space for temporary theatrical use is unique. And for all its temporariness, its influence and legacy on directors, designers and other theatre-makers has been profound. The effect has been both concrete and intangible. Tramway is one of eight spaces first converted, usually for a matter of weeks, to host Brook's work but which have survived and developed full-time and flourishing artistic lives of their own. (Often, as in Tramway's case, these have been used by Brook for other productions.) These buildings include Les Halles de Schaerbeek (Brussels); the Mercat de los Flors (Barcelona); the Bockenheimer Depot (Frankfurt); the Ostre Gasvaerk (Copenhagen); the Gessnerallee (Zurich); the Kampnagelfabrik (Hamburg) and Brooklyn's Majestic Theatre. Most, but not all, of these buildings have dedicated themselves to new, adventurous work by artists and companies from their own countries and abroad. Often, especially in the case of Tramway, Kampnagel, the Bockenheimer Depot and the Mercat de los Flors, the allure of large and exciting space has inspired new production or experiment of a site-specific kind. Frequently, it is the policy of these buildings to encourage or commission it. The artistic lives of these buildings revolves around creative relationships with existing companies or directors, and often attaches importance to helping and encouraging new or younger ones. None of them has a resident company of its own. It is interesting that Jean Guy Lecat, though responsible in large measure for the successful first use or conversion of these buildings, doesn't see creative after-life as especially important. This has, in his view, destroyed rather than enhanced their quality as performing spaces: when municipalities decide to keep on one-off spaces, their raw and 'found' quality disappears, developed out of recognition in the interests of safety, public comfort and the cause of a permanent role in the cultural infrastructure. Nevertheless, municipal interest in retaining and investing in these or other cultural spaces is substantial progress by any standards and should, on the whole, be welcomed.

The intangible impact of Brook's work and thinking in theatrical space has been immense. A generation of directors and designers has been influenced by the possibilities which environment, rather than set or even theatre design offers their work. Increasingly, set designers work with found space in mind, using environments as a visual and aesthetic foundation or reference for what they design. Collaborations between artists of different disciplines have become more common. Found space has offered new challenges and opportunities to lighting designers. Some directors, like Deborah Warner, Bill Bryden, Mike Pearson, Barry Rutter, John Fox as well as many ensembles overseas like the Wooster Group, Reza Abdoh, Baktruppen, Theatre Acco, La Fura dels Baus find it almost impossible to make their work in conventional theatres. Ariane Mnouchkine in Paris and Hollandia, in the Netherlands, never do, only performing site-specifically. Companies in

Interior of the Tramway Theatre, Glasgow, being converted for performance. (Photo: Alan Crumlish)

search of permanent homes (Toneelgroep Amsterdam in the city's Westergasfabrik, CBTO in Birmingham) choose empty, non-theatre or industrial spaces in preference to new-built or even 'professionally' converted ones. An international field of technical expertise in light, sound and space conversion has appeared.

Gradually, a new vocabulary connected with the complex aesthetics of found space is emerging. This raises intricate dramaturgical questions . How do we deal with concepts of memory in historical space? Does space have a narrative? Can one 'write' with, or in space, for example in contemporary dance? And when space has been used once and goes on being used, does it merely become an 'unconventional' theatre, or can its virgin condition be re-found, re-used, renewed?

Perhaps what Brook has shown us, in spite of all that his work has left behind, is that these are, and will remain, rhetorical questions. Even space is an evanescent phenomenon of the theatre – always capable of being better, constantly open to change, and in itself nothing without the other essential components of theatre, which it both enlivens and, in turn, which bring it to life. As Ritsaert ten Cate expressed it: '...theatrical space begins in the mind. There can be no structural space – however perfect – that comes before this. This has nothing to do with architecture for its own sake, but with perceptions of space, of thought, of imagination'.[1]

---

1. Ritsaert ten Cate, 28 vii 1991, reproduced in *The Written Space, Theaterschrift*, page 51 Kaaltheater, Brussels, 1992

A SHORT DIARY OF SCOTTISH THEATRES

November 1994 – February 1995

Joyce McMillan

Joyce McMillan was born in Paisley in 1952 and brought up in Renfrewshire. She was educated at Paisley Grammar School, St Andrews University and Edinburgh University. In 1979 she began to review theatre for BBC Radio Scotland and The Scotsman, and has been working as a freelance journalist and broadcaster ever since, specialising in cultural, social and political commentary. Today, she is political columnist and leading theatre critic for Scotland on Sunday, and radio reviewer for the (Glasgow) Herald. She is also involved in Scottish and European campaigns for democracy and human rights, and is Vice-Chair of the Freelance Council of the National Union of Journalists. She lives in Edinburgh, from where she broadcasts frequently on Radio Scotland and Radio 4.
(*Photo: Chris Hill, NUJ*)

9th November 1994:
The Arches Theatre, Midland Street, Glasgow

In Scotland, as everywhere else, there are three kinds of theatres: old theatres, new theatres, and 'found' spaces like the one I am sitting in tonight. The Arches Theatre is a dark, dank series of old stone tunnels beneath Glasgow's Central Station, first opened to the public – for a huge exhibition of Glasgow history – during the city's *annus mirabilis* as European City of Culture in 1990; and still miraculously alive five years later, as a theatre, a bar, and an occasional rock venue. The Arches is still here partly because of the passion of its director, Andy Arnold, who came back from London to run the little Arches theatre-space in 1990, and simply refused to leave it. But it has also survived, I think, because of the extraordinary quality of the space itself, which seems to bring the business of theatre-making hard up against some of the toughest realities of our times. The entrance to the theatre – a heavy narrow steel door, protected in turn by a metal grid – lies in Midland Street, itself a dark, dripping tunnel of a thoroughfare, under the station, that often acts as a shelter for a homeless people and down and outs; the streets round about, commercially devastated by the opening of a huge indoor shopping mall at St. Enoch's, are a grim patchwork of gap-sites, junk food outlets and bargain stores, punctuated by the occasional magnificent Victorian pub. Overhead, the trains rumble to and fro on the thirteen platforms of Central Station, clearly audible even inside the theatre; every few minutes, performances are shaken and stirred by the long, heavy, rhythmic thunder of an inter-city slowing as it pulls into Platform One, or the slightly lighter roar of an ordinary commuter train. And in this space, Arnold has created a stream of memora-

ble productions, leaning heavily on the Irish and American connections that are written into the grain of this city. O'Casey, Mamet, Sam Shepard, the odd Irish-looking Joe Orton thrown in for luck; and tonight, Arthur Miller's *The Crucible*, in what turns out to be one of the most memorable productions I have ever seen. For this show, Arnold has even abandoned the usual theatre-space, a welcoming little end-on auditorium with a neat rake of about sixty seats. He has pushed us back into one of the farthest tunnels, a long stone arch receding into darkness, candles guttering in sconces on the walls, an oblong of old church pews for seats; and here, in the week of the American congressional elections that swept the new anti-liberal ascendancy to power, we watch a young Scottish cast unfold Miller's terrible, definitive drama of witch-hunt with a passion that breaks the heart. We weep, as well we might, and around us all, the dangerous unreason of our own society presses in around us, impossible, here, to ignore.

Ever since the early 1960's, when the Traverse Theatre was founded, just off Edinburgh's Royal Mile, in a long, low-ceilinged parlour of a room said to have been part of a brothel called Kelly's Paradise, some of the most thrilling theatre spaces in Scotland have been those never meant for the theatre at all; the sail maker's loft in the Grassmarket that became the second Traverse, the great Tramway in Glasgow (p. 57), the stripped bingo-hall floor of the Edinburgh Empire – now the new Festival Theatre (pp. 96, 152) – when Frank Dunlop had the inspiration of using the space, raw and transitional as it was, during the Edinburgh Festival of 1991. Our need for these places, with their insistent, hard, post-industrial reminders of work and of life itself, of real effort, real achievement, and real transience and loss, tells us something about the condition of theatre now; something I am constantly trying to understand.

14th January 1995:
The Royal Lyceum Theatre, Grindlay Street, Edinburgh

The Royal Lyceum is a beautiful, formal Victorian theatre, the kind often described as a 'gem' (p. 96). Opened by Howard and Wyndham in 1883, designed by C.J. Phipps, and generously refurbished by Edinburgh District Council in the late 1970's (for the auditorium and seating) and again in the late 1980's (for new backstage and front-of-house facilities, including a glittering glass foyer), the theatre sits in a part of Edinburgh, in the western lee of the Castle, that has always been associated with entertainment and the arts; the Usher Hall stands beside it, the imposing new Traverse is in the business centre behind it, and its site was occupied, before it was built, by the famous Cooke Bros. Circus. Today it has a 773 seat auditorium, including its rarely used upper circle, decked out in a lush colour-scheme of deep blue and gold with dark red upholstery, facing a fine traditional proscenium stage, and lit by an exceptionally beautiful modern chandelier donated, fifteen years ago, by the Carlsberg Company. Empty, the space has an extraordinary, breathtaking atmosphere, full of theatrical ghosts. Henry Irving and Ellen Terry opened the theatre on the evening of September 10th 1883, with a performance of *Much Ado About Nothing*; and tonight, in the post-Christmas doldrums of 1995, the Lyceum Company – led by the much loved Scottish actress Eileen McCallum – are tackling Ernest Thompson's soft-centred American family drama *On Golden Pond*, to pretty good effect.

And yet despite, or perhaps because of, its distinguished history, the Lyceum strikes me as a house that bears down heavily on the business of theatre-making in the late 20th century. During my time as a critic, four directors – Stephen MacDonald, Leslie Lawton, Ian Wooldridge, and now Kenny Ireland – have tussled mightily with the space and its demands, without ever quite transforming it into the kind of

Interior of the Dundee Repertory Theatre
(*Photo: Fotopress, Dundee*)

forum for contemporary Scottish life and art that the country's leading repertory theatre needs to be; indeed it seems to take a huge scale, passion and physical depth of production – like the bold assault on Tankred Dorst's German epic *Merlin* staged by Ian Wooldridge in 1992–3 – even to begin to shift the balance of energy from that glowing auditorium to the stage. In the Spring of 1994, Kenny Ireland tried the ultimate challenge to the space, building a floor over the stalls at stage-level, and turning the entire area into a reconstruction of the palace forecourt at Thebes, for a promenade production of *Oedipus Tyrannos*; but it sat uneasily on the old auditorium, which peeped out from behind the plastic rocks like a genteel old lady forced, against her better judgement, to get herself up in fancy dress.

The Lyceum, in other words, seems like a space that has learned to set its own terms; a space that allows plays to be staged in it, little brightly-lit worlds behind the proscenium arch, but is somehow unchanged by them. Unlike the cheerful old tub of the Edwardian King's Theatre up the hill at Tollcross – just as historically interesting, in its way just as beautiful, traditional home of Edinburgh's huge annual pantomime – it has no ethos of free-flowing, rollicking popularity. It has often in its artistic history fallen into the trap of reflecting Edinburgh's fierce

social divisions – genteel versus popular, anglicised culture versus Scottish – rather than challenging them; today, economic necessity requires it to market itself partly as a historic building, and an upmarket venue for social events. I have seen great performances in the Lyceum, and had wonderful evenings there; it remains Scotland's most active and best-attended repertory theatre, its own productions playing to well over 100,000 people a year. But when it comes to the development of artistic policy, it often seems that the Lyceum Company is trapped by the sheer weight of the building, encrusted by a century's worth of class and cultural assumptions about what theatre is, and whom it is for. Whenever I read the first chapter of John McGrath's great radical theatre manifesto *A Good Night Out*, with its brilliant description of how the unspoken 'language' of a theatre event – the atmosphere of the building, the architecture, the location, the formal assumptions – can dominate and overwhelm what is actually said on stage, the Lyceum is one of the theatres I think of. This old lady eats directors of a radical and populist mind for breakfast; and few have managed to stage more than a token resistance.

9th February, 1995:
Dundee Rep, Tay Square, Dundee.

Peter Shaffer's *Amadeus* is not my favourite play. For all its wit, it's one of those parasitic, parodic efforts, dependent on a notion of 'high culture' that people defer to but increasingly resent, that strike me as a gloomy harbinger of a culture in decline; and it is a good twenty minutes too long. But here in Dundee, in the modern rep theatre in Tay Square (*see above left*), I am watching one of the most enjoyable productions I ever hope to see, an elegant, exuberant staging by rising young director Richard Baron in which Michael Mackenzie and Jimmy Chisholm strike powerful dramatic sparks off one another in the roles of Salieri and Mozart; and I am not surprised. Of all the purpose-built theatres in Scotland, this is the one where the atmosphere is most down-to-earth and uncluttered, most likely to cut through fanciful bullshit and hyper-aesthetic

posturing, most likely to compel actors into strong, disciplined performances, well-founded on the world outside the theatre. Dundee, in the 1990's, remains the most socially homogeneous of Scottish cities, a fine grey strand of a town lying gravely under the hills on the cold north shore of the Tay, a place that has its share of post-industrial decline, unemployment and despair, but always remains warm-hearted, well-centred in its own identity; and the audiences in the theatre – whether they're watching Chekhov, Eugene O'Neill, or a play about the long-gone world of the city's whaling fleets and jute mills – tend to reflect that character, cheerful, sensible, warm. And the great achievement of the Dundee Rep building – a vaguely circular chunk of modern concrete construction, with an attractive glass frontage that does a minimum of violence to the grave early Victorian order of Tay Square – is that it provides a dynamic, practical modern space in which the relationship between this town and its actors can flow on unimpeded, a theatre-place that is full of comfort and technical capacity, and yet somehow unobtrusive when it comes to the business of theatre itself (p. 65). The theatre, financed jointly by Dundee District Council, Tayside Region and the Scottish Arts Council, and designed by local architects Nicholl and Russell, opened in 1982, and had the advantage of being built not just for 'theatre' in the abstract, but for an existing and good-going repertory company which had been operating, with some difficulty, out of a former church hall in Lochee Road; and its 450-seat auditorium, rising like a miniature Olivier Theatre from first floor level, above an open ground floor of foyer space and bars, is a noticeably elegant and well-realised effort to take the concept of theatre-space back to the basics that preceded Victorian rococo and plush, and forward into the next century. In concept, it is like a small Greek amphitheatre, with a steep semicircular tier of seats rising above and around a large, beautiful stage

Stalls Studio, Citizens' Theatre, Glasgow, 1992.
Performance of *Oedipus Rex*, 1994, directed by Clare Venables and designed by Stewart Laing.
(*Photo: Ivan Kyncl, courtesy of the Citizens' Theatre Archive*)

whose shape completes the circle. The front row of seats is almost on a level with the low edge of the stage; and the dark upholstered seats sweep round like continuous benches with no armrests between them, so that the audience sits companionably shoulder to shoulder.

And time and again, the shape and proportions of this space seem to create possibilities of communication, of immediacy, of intimacy combined with a sense of scale and grandeur, that draw the best from both actors and plays. I have seen productions fail here of course. Performances that sit far back on the stage lose all power and impact; conventional 'fourth wall' dramas can look a shade uncomfortable. But it's a design that truly brings actors and audience into the same space, to share their world and their story. It welcomes and does not intimidate; it opens channels of communication; it is easy, in the 1990's, to feel at home here.

February 23rd 1995:
The Citizens' Theatre, Gorbals, Glasgow.

And so to the one that got away, the battered 19th century theatre, among the tower blocks, wastelands and new development projects of what was once Glasgow's working class heart, that somehow feels less 'old' than any other Victorian or Edwardian theatre in Scotland. I suppose this gorgeous old space does start with some powerful structural advantages; opened in 1878 as Her Majesty's, swiftly renamed The Royal Princess's, and known as the Citizens' after the company that moved there in the late 1940's, it has a wonderfully energetic, tip-tilted auditorium – seating 570 without its rickety upper circle – in which the stage and the seating seem to lean hungrily towards one another. The stage – like the huge set-making and costume workshops behind – was built with pantomime in mind, the powerful direct interaction with the audience, the jokes, the topicality, the local references, the great walk-down

Circle Studio, Citizens' Theatre, Glasgow, 1992.
Performance of *La Ronde*, 1994, directed by Matthew Lloyd and designed by Kenny Miller.
(Photo: Ivan Kyncl, courtesy of the Citizens' Theatre Archive)

finales in which the stage opens out to the audience; the opening production, on 28th December 1878, was a resplendent version of *Ali Baba and the Forty Thieves*, and I have certainly never seen a conventional proscenium-arch stage that looks less like a high-and-mighty platform, more like a part of the auditorium space.

But it seems to me that this theatre could, nevertheless, have been in the same plight as many other old houses in Scotland – loved as artefacts, increasingly irrelevant as places for making modern theatre – if it had not, 25 years ago, met its match. Perhaps it was fortunate, in a sense, that when the present triumvirate of directors (Giles Havergal, Philip Prowse, Robert David MacDonald) arrived at the Citizens', in 1969 and 1970, the theatre building itself was at something of a low ebb. The dense tenement streets around it had been pulled down, the theatre had lost its fine classical frontage and looked pretty much like a carpet warehouse, the foyer space was unglamorous and basic, the auditorium was charming but shabby. There was nothing, in other words, to inspire an attitude of reverence or awe towards the old place; and within a couple of years, the new team had taken it by the scruff of the neck and stamped their personality and style all over it. So far as the exterior was concerned, they played up the warehouse look, painting a huge 'all seats 50p' sign on the wall facing north across the river, and using the unassuming look of the place – as well as those rock-bottom prices – to break down social barriers around the idea of theatre-going. Inside, they ran a blood-and-thunder Jacobean colour scheme of black, gold and red through the whole place, decorating the spartan foyer with huge, grainy production photographs, and turning the auditorium into a cleverly-lit bordello of red and black paint and gilt plaster work.

And in this space – transformed, remade to express their own aesthetic and perspective – they created during the 1970's and 80's, one of the most exciting repertory theatres in Europe, running a mind-blowing programme of Jacobean horrors and European classics produced with astonishing visual flair, winning over a city that had always had a tremendous love-affair with the visual arts and theatrical spectacle, spearheading Glasgow's development as an international 'city of culture', shocking the bourgeoisie, having tremendous fun. In the early 1980's, when the company tackled the Genet trilogy of *The Maids*, *The Screens* and *The Blacks*, Prowse even demonstrated his mastery of the space by building a set which continued the red-black-and-gold-pillared architecture of the proscenium straight round the back of the stage, annihilating the gap between stage and auditorium, and raising the most challenging questions about the audience's own role in the real-life theatre of hypocrisy and compliance. The company faltered a little in 1989, when the burst of investment associated with Glasgow's year as City of culture brought the Citizens' a hideous new frontage in Sainsbury's-post-modern style, all yellow brick and blue hi-tech tubing, along with a vast new white foyer like the promenade deck of a liner; the triumvirate seemed, briefly, a little overwhelmed by it all.

But by the beginning of 1992 they had worked out what to do; in the teeth of recession, poverty, post-modern architecture and the penny-pinching spirit of the times, they would fill up the wide-open spaces of their new foyer with little studio theatres, a tiny black-box 60 seater to the right of the door at stalls level, a slightly more spacious 120 seater directly above it; and fill the little theatres with shows (pp. 66, 67). And after a shaky start, the amazing chutzpah of this move began to pay off. Through the studios poured a stream of young directors, new writers, odd experiments, Robert David MacDonald fragments, visiting companies and, eventually, new young audiences; the main stage thrived on the new talent and energy they brought into the building; and the foyer, on a good evening, seethed like the entrance to a multiplex cinema, with three audiences queuing at the bar, criss-crossing in front of the long ticket desk, exchanging notes in a roar of conversation.

Which is how I come to be sitting, this Friday night, among a packed 120-strong crowd on fiercely uncomfortable makeshift seating modules in the Cits' Circle Studio, watching a searing stage version of Irvine Welsh's *Trainspotting*, a cult novel about the drug culture of unemployed Edinburgh kids in the 1990's. It's rough-edged, it's foul-mouthed, it's Scottish, it's adapted and directed by a sometime Cits' actor called Harry Gibson, it's full of young acting talent; Philip Prowse lurks in a high corner of the audience like an aristocratic hawk, talent-spotting, revelling in the sweaty theatricality of it. In the main auditorium, a few yards away, his stunning production of Middleton's *Women Beware Women* is storming towards the end of its short run, great washing lines of ragged rotting corpses hanging in the sky of Middleton's Florence above the stage, the cast punching out contemporary sexual politics with a force you can almost taste; downstairs, the little Stalls Studio is preparing to receive Empty Space Theatre's touring version of *To The Lighthouse*.

And does it matter that all this is happening here, in this particular old building, in this particular place just beyond the river, beside the mosque, opposite the tower blocks? Of course it does: the Cits' auditorium was built with flair and affection by people who knew and loved popular theatre; and its location, on the dramatic front line of Glasgow's recent history, has always kept its feet close to the ground. But what matters most, beyond all that, is that the place is in the hands of people who know that theatre is an art and an action, not a place; an art that must always find and shape the spaces it needs for the time it lives in, and not be limited by the spaces it inherits, an art that in changing, has to change the bricks and mortar, lath and plaster with which it surrounds itself. If this old place fell into the Clyde tomorrow, in other words, Havergal, Prowse, and MacDonald would probably stage a floating opera on the wreckage, and attract their biggest audience yet. Because that's how it is, in the heart of theatre. Buildings rise and fall; the show goes on.

WARWICK ARTS CENTRE

Jodi Myers

Jodi Myers has been Director of Warwick Arts Centre since January 1991. Prior to that she was Deputy Director of Touring at the Arts Council of Great Britain, having spent a number of years in arts marketing and stage management. Currently she serves on the Council of the Theatrical Management Association, is a member of the Arts Advisory Group of the Royal Society of Arts and a member of the Touring Music Sub-Committee for the Arts Council of England.

Main Auditorium, Arts Centre, University of Warwick (*Photo: courtesy of the University of Warwick*)

Arts Centres provide some of the most active theatre spaces of recent decades, largely as touring venues for professional theatre, music and dance.

The largest arts centre outside London is to be found in Coventry. Warwick Arts Centre, which is part of the University of Warwick, was designed by Renton Howard Wood Levin, and won an award for its innovative design when it opened in 1974. The first phase of building included a Theatre, which quickly became one of the most popular venues on the national touring circuit.

The Theatre combines a sense of space, both on stage and in the auditorium, rare in a venue having a capacity of 543, with a high degree of intimacy, and an excellent performer/spectator relationship. It offers considerable staging flexibility, through a number of features, notably a series of moveable towers which replace the traditional fixed proscenium arch. The forestage, which brings the stage into close contact with the audience, converts easily into a sizeable orchestra pit or can be seated with 30 additional places.

No seat feels far from the stage and everyone has a clear view; good sightlines are appreciated by all members of the audience, but children are particularly well catered for, as the auditorium's rake means no one has to peer over the seat back or head of the person in front of them. The acoustic is most suited to speech, but is also sympathetic to opera and chamber music.

As well as hosting a wide range of established companies – many of whom, including the Royal Court, Cheek by Jowl and the Richard Alston Dance Company, have chosen to premiere work there – in the early 1990s the Theatre also presented the work of the acclaimed Welsh theatre company, Brith Gof, and the visual theatre group. I.O.U., which made the most of the Theatre's generous dimensions. In 1994, to celebrate the twentieth anniversary of its opening, the Arts Centre commissioned three pieces specifically for the Theatre programme, which then toured nationally.

The first phase of the Arts Centre also included a fully flexible Studio, which affords the possibility of a variety of staging and seating configurations. In 1981, the Concert Hall, with a marvellous acoustic, was opened and, while its first decade featured music of all kinds, in the early 1990s its potential for theatrical presentation was explored, which resulted in some very unusual theatre being staged in it, including a piece which was specially commissioned.

The Arts Centre also includes a Film Theatre and Gallery, where on occasion theatre companies can be found in residence, running workshops in and around sculptures and other artworks, proving that drama is not confined to stages.

Warwick Arts Centre is still evolving two decades after it opened and 1995 will see the opening of a new foyer to accommodate nightly audiences often well in excess of 2,000. No doubt the performance possibilities of this new foyer will be explored in due course.

THE HAYMARKET THEATRE, LEICESTER

John Blackmore

John Blackmore is Chief Executive of the Haymarket Theatre, Leicester. He has directed over one hundred professional productions, and has run theatres and theatre companies for twenty-eight years, including the Library Theatre, Manchester, the Young People's Company at the Midlands Arts Centre, and the Duke's Playhouse, Lancaster. He was founder-director of the Tynewear Theatre Company, later the Tyne Theatre Company, and has been responsible for two Theatre in Education teams. Before moving to Leicester, he was director of the University of Warwick Arts Centre, and Executive Producer with the English Shakespeare Company.

Information from John Blackmore, Chief Executive

The Leicester Haymarket is one of a series of major Repertory Theatres which in the early 1970s received local authority support as a way of regenerating the inner city.

The Haymarket, completed in 1973, is unusual in the extent to which its building is so fully integrated into the commercial life of the city. The Haymarket forms part of a town-centre scheme of about 4.3 acres, including shops and offices, with parking for five hundred cars. The subject of a redevelopment proposal (in March 1995) that involves a £12m rebuild and refurbishment of the immediate area, the theatre is likely to become even more part and parcel of the civic and commercial heart of Leicester.

Designed by Building Design Partnership in collaboration with the Leicester City Architect's Department, the theatre draws clear benefits from its civic origins, especially in ease of access by car and on foot. The theatre entrance and main foyer are at first floor level over shops, and can be approached along shopping galleries from the central square. The upper foyer can be reached directly from the city-owned car park.

Constructed in reinforced concrete with red-brick cladding, the building is from the exterior almost indistinguishable from surrounding commercial properties. A design study to give it a more distinctive appearance is currently under way.

Inside, the foyers are spacious and inviting. The auditorium seats about 750, in two tiers, with a large proscenium opening and a fixed thrust stage and side stages. It retains a comparatively intimate feel, almost like a Greek theatre, despite the existence of the gallery. Leicester has made its name producing large musicals. *Me and My Girl* went to Broadway. *Madam Butterfly* with Antony Hopkins, *My Fair Lady*

Auditorium of the Haymarket Theatre, Leicester
(Photo: Courtesy of Haymarket Theatre)

with Tony Britton, *West Side Story, High Society,* the Sondheim musicals have all been performed on the Leicester stage. Yet the auditorium provides a comfortable space for plays too.

Recent theatres have experienced a problem in retaining the intimate wrap-around feel of earlier theatres such as Matcham's, but Leicester is perhaps, with the West Yorkshire Playhouse, the most successful of its generation of major Reps in solving or almost solving that problem.

THE NOTTINGHAM PLAYHOUSE
Space for Art or Art for Spaces

Ruth Mackenzie

Thirty years after Peter Moro's Nottingham Playhouse was built, and in the year it was listed Grade II* for being 'stylistically a crucial link between the Royal Festival Hall and the Royal National Theatre', we installed an elegant glass lift in the foyer to give everyone, but particularly those in wheelchairs, access to all floors of the theatre. Architect Julian Marsh's design for the lift got Listed Planning consent, and the local Coalition for Disabled People worked closely with him to ensure the lift would meet the needs of disabled people (*see* below).

It does, but it also meets some other quite unforeseen needs. It opened in November 1994 and in each interval of the 80 performances of our Christmas pantomime *Cinderella*, the lift offered children a new and hugely entertaining ride up and down the building. For Nottingham Playhouse's Christmas party, the lift provided Artistic Director Martin Duncan with a surprising entrance descending down this glass chimney as Father Christmas. For the launch of his first artistic season, it was the focus for his plan to make a piece of performance art celebrating our third partnership with the London Interna-

tional Festival of Theatre (known as L.I.F.T).

The best laid architectural plans for spaces for theatre cannot anticipate the audiences' and artists' creativity. The history of theatre buildings is littered with the recriminations of artists who have found themselves unreasonably restricted by the imagination of architects who failed to consult them adequately. Even more annoying are the recriminations of subsequent generations of artists about the failure of the artists who preceded them to anticipate their needs. Often forgotten are the feelings of audiences, stuck on backless benches in the hot and uncomfortable studio black boxes that excited artists 20 years ago, for example.

Yesterday's good ideas for theatre spaces often seem dismal to the artists and audiences of today – like yesterday's fashions, they are not yet old enough to have heritage value and just old enough to be hopelessly out of date. This is a challenge for those of us working in recently built theatre spaces, and especially a problem for those who wish to work with the most exciting contemporary artists who are driven to make their work without compromises. They are often not interested in making their art to fit existing spaces. They would like the space to be made to fit their art.

One current solution for some artists is to develop their art in a space especially conceived for that piece of art. In arts jargon, this is known as site specific work. Sometimes, the specific site is a warehouse, sometimes a quarry, in Nottingham recently a nightclub for our premiere *Dirty Reality* led by Denise Wong and a ruined castle in Newark for Michael Eaton's *Leaves Of Life*. These spaces are by definition non-theatre space, although with outstandingly successful non-theatre spaces such as Glasgow's Tramway, converted initially to house Peter Brook's

Ruth Mackenzie is Executive Director of Nottingham Playhouse. She was previously Director and Co-Founder of Moving Parts Theatre Company, Fellow in Theatre at the University of Bradford, Artistic Director of Bradford Multicultural Festival, Drama Officer at the Arts Council of Great Britain and Head of Strategic Planning for the South Bank Centre (London). A graduate of Newnham College, Cambridge, and the Sorbonne, she holds an honorary D.Litt. of Nottingham Trent University and an Honorary Fellowship of the University of Nottingham. Among many public appointments she has been a member of the Arts Council Touring Advisory Board, the British Council Drama and Dance Advisory Committee and the Arts Council National Lottery Advisory Committee.

Right:
The glass lift, foyer, the Nottingham Playhouse, 1995.
(*Photo: Mark Enstone*)
Overleaf:
Auditorium of the Nottingham Playhouse, as adapted for Goldoni's *The Servant of Two Masters*, directed by Martin Duncan.
(*Photo: Frazer Ashford*)

71

Mahabarata, it is intriguing to wonder when a 'non-theatre space' that has been housing theatre non-stop for five years becomes in fact a theatre space.

It is a tribute to Peter Moro's achievement in Nottingham that Peter Brook brought his production of *The Man Who* to Nottingham Playhouse in 1994. Peter Brook is notoriously fussy about the physical conditions in which he will work, and Nottingham Playhouse does not strikingly resemble the Bouffes du Nord for which *The Man Who* was created.

Peter Brook's production manager, John Guy Lecat, has amongst his many jobs the task of visiting theatres and spaces to see if they have the right site-specific ambience for Peter's work. Peter Brook is a pre-eminent example of an artist whose demands for space for his art have led to the creation of a host of non-theatre spaces round the world. When he visited Nottingham Playhouse (p. 131), the physical aspects of its auditorium were entirely wrong: it was too big, the audience were below the level of the stage, it had a proscenium arch. It would not work. They could not come.

But they did. We found that we shared the same determination to get the creative conditions right in our companies, central to which is the passion to create and share with a community, and these shared values created the right 'specifics' for the visit, even though the physical 'site specifics' had seemed to be against us. So when Peter Brook and his company visited Nottingham Playhouse, as well as their performances in the Playhouse, the company offered workshops within our community to local students from both universities, local adult education classes, local professional artists, local musicians, local inner city African and Caribbean young people, local schoolchildren, with Peter Brook himself leading workshops for Toothill Comprehensive and severe learning difficulties children from the Shepherd School. They led a formal programme of talks and receptions, and they also chatted to audiences before and after the show in our outside bar, idyllically Parisian in uncharacteristic sunshine.

One of the most significant aspects of Peter Brook's visit was the involvement of the City of Nottingham and the regional inward investment agency the East Midlands Development Company, both of whom enthusiastically supported his visit in the form of substantial sponsorship. They did this because they believed that enabling an international artist of the status of Peter Brook to work in Nottingham would signal to international businessmen and inward investors that Nottingham had an European quality of life and standards of excellence which make it a brilliant place to live and work. It is for this reason that Nottingham and Nottinghamshire invest in Nottingham Playhouse, finding over £600,000 a year to help Martin Duncan achieve his ambitious ideas for the Playhouse's artistic programme, and Nottinghamshire have doubled their resources for Roundabout's programme of artists in schools over the last four years.

Much in the same way, 30 years before, the City of Nottingham had backed the then enormous investment in Peter Moro's new Playhouse. Their understanding of the importance of a local theatre in developing and reflecting the culture of their communities, and providing a positive and inspiring way of projecting the City's name nationally and internationally was then ahead of its times.

However, as well as the role of the local community leaders in providing the resources and buildings for theatre, the role of the community themselves in enabling a piece of art or a place to make art is crucial. Nottingham has taught us all in the Playhouse a great deal about the way in which the individuals in the community shape the provision – the bricks and mortar. The original Nottingham Playhouse was created by community members in a converted cinema in 1948, with the community and City and the Arts Council raising the money for the new theatre in 1963. Right from its beginnings, the Playhouse was shaped by the community members' desire for excellence and innovation, and the spirit of adventure has continued throughout the highlights of its distinguished history under directors such as André Van Gyseghem, John Neville, Frank Dunlop, Stuart Burge, Richard Eyre, Pip Broughton and now Martin Duncan. Unlike some other cities where their theatres were initiated 'top down' by the local government, the commitment of Nottingham's people to their theatre and to its distinctiveness creates a very different atmosphere. The theatre is not something imposed upon the community; it was created by the community and is sustained by them.

In Nottingham, that commitment today is clearest in the way in which community members shape the actual art in each night's performance or each day's workshop. As the Sunday Times recently quoted, over 40 per cent of Nottingham Playhouse's audiences are under the age of 30 and see the Playhouse's programme as a way to develop their own skills and explore theatre which might involve innovative comedians making plays such as the Comedy Store Players, international African dance artists or the most demanding theatre, with surtitles, by Lev Dodin or Robert Lepage.

Peter Brook said that Nottingham audiences laughed at the right places and in the right way at *The Man Who*, and that was a great compliment to Nottingham. The development of audiences who 'laugh in the right way' comes from the creativity of the community in creating and owning the art led by the Playhouse. The innovative live artists Lee Simpson and Phelim McDermott, for example, demonstrated the creativity of Nottingham in radical fashion with their commissioned *Improbable Tales* where each night they and the audience improvised a different play with a different cast, and with different set, lights, music, technical support. Only the stage and auditorium remained the same, but the atmosphere changed completely each night as artists and audience created a new world. It was 'site specific' in the sense in which only through the growth of rapport and experiment between those artists, the Playhouse staff and audiences of Nottingham, through a series of previous experiments, could the project happen. Or as Lee Simpson and Phelim McDermott put it, it was hard to imagine another theatre and community mad enough to allow them to create so impossible a project.

It is this quality of shared adventure which drew

Martin Duncan to leave the freelance opera directing world and take on the running of Nottingham Playhouse. In his new three year plan *See Change* he says: 'Our first ambition is to work in an atmosphere where the art we make is a vital part of everyday life, where everyone in Nottingham and Nottinghamshire feels art is as important and necessary to them as a daily cup of coffee is to the process of waking up'.

It is important that the three year plan focuses upon atmosphere, and it is the creation of and creativity in that atmosphere that leads the work at the Playhouse, rather than the physical aspects of the building.

Of course, the building itself offers him the challenge of finding new ways for his artists and audiences to play with the space – extending the stage through the proscenium arch, or playing with the orchestra pit, which Martin has used in celebrated past productions such as *The Servant Of Two Masters* (see right) as a way of subverting the expectation of the pit as a barrier between stage pictures and audience. In that production, the musicians in the pit made coffee and spaghetti and served the audience in the interval, and throughout the play itself acted as a link joining audience and actors together. That production too played with action in the auditorium, in the foyers and even in the streets around the theatre.

His first production for Nottingham Playhouse brings together creative collaborators across art forms – writer Alistair Beaton with a new adaptation of Gogol's *The Nose*, designer Tim Hatley, lighting designer Wolfgang Göbbel, Peter Salem creating a new sound score and Linda Dobell as choreographer, working with an ensemble of ten performers. Conceived for Nottingham Playhouse, squeezing the distorted perspective of St Petersburg's main street into the entire depth of the auditorium, with runaway noses created by community members in education workshops, by established visual artist

Duncan MacAskill in the foyers of the Playhouse, and by community participants in the streets and shopping centres of Nottingham, the anarchy of Gogol's original story is created with and for Nottingham specifically.

In the best sense, the piece is 'site specific': made with and for our community, it involves a family of artists including young people in schools and communities, artists familiar to Nottingham such as Lee and Phelim and international artists such as Wolfgang Göbbel making a world premiere for the physical space of Nottingham Playhouse's auditorium and the creative space that the community have built up. Although it is made specifically for Not-

tingham, it has also been invited as a flagship production of a theatre festival in Bucharest.

Nottingham Playhouse's production manager has learnt from our international partnerships that his priority in Bucharest will be to find the theatre with the right creative atmosphere and not to despair when he cannot find a theatre with the right dimensions.

Over the last few years of experiment in Nottingham and work with a range of demanding artists, our own Artistic Directors Pip Broughton and now Martin Duncan, as well as international artists from all over world, we have learnt that the most important quality in a building is a determination to make the impossible possible.

When the extraordinary director of the Rostevelli Company of Tblisi, Robert Sturua, created a production of *Hamlet* for Thelma Holt, he was adamant that he wanted it to play in warehouses specially adapted for the production. We persuaded him that we could floor over the auditorium, bring in temporary seating and scaffolding (as you do for a warehouse converted to a temporary theatre), and turn Nottingham Playhouse into a warehouse. The company led by Alan Rickman were very doubtful, but when they came they found the space had an entirely different feel, and the transformation of a familiar auditorium into a rough warehouse interior added to the excitement of the production. More mundanely, for the acting company, the advantages of this warehouse feel in a space with heating, dressing rooms, hot water, acoustics, and an artist-friendly bar and restaurant made up for some of the disadvantages they had been discovering in real warehouses in wintry regional towns.

Again, as our three year plan says: For us and our communities, the word RISK should be positive, as we hope it means joining together to make and share a piece of art which should be exhilarating, daring, mysterious, inspiring, dazzling, entertaining, eccentric, intriguing, in a creative atmosphere that instantly makes us all look forward to the art.

That atmosphere starts at the front door of all the spaces where we perform and embraces all the workshops, schools work, community work, special events that we make. It should inspire everyone who works with us, all of us and all the artists from young people in schools doing workshops to members of the community creating their own art with us to the most famous actor creating a performance.

Our theatre in education company, Roundabout, recently took their Caribbean version of *Peacemaker* by David Holman to Okinawa, representing Britain in an international festival. The piece was carefully programmed into a suitable space, and they insisted that the usual festival audience had to be supplemented by school parties. This was lucky, as the set flew round the world and landed thousands of miles away from them. With the children, they improvised a set for the show, and created both the atmosphere they needed and the performance they had been invited to give.

The importance of the atmosphere of the space leads the work of Roundabout, now Britain's oldest surviving Theatre in Education Company. In an unique partnership with Nottinghamshire Education Authority, Roundabout's funding has doubled over the last four years, and over this year artists will create over 500 performances and workshops with and for young people in Nottinghamshire schools. The artistic work is entirely specific to the needs of those young children and the educational values of Nottinghamshire. The commitment to the cultural values of our communities and artistic standards that led to Roundabout representing Britain at an international festival in Japan are shared by the schools. The schools' buildings are, of course, all different, but with shared values and commitment, the artists and young people can create the same atmosphere in each school around the county.

In Nottingham, we cannot achieve the ideal of creating a physical space for each piece of art we make. The ideal of literal 'site-specific art' is beyond us. What we can try to achieve is the atmosphere and values of site-specific art, and work with the creativity of artists and audiences to create a specific atmosphere which overcomes the restrictions of physical buildings, even one as beautiful as Peter Moro's Playhouse.

In the end, making space for artists and art is as much about the process and atmosphere in which creativity can thrive as it is about the physical conditions. Making space for art is a metaphor about creating opportunities as much as a description of bricks and mortar. It is about celebrating the creativity and 'play' of art and artists, from Peter Brook to the children in Nottingham Playhouse's lift.

THE WEST YORKSHIRE PLAYHOUSE

Jude Kelly

Jude Kelly took up her appointment as Artistic Director of the West Yorkshire Playhouse, Leeds, in January 1989, and was appointed Chief Executive in April, 1993. She has been Artistic Director of Solent People's Theatre (1976–80) and Battersea Arts Centre (from 1980), a venue which she successfully developed as a multi-functional centre with two theatres, cinema, restaurant, art gallery, potteries and disabled dark room. She has been Director of the National Theatre of Brent, has directed a four-part series for Channel 4 television, and has also directed for the Royal Shakespeare Company, where her production of *Sarcophagus* (about the Chernobyl disaster) was transferred to the Mermaid Theatre, and was nominated for two Olivier awards. She has also directed at Bristol Old Vic, the Lyric Hammersmith, the Abbey Theatre, Dublin and in New York, and has been Festival Director for the York Mystery Plays.

Based on a conversation with Ronnie Mulryne

The Citizens' Theatre, Glasgow, offers a very interesting parallel and contrast to the West Yorkshire Playhouse. At the Citizens', they have divided their playing areas into three, as a way of breathing new life into the work of the Company. They have found that some of the most enterprising work is now going on in the little studio spaces rather than in the main auditorium (pp. 66, 67). It seems as if the public has decided that the two small spaces are adventurous, while the established space is conventional. I don't think the Company felt that would be the case. Small is beautiful seems to have been the public's instinctive reaction. The red plush seats and the red plush curtains don't seem to be inviting to today's audiences. Peter Brook appears to be right in saying that rough theatre will save the day. The Citizens', a marvellous community theatre, clearly felt that the spaces they had weren't appropriate for the work they wanted to do.

The Tramway [in Glasgow] is another kind of alternative (p. 57, 61–63). What is interesting about such spaces is that they already have a human history in the very bones of the building, a certain kind of authenticity. This may sound a little poetic and spiritual, but for theatre it makes a difference. You want in such spaces to join the forward march of history. Places like the Tramway inspire you to follow the echo of the voices that remain in that space. There are no holds barred. Nothing dictates to you the way to make theatre, as the proscenium arch tends to do. The space allows you to create a theatre language for contemporary experience. In the same way, a theatre like the Bouffes du Nord [in Paris] encourages you to think in terms of a gathering of people who want to talk together through imaginative means.

The West Yorkshire Playhouse is sited on Quarry Hill. On that Hill a most important social experiment took place, but one that failed. The Quarry Hill flats were built on the Corbusier model. They provided inner city living for a great many people, in an attempt to create a community. But many of the essential aspects of community, many of the things that would have made it a city within a city, the parks, the laundrettes, the little shops, just weren't provided. When you knock all that down, and you are left with the hill, part of me thinks that all that idealism, all those people's lives, don't go away. I walked around the theatre site when only the first row of bricks was down, and I knew the project would work. The place felt right as a place people would come to. Sometimes the planners talk about purpose-built theatres in terms of *need* – a fly tower, a club space, a certain size of auditorium – but to talk about need in this way is to ensure failure in terms of a place where art will happen. Art awakens desire. You have to give people more than they need, practically, indeed more than the architect can imagine. The brief for a new theatre should not merely be one of practical needs, though of course these are important. The governing question should be, 'How does one find the heartbeat of this building? How do you encourage the reaction, "I could do something with this place"?'

The building of the West Yorkshire Playhouse strikes me as quite special. The history of the theatre building really started as part of that movement in the 1950s that was about the wider establishment of repertory theatre. It began with a non-professional group of theatre devotees saying, 'We must have a space for professional theatre.' There was then only a temporary space at the University. Twenty years later, the money was raised for a purpose-built building. In that time, there grew up an accumulation of ideas and ambitions as to what could happen in a theatre building, and a wish to go beyond what was then current taste. The building was created for the future and not for the present. Happily, the thinking was entirely opposed to a multipurpose series

The Courtyard Theatre at the West Yorkshire Playhouse
(Photo: Paul White Photography and Design)

The Quarry Theatre at the West Yorkshire Playhouse
(Photo: Paul White Photography and Design)

of spaces. In the building of the Playhouse, *passion* was a definite ingredient. The husband and wife architects who built it, Marjorie and Ian Appleton, became just as obsessed with the building as the people who commissioned it, and the people like myself who have inherited it. That obsession brought its own minor strife, but only because people cared so passionately about it. Not because they wanted it to look nice, but because they wanted it to have a long-term meaning.

The outside of the Playhouse is built of Leeds brick. Originally, when people saw the outside of the building, they thought it was a great disappointment – too like an Asda supermarket. It's rather a pleasant building which fits in with the general look of Leeds. In a hundred years time, this will simply be one version of a 1990s building, and will be absolutely fine. Its great advantage is that people have already made it part of the community, because they feel they understand it. They feel comfortable with it, and so they come in. Inside, the use of light is splendid. We need to photosynthesise, as creatures of nature. Every space, every dressing room, every office, every rehearsal room has natural light. That represents an intuitive understanding of what we desire. Not only do we need electric light, but the provision of natural light in this way allows us to tap into something that is fundamental to our desires.

The audience has a sense of freedom in the foyer spaces outside the auditoria. Of course we want beautiful auditoria, and this we have secured, with each of the two auditoria well adapted to the productions we do there. But the artists coming into the building want to be in all the spaces. They actually *like* being in the foyer, and they *like* being in the Congreve room, and they *like* being in the rehearsal room. There is no sense that the artist closets himself or herself in the auditorium. The connection between what the artist makes, which is a very private and personal process, and the fact that it only has meaning if it is given as a gift, the generosity to accept that it only has meaning if there is a receiver – that vital circle between art making and giving has to have space for its realisation. If you were a

David Edgar's *Pentecost* in the new Other Place, Stratford-upon-Avon, 1994–5. Directed by Michael Attenborough, designed by Robert Jones
(*Photo: Clive Barda*)

Royal Shakespeare Theatre,
Stratford-upon-Avon,
refurbished 1993
(*Photo: Colin Willoughby*)

The Auditorium of the Lawrence
Batley Theatre, Huddersfield.
For description see pp. 170–171.
(*Photo: Peter Rourke*)

The set for Tourneur's *The Atheist's Tragedy*, directed by Anthony Clark, designed by Patrick Connellan, 1994 at the Birmingham Repertory Theatre. (*Photo: Courtesy of Bob Wain*)

The set for Lynn Ahrens' and Stephen Flaherty's *Once on This Island*, directed by David Toguri and Gwenda Hughes, designed by Kendra Ullyart, 1994 at the Birmingham Repertory Theatre. (*Photo: Courtesy of Bob Wain*)

Greek citizen, and you attended the play, you might well bump into the playwright, and you would talk to him about all the issues the play raised. If you were a member of a tribe, hunting for ten days while someone else was creating an important piece of theatre, one that would affect your tribal taboos and customs, you would discuss it with him. In every context, meaning, form, skill, personality, you must as an artist *belong*. I'm not saying that every member of the audience has to rub shoulders with every artist, but there has got to be some sense of a meeting place. In the Playhouse, there is no stage door, so you have to leave through the front door, with the audience. There is an acceptance that your work is for other people. Inside the auditorium, there is a respect for the ordinary moments of human exchange. When you come out into the foyer spaces, you must be allowed to exchange and debate. The attractiveness of other spaces in the theatre is not about how to make money at the coffee bar, it is about how to get that sense of community.

There's another issue about the Playhouse. In Britain, we have very little sense of our real collective history. In this rather turbulent, uneasy moment, a time of economic insignificance as a nation, we need to find the courage to embrace a lot of new thinking. We have to reassume some pride in Britishness. We have to know what that could mean to us. We are very good at looking at other people's art and saying that's a marvellous example of their cultural inheritance. We don't know what ours means to us. We don't know our own culture. We're not sure whether it's class-ridden, whether it's imperialist and xenophobic, or whether it comes from a quite different direction, like the Yorkshire brass band and clog dancing. We don't know whether to be patronising about it or proud of it. We are just very confused. One thing we must do is realise that the region we are in is just as worthy of respect as any other region, including the metropolis. There is no reason why the West Yorkshire Playhouse should not at this point in time take off on behalf of the nation. You have got to go through a glass ceiling which sits over the head of regional theatre. This

need only be a mental problem. The West Yorkshire Playhouse has everything we need in a physical sense. The only thing that prevents us piercing that glass ceiling is that we can't believe that different parts of the nation can have equal resources. It never occurs to anyone that it could be more important to the nation if the kind of energy we associate with metropolitan work was happening in ten places *outside* London. Here you can harness the energies of a whole community. The fact that the building can be used for health care meetings, disability groups, and all the things we sagely approve of, actually educates people into the realisation that their community is composed of all these people, whom they don't know and don't understand and haven't honoured. That process is a creative process, and could happen throughout the nation. In terms of art, and an art space, and a cultural mixing point, it's important for the theatre to be there to allow these meetings to happen.

If you think of theatre in terms of a sacred space, and ask why we have these special buildings for theatre, it must be because we need theatre to happen, we need imaginative versions of our own situation. In a secular society, I would say that we need theatre even more desperately. Building a special place is at the root of recognising the need for theatre to happen. The theatre building should show the kind of beauty that recognises the special nature of the well we go to drink from. But it must also include the idea that everyone must be made welcome at this well. The energy that people bring into the theatre will change everything, not in some generalised watered-down way, but in ways that genuinely affect our humanity, and not only as it is now but as we'd like it to be.

Neither of our spaces at the West Yorkshire Playhouse is a conventional proscenium arch theatre. That is quite significant, because on an unconventional stage, an open stage, one recognises that theatre is more democratic and dangerous than simple picture-creation (though wonderful work can be done on proscenium stages too). The Quarry is basically an epic arena (p. 75). It works best presenting

big human ideas. It can show the collision of the personal and the great, when you see that one person's life is a small thing in comparison with the totality. The Quarry lends itself to major plays of that kind and to the major musicals. It never confines anything. The Courtyard is much more flexible (p. 75). It always says, 'I'm in the same room as you.' It allows for quite small, intimate, domestic situations where the actors and the audience together take in whatever is happening on stage. If you are doing comedy or satire, there's a definite agreement that you are in the same club. The Quarry is somewhere you are invited to wallow in the grandiosity of it all, or you can think quite selectively, in quite a detached way, about the work that is in front of you. In the Courtyard, by contrast, you are drawn into the sometimes quite subtle rhythms of the performance. In terms of how directors want to approach work, the two theatres allow you to say, 'What scale of feeling is this piece?' The artist can then make a choice of the more suitable space.

THE BIRMINGHAM REPERTORY THEATRE

Directing at the Birmingham Rep

Bill Alexander, Anthony Clark, Gwenda Hughes

Gwenda Hughes. Since becoming an Associate Director of the Birmingham Repertory Theatre Gwenda has directed among other productions *Loot, Romeo and Juliet, Big Maggie, Translations,* and *Hobson's Choice;* as well as plays on tour, and *Travelling Light* and *Worlds Apart* for children with severe learning difficulties in the Studio. Her co-directed *Once on This Island* (also in West End) won an Olivier Award (1995). Gwenda worked as an actor in theatre and television before being awarded an Arts Council Trainee Director's Bursary to work with Theatre Centre in 1982. She was then appointed Artistic Director of Watford Palace Theatre-in-Education Company, and from January 1987 worked as a freelance director with the Perspectives Theatre Company, Unicorn, M6, Red Ladder and Women's Theatre Group. She has also directed for the Young Vic and the Oldham Coliseum.

Based on a conversation with Ronnie Mulryne and Margaret Shewring

Bill Alexander: I'd like to begin by contradicting the common perception that Birmingham Rep is an awkward space. It is a *large* space, and has the normal problems of large spaces.

The fundamental way *not* to use a large space is to fill it with set. You do not want the set to compete with the actors. The best use for a large space is classical and non-naturalistic. The key is to use as little set as possible, but to know how to use the actors in relation to it.

Problems arise with naturalistic pieces. For example, in *Awake and Sing* the set was a series of rooms for a poor family. But the stage space suggested a room that was, in naturalistic terms, too big for such a poor family to live in. For *Playboy of the Western World* Tony [Clark] used, very successfully, a small naturalistic space within a large abstract space.

The Rep's auditorium is democratic, in that almost all of the audience has a good view. And the auditorium is not too wide. Some questions do arise. Is it too sharply raked? Too precipitous?

There are some potential limits on the kind of programme you can perform. The stage is best used for epic. Yet it is not impossible to stage a domestic play successfully. For example, we staged *Old Times* [by Harold Pinter] very successfully. You need to find the plays that go best in a large space, artistically, politically, in terms of design.

The Rep definitely works best when the stage is extended out over the first three rows. When these rows are left in, people sitting in them are below the level of the stage. When you build out over these rows, the actors' feet are on the same level as the audience, forming a real meeting point between the spectators and the stage.

Bill Alexander was appointed Artistic Director of Birmingham Repertory Theatre in November 1992. He began his directing career at the Bristol Old Vic, after which he joined the Royal Shakespeare Company (in 1977) with a special brief for new plays. In 1984 he was appointed Associate Director of the Company. His RSC productions include Antony Sher in *Tartuffe* and *Richard III, The Merchant of Venice* (Antony Sher and Harriet Walter) and *The Merry Wives of Windsor* (Nicky Henson and Lindsay Duncan), which won him the Olivier Award for Best Director. He has directed at the Nottingham Playhouse, the Royal Court, the Victory Theatre, New York, and the Shakespeare Theatre, Washington. His productions at Birmingham include *Old Times* (with Tim Pigott-Smith, Carol Royle and Estelle Kohler), *The Snowman* and *The Tempest.*

Anthony Clark joined the Birmingham Repertory Theatre as Associate Director in 1990. Among his productions for Birmingham are *Cider with Rosie, The Atheists' Tragedy* (for which he won the Martini Regional Theatre Award), *The Playboy of the Western World* and new plays *Rough, Playing the Rules* (Menthorn First Night Production Award), *Nervous Women* and *Syme* (a co-production with the Royal National Theatre Studio). A graduate of the Manchester University Drama Department, Anthony was appointed Artistic Director of Contact Theatre, Manchester, in 1984, and has directed freelance at the Young Vic, Greenwich Theatre, Bristol Old Vic and the Royal National Theatre. He has written more than a dozen plays and adaptations which have been produced by the Orange Tree theatre, the Royal Shakespeare Company, The Royal National Theatre, Contact theatre, the Bolton Octagon, Bristol Old Vic, the Leicester Haymarket and Birmingham Repertory Theatre.

Tony Clark: A director has to find a dynamic between the actors that can be translated spatially. The proportional balance between actors in space is what is needed to tell a story. The actors discover these spatial relationships in rehearsal. The stage design should be such as to allow the spatial relationships to be expressed in performance.

The relationships are often not naturalistic. So, in *The Atheist's Tragedy* (p. 78), in order to project the dynamics of the narrative in spatial terms, the dynamics used were not those of real space but of fictional space. Emotional distance parallels physical distance. Ideally, one shouldn't design too much before rehearsal establishes the play's relationships.

Bill: If only we could restructure the way we prepare for a show! We would have three weeks with no set or design, then a five week design period, and then a six week rehearsal period in the designed space.

It is, as I say, important not to overwhelm the stage with a very large set. It may be good to have a simple set with not a lot of detail. You can fill the space with light or fabric. Just don't complicate it.

Tony: Yes. A set can easily become decorative, and not essential.

Bill: Avoid doing something in designing the stage space that *defines* the play or *describes* it. The design should at best provide a context within which the play is allowed to describe itself. Design obviously means different things in different theatre spaces. The experience of watching the Rep stage is not pictorial. If stage space reproduces the experience of looking at a screen, then the uniqueness of theatre is not happening. The Rep is not a picture-frame stage, and in this it differs from, say, the Lyttleton.

Gwenda Hughes: The Rep auditorium doesn't bring the audience on stage.

Tony: A lot of rubbish is talked about the value of the actors being in the same room as the audience.

Gwenda: A wonderful contemporary play such as [David Edgar's] *Pentecost* (p. 76), currently at The

Left: The Auditorium of the old Birmingham Repertory Theatre (S.N. Cooke, 1913) (*Photo: Courtesy of the Birmingham Post and Mail*)

Below: The Auditorium of the new Birmingham Repertory Theatre (Graham Winteringham, 1970) (*Photo: Alan Wood*)

Other Place in Stratford, would actually go better on the Rep stage.

Bill: Yes. The RSC are doing [Anne Devlin's] *After Easter* at The Other Place (p. 91). But to have the audience on three sides, as they are at The Other Place, is by now as conventional as using a proscenium arch – but much more limiting. My own production of *After Easter* at the Lyric [in Belfast] used a proscenium arch. With a proscenium it was possible to do more to shape the play, to compose it.

Tony: We have lost the compositional sense of theatre that helped to elucidate narrative.

Bill: Aesthetically, either a picture-frame or a courtyard theatre is more limiting than the Rep auditorium. People drool over the Swan [in Stratford] (p. 168). But it is arguably the most limiting theatre I have ever worked in. It tells you *how* to approach a play. It tells you what it, the space, will sustain. I hate that. I was uneasy working in it as a space.

The notion that courtyards encourage audience engagement more than other spaces is spurious. What does engage an audience is truth, emotional reality and aesthetic inventiveness. Moreover, it is far easier technically to direct for a courtyard theatre than for a proscenium arch. You can't get it wrong in a courtyard. If you keep moving the actors you can create something interesting. You can get it very wrong in a proscenium, but you can also get it very right.

Gwenda: So far as a theatre space making a political statement is concerned, it is true that, for example, on our small-scale tours [to schools, colleges, clubs] the three or four sided space does often in itself make a political statement with a genuine educational meaning. The space echoes the audience-actor relationship, after a period of working or discussing together.

Tony: So much proscenium arch theatre is voyeuristic.

Bill: The Birmingham Rep is, one has to agree, a difficult space. But that is precisely what makes it so exciting. Theatre space is really a matter of fashion, isn't it? When critics so much admire experimental Shakespeare, they are often really responding to the novelty of smaller space for Shakespeare.

Tony: We should make it clear that the Birmingham Rep is not really a proscenium theatre. It's an *arena* theatre.

Gwenda: Actors occupying the same space as the audience *can* immediately engage the audience. Equally, they can have the opposite effect. Actors can make plays happen, can energise them in a large arena space. I'm thinking for example of Polly James in *Cider with Rosie,* or Gillian Hanna in *Big Maggie,* where the sense of engagement went right to the back of that big auditorium. Acting in a large space, the actor must *want* to communicate, to tell a story, in order to energise the space.

Bill: There needs to be an understanding of the interaction of subjective narrative and objective narrative. The subjective narrative must be told in an objective context, that is that 900 people are watching. The truth of theatre lies in this paradox. Like all true paradoxes, it is more interesting than simple truth.

To talk admiringly about theatre as a 'community' event is another fashionable convention, but little more than that.

Gwenda: It came out of the sixties, emerging from a political situation, and finding expression in taking unconventional theatre out to unconventional spaces. But the sixties *did* make important discoveries about space, such as the work of La Mama and the Fringe and physical theatre. Some current groups think they are discovering what has already been discovered. Some of their work is curiously old-fashioned.

Tony: The fact is that if you want to engage with an audience, you have to keep on redefining the relationship between actor and audience. For me, there is no such thing as a consistency of convention. That notion is born of the concept of theatre as passive spectacle. Convention reaffirms passivity.

Gwenda: Unfortunately, these conventions become assimilated into buildings, as for instance recently the Swan.

Bill: In making audience-members more aware of each other in small theatres, you greatly increase a sense of self-consciousness. What makes for shared experience is not size of space, but shared truths passionately communicated, so that the whole space is energised.

Gwenda: Most people's sense of space and perspective is now through TV. The camera angles of, for instance, *Hill Street Blues* help to define how people relate to visual experience. Their relationship to theatre work can be affected by this too. But the classic form is distant from us. It has its own visual logic. What the audience demands of it is extraordinary, and this must affect stage direction and design.

Tony: Visual conventions *have* changed. It used to be shocking in the theatre to turn one's back on the audience, and behave as if there was a fourth wall. Now it's no longer shocking to do just that. It has become commonplace, and meaningless.

Gwenda: Theatre demands the active engagement of the audience's imagination. Some plays come across as insincere unless they are presented in a space of epic proportions. You *need* distance. You *need* a large space. The Rep auditorium has 'wedges' where the auditorium doesn't work for a small number of seats, twenty but no more. The rest is a strong space. I like working in it. It's good to play to.

PART THREE

THEATRE SPACE

Writing, Directing, Designing and Acting

Theatre space stimulates and influences the work of artists across the spectrum from the writer and the director to the designer and the actor.

In Part Three, artists from many parts of the theatrical profession specify the ways in which a wide variety of theatre spaces has shaped their work, opened up opportunities, closed down options and offered both continuing frustrations and enhanced perspectives.

HOUSING THE NEW

Post-war British Theatre Architecture and New Writing

David Edgar

David Edgar was born in Birmingham in 1948 into a theatre family. He read Drama at Manchester University, and after a short career in local journalism, he took up playwriting full time in 1972. His work for the National Theatre includes *Entertaining Strangers* (1987) and *The Shape of the Table* (1990). For the Royal Shakespeare Company, he wrote *Destiny* (Other Place, Stratford, 1976; Aldwych, London, 1977), *The Jail Diary of Albie Sachs* (Warehouse, London, 1978), an adaptation of *Nicholas Nickleby* (Aldwych, 1980; Plymouth Theatre, New York, 1981), *Maydays* (Barbican Theatre, London, 1983), a version of *Dr Jekyll and Mr Hyde* (Barbican, 1991) and *Pentecost* (Other Place, 1994). His screenplays include *I know what I meant* (Granada TV, 1974), *Lady Jane* (Paramount, 1986), *Buying a Landslide* (BBC2, 1992), *Citizen Locke* (Channel Four, 1994) and the three-part serial *Vote for Them* (with Neil Grant, BBC2, 1989). He founded and directs Britain's first post-graduate course in playwriting, at the University of Birmingham, where he holds an honorary Professorship.
(*Photo: Chris Davies*)

The angry young playwrights of the mid to late 50s were not particularly exercised by architecture. The two great sites of the 1955–6 dramatic revolution were both smallish 19th century theatres, of conventional if homely appearance, with monarchist titles. True, Stratford's Theatre Royal was in proletarian east London, and Sloane Square's Royal Court had a tradition of theatrical radicalism (under the management of Harley Granville Barker and Bernard Shaw in the early years of the century). But neither George Devine, Joan Littlewood, nor the playwrights they nurtured were concerned – at that time at least – with revolutionising the nature of the playhouses in which their work was presented.

The playwriterly challenge to the conventional playhouse was left for the next generation – that group of radical young dramatists who came into the theatre in the late 1960s. There were three factors enabling young writers to enter the theatre in large numbers at that time: the global youth revolt against the Vietnam War which gave them a message; the abolition of stage censorship which allowed them to express it; and the expansion of subsidy which created a whole new theatre sector (first dubbed the 'underground', then – anent the Edinburgh festival – the fringe) in which their work could be performed.

Of the three, the abolition of the censor seems the most tangential, but in fact it enabled all the others. Stage censorship in Britain had been enshrined in statute law in the early 18th century, as a function of the office of the Lord Chamberlain, who had the right and duty to approve every word spoken – and every stage direction realised – on the British stage. The most notorious – and risible – effects of censorship related to sexuality (Joe Orton in particular enjoyed publishing the changes that would be re-

quired for his uncensored playtexts to be legally performed), but the censor also severely restricted the portrayal of violence and indeed the discussion of politics (the last Lord Chamberlain not only described the RSC's mild and liberal Vietnam War play *US* as 'bestial, anti-American and leftwing' but also threatened to deny it a license on that account: he said at one point he would only license the play if he could be convinced the American ambassador would not walk out of it).

But the reason why the August 1968 abolition of theatre censorship changed theatre irrevocably was actually bureaucratic. The requirement that dialogue and stage directions be approved in advance effectively proscribed street theatre, improvised theatre, topical theatre and indeed theatre that interrelated with its audience. The fringe as it developed would have found restrictions on what it could say irksome; it would find restrictions on when, how and whether it could change it impossible. Not only would the Living Theatre have been unable to take their own clothes off at the end of *Paradise Now* (performed at the Roundhouse in 1969), they would have been unable to invite the audience to join them.

The two defining characteristics of the fringe theatre of the late 60s and early 70s were its distrust of the establishment in all its forms and its hostility to theatre buildings. The nature – and spirit – of the time was brought home to me vividly by a particular event. I lived in the late 60s and early 70s in Bradford, which for reasons best known to itself had become a kind of northern outpost of the late 60s counterculture, and which played host to a veritable garden of exotic theatrical blooms during the two immensively successful Bradford Festivals of 1970 and 1971. (So successful were they, by the by, with so many people having such an obviously wonderful time,

that the City authorities refused to finance a third, on the grounds that giving so many people so much unambiguous pleasure was clearly a gross abuse of public funds). Here, you would find performance artists careering around the city on pink bicycles ridden in Red Arrow formation; there, my friend Howard Brenton's play about *Scott of the Antarctic* was being performed in the ice rink, with myself essaying the small but nonetheless significant role of the Almighty; while, somewhere else, Portable Theatre were presenting an early play by David Hare or Snoo Wilson, as like as not involving loud bangs and dead dogs, the Welfare State troupe were

Above left: The old Other Place, Stratford-on-Avon, under demolition, 1989. (*Photo: Shakespeare Centre Library*)

Left and Above: David Edgar's *Destiny* in the old Other Place, Stratford-on-Avon, 1976, directed by Ron Daniels, designed by Di Seymour (*Photo: Shakespeare Centre Library*)

enacting a pagan child's naming ceremony – with fire-eaters and real goats – in the Wool Exchange, and Albert Hunt's Art College Group were staging a full-scale mock-up of an American Presidential election, with live elephant, in the streets of the city. And, somewhere else again, in clubs and pubs, agit-prop groups with names like Red Ladder and The General Will were relating contemporary labour history, and joining, in their own way, the general and universal call for the overthrow of all fixed things.

What will be immediately obvious from that description is the wide variety of performance spaces employed, and the fact that none of them was a purpose-built theatre. The street itself probably proved the most ephemeral of the new theatre locations (the British discomfort with street theatre was demonstrated to me – once again in 1969 – by the sad retreat of New York's processional Bread and Puppet theatre from the vibrant accessibility of Sloane Square into the unwelcoming bowels of the Royal Court: when the performers encouraged dress circle and gallery dwellers to come downstairs to fill up the stalls, the ushering staff staged a walk-out). Site-specific theatre on the other hand proved surprisingly resilient: Chris Parr, who produced and directed *Scott*, also presented a Brenton play about Wesley in Bradford's Methodist Hall and a new version of the life of King David in the Cathedral, while the Welfare State have continued to tailor their work to specific locations (from the seaside at Barrow to dockland Thames).

Further, the early 70s did see an emergent circuit of venues for touring work. A good deal of the journey away from conventional theatre buildings was in pursuit of the Holy Grail of the working class audience for politically engaged theatre. Lenin classically defined agitation as saying a few things to large numbers and propaganda as saying more things to fewer; if street theatre was agit then prop required the greater comfort and concentration of an interior space. Because of the perceived off-puttingness of conventional theatres, it was felt that audiences were best addressed in places they knew, and considerable efforts were made to tailor prod-uct to the expectations of audiences in community centres and working men's clubs in particular. The most successful companies in this regard were probably Red Ladder (working from Leeds) and John McGrath's English and Scottish 7:84 companies, whose work was particularly successful in the Scottish Highlands and working-class cities with strong regional identities like Glasgow and Liverpool.

But the generic fringe theatre location was either a room above a pub or a cellar below, roughly converted for home-produced theatrical presentation. My first London work – the two-hander *Two Kinds of Angel* – was performed in a basement theatre (imaginatively called The Basement Theatre) actually beneath a Greek Street strip club; my second was presented in a little theatre (eccentrically dubbed The Little Theatre), somewhere near St Martin's Lane. Indeed, almost all of my non-touring early work was presented in small, low-ceilinged rooms, their architectural, electrical and plumbing peculiarities obscured (but, happily, never entirely hidden) by ubiquitous black emulsion, including the now sadly defunct Pool Theatre, Edinburgh, the still thriving Bush Theatre and the much-relocated Soho Poly (for which, when in Ridinghouse Street, agents prepared special lists of short actors; I am six foot four, and had to attend rehearsals on all fours).

The capacity of such spaces to embrace elements of their own architectural character – and in that sense to become site specific manqué – was most dramatically illustrated for me by a lunchtime play I wrote for the Open Space in 1975. The play was called *The National Theatre*, set in a strip club, and led to considerable confusion among its passing trade, some of whom thought it *was* a strip show, while others thought it *was* the National Theatre. It's a moot point which sector of the audience was more disappointed.

As the 70s developed, the fringe became both more divided and more institutionalised. Divided, in that the performance artists quickly split away from the political theatre movement, to form their own circuits with their own devotees; at the same time, the touring political theatre groups, still com-mitted to playing to working-class audiences in non-theatrical spaces became increasingly distinct from those playwrights, directors and actors who wanted to work with producing theatres. Sensing the energy of the upsurge of work that had emerged since the late 60s, producing theatres in the early 70s responded architecturally as well as programmatically. The decade between 1965 and 1975 saw the greatest sustained period of British theatre building this century. Many of the provincial playhouses built in this period were planned with one large auditorium, to cater for what was expected to be an exponentially expanding audience for serious theatre. As the fringe exploded into life all around them, theatre managers sought ways to tap into the growing market for small scale, alternative theatre, either by adding purpose-built studios to their plans, or by converting what were intended to be rehearsal rooms or scene stores into flexible studio spaces.

The model of the studio space was a purpose-built flexible-seat version of the found architecture of the pub theatre: small, square or rectangular, with flexible seating configuration, and painted black. Similarly, the arts centres which began to mushroom at the same time imitated the atmosphere of the community centres and working men's clubs for which they quickly substituted as touring theatre venues. So although there were still non-theatre touring venues (though by no means throughout the country) and a large number of London pub theatres survived, the main move of the mid-to-late 70s was towards purpose-built small spaces attached to arts centres and reps.

To a certain extent, this development represented a surrender by those who sought new audiences (no one had any illusions that the working class was going to flock to repertory theatre studios). This was by no means the only deleterious effect of the studio movement. In May 1973, I wrote a piece in *Plays and Players* noting that theatres with studios did less new work in their main houses than theatres without (and not many more overall). Studios quickly became ghettos for new work, which was particularly frustrating for those of us who had moved out of the fringe in order to be able to write large-cast plays on big themes. The battle to get plays by writers of our generation out of the Royal Court's Theatre Upstairs (*see* below, right) and on to the main stage downstairs was particularly bitter, and not really concluded until Max Stafford-Clark took over as artistic director in 1979.

My own experience was reasonably typical. Increasingly disillusioned with the potential of small-scale touring theatre (and indeed alienated from the company I'd done most of my agitprop work with, The General Will), I found myself more or less commuting between the London fringe (notably in my case the Bush and the Soho Poly) and my local studio theatre in Birmingham. Wanting to write a large-scale play about the rise of British fascism in the 1970s, I sought and gained a commission from Richard Eyre, then running a policy at the studio-less Nottingham Playhouse (pp. 71, 130)which looked exciting enough at the time and now seems positively arcadian (mainstage new plays included Brenton and Hare's *Brassneck* and Trevor Griffith's *Comedians*). The draft I produced was certainly large-scale, and Richard didn't feel, in the usual phrase, that it was right for him. I then won a residency at the Birmingham Repertory Theatre (pp. 80–82), for whom I agreed to write two plays. One was a piece for the studio (called *O Fair Jerusalem*, it was set in a church, had a brilliant environmental set by Chris Dyer, and a now utterly inconceivable cast of 15). The other was a reworking of the fascism play, of which I produced a much more manageable draft, but which nonetheless became the only play in the Birmingham Rep's history to be specifically and individually pulled from the programme by the Board.

I then sent the play round all the other large theatres in the country – including the National and the RSC – all of whom rejected it. It was however read by Ron Daniels, who had just himself moved from a basically fringe career into the RSC. He sought to persuade me that the ideal location for a play about urban racism, with a cast of 20 and covering 30 years of history, was a small tin hut in rural Warwickshire. The Other Place was a kind of large shed on the edge of an RSC car park, was indeed made of corrugated metal, and had been used as a wardrobe store before Michel St Denis acquisitioned it for internal developmental work with the company in the late 60s (p. 85). The fact that Peter Brook's *A Midsummer Night's Dream* was rehearsed there perhaps added to its mythology. In the way that theatres up and down the land were converting rehearsal rooms into studio theatres, the RSC handed it over to their young star director Buzz Goodbody, who presented a justly feted programme of intimate readings of classical and contemporary plays.

My play *Destiny* was the first individually written new play to be presented there (p. 85), in a season which also included a revival of Charles Wood's *Dingo* and Trevor Nunn's legendary *Macbeth*. It is possible to be romantic about some aspects of the old Other Place: it *was* freezing in winter and baking in summer, the rain *did* interfere with certain performances and the superficially democratic first-come-first-served ticketing was in effect discrimination in favour of Stratfordians without children. (The seating policy was not the only aspect of gloomy puritanism; the squelch across the car park to buy soggy drinks from an occasional caravan became known colloquially as the Passchendaele Run).

What the theatre did have was an immediacy that resulted partly from its geometry but also from the closeness of the world outside (one exit opened into a short corridor to the car park, another directly into the night). Paradoxically, this sense of the imminence of the surroundings served to concentrate attention inside (in the manner, I suppose, of a circled wagon train). The transparency of its architecture (open scaffolding, undisguised entrances, open stairways) made it both an empty and a rough theatre space. Anything could be imagined, but the best things were raw and direct. It was never a place to be diverted or indulged, but it was certainly a place to be moved and to be scared.

As a result, my warning of incipient British fascism (by no means as empty a warning as it was then thought and now might appear) was more directly chilling and perhaps less politically grand than I had expected (the actual appearance of Adolf Hitler on the stage at the end was an example of misplaced rhetorical zeal – he disappeared on to the sound tape for the second preview). For reasons partly of bravery and partly of scheduling pragmatism, the play transferred not to the RSC's small London theatre (the Warehouse), but to its then large space, the Aldwych theatre in the Strand, where it shared a short season (and a basic set) with Donald Sinden's underestimated *Lear*. This juxtaposition helped to up the grandeur of the piece, as did the fact that we opened during the celebrations of the Queen's Jubilee, and these two plays of nationhood gone rancid automatically called the *ersatz kitsch* of that event into question. I think it *was* less scary (except perhaps for the night when it was picketed by the National Party, who physically assaulted some members of the audience). But it certainly did feel that what was happening on the stage had both a historical sweep and scope and a purchase on the heart of the times.

I was to work in the Aldwych once more, when the theatre was transformed by John Napier into a magical approximation of a found environment, for Trevor Nunn and John Caird's production of my adaptation of *Nicholas Nickleby*. Napier decided to take advantage of the Aldwych's great architectural drawback – its over-forward dress circle – to build a rickety walkway over the heads of the stalls audience, umbilically connecting the auditorium with

The Royal Court Theatre Upstairs. (*Courtesy: Strand Lighting Archive*)

The Auditorium of the Aldwych Theatre, London, (W.G.R. Sprague, 1905), as set out for the Royal Shakespeare Company's production of *The Life and Adventures of Nicholas Nickleby*, adapted by David Edgar, directed by Trevor Nunn and John Caird, designed by John Napier and Dermot Hayes, 1980. (*Photo: Laurence Burns*)

the junkyard set on the stage (*see* above).

Shortly after *Nickleby*, the RSC moved into the purpose-built mausoleum of the Barbican (p. 95). It was perhaps symbolically significant that what was then and I think remains Britain's greatest theatre company should choose the early 80s to move into a building that represented the limitations of post-50s British theatre architecture in the starkest terms (p. 122). Like many a rep, the Barbican is in an under-populated part of town, difficult to find, and, once found, difficult to get into. The front of house is unwelcoming and bleak, there are no proper facilities for selling books (or indeed drinks), and it is impossible for a group of more than four comfortably to meet together. Most importantly, for anything but major Shakespeare and musicals the Barbican's large stage is too big, and for most of its highly popular studio work the Pit is too small (and – for it too is a translated rehearsal space – too low).

Through the 80s, as non-purpose-built spaces withered and closed (along with the touring groups that sustained them), British theatre architecture was increasingly dominated by postwar buildings that – through over-optimism on the one hand and lack of imagination on the other – were either too big or too small. This is not just a problem for new plays: indeed, David Hare, Alan Bennett and Tom Stoppard have recently proved better able to fill the National's large spaces – in all senses – than George Farquhar, Anton Chekhov and William Shakespeare. As Max Stafford-Clark points out, playhouses above a certain size have always found themselves restricted to certain sorts of large-scale spectacular. The good citizens of Birmingham decided to finance the removal of their repertory theatre from a 450 seat to a 900 seat theatre for the best and most culturally democratic of reasons (p. 81). But it may be that a 600 seater – or even a flexible theatre seating between 400 and 600 – would have been preferable.

In late 1994 I was faced with the consequences of this imbalance in the starkest sense. When the RSC accepted my play *Pentecost* for production at Stratford, we debated long and hard about whether it should go in the Swan or the (now new) Other Place (p. 76). The decision to go for the Other Place partly reflects the limitations of the Swan (a brilliant space for rumbustious comedy, the theatre seems to embrace you as you enter it. This was not a sensation we wished *Pentecost* to provide). But it was also a response to the extraordinary effectiveness of the rebuilding of the smaller theatre. The new Other Place preserved the geometry of the old (including its three-sided balcony and exits into the darkness), while adding the sybaritic indulgences of proper dressing rooms, effective climatic controls, and a bar (p. 27). Happily, the chill has not fallen victim to the central heating: the theatre remains a space in which you can feel – as the play on occasions requires you – that it's you and it against the world outside.

Faced with the decision of where to take the play on its 1995 London outing, we found ourselves trapped between the rock of the Barbican (too big, too far) and the hard place of the Pit (too small, too low). It's to the great credit of the RSC that it took the bold decision to hire another theatre – which combines a reasonable audience size with the intimacy and involvement of a small theatre.

The Young Vic, like the Cottesloe and the smallest handful of other theatres in Britain, is a tiered flexible space with an audience of around 400 (p. 172). Under David Thacker's direction, it proved a more or less perfect space for Ibsen and Arthur Miller: it has also effectively accommodated Sean O'Casey, chamber Shakespeare (Trevor Nunn's *Othello* and *Timon of Athens*) and indeed contemporary plays. To say that this type of playhouse is the only type of playhouse that can work in the 1990s is as restrictive as the opinion that all playhouses should be three-tiered raked auditoria facing endstages. But if every major city in Britain built a flexible 400 seater – and London built half a dozen more – the future of classical, contemporary and new play production would look brighter than it does now.

DIRECTING FOR THE RSC

The Classic and the New

Michael Attenborough

Based on a conversation with Ronnie Mulryne and Margaret Shewring

One of the things that is interesting for me in working for the Royal Shakespeare Company is that you have a choice of spaces. If you decide to do a production of *Measure for Measure* in The Other Place it's fairly obvious the kind of influence this decision is going to have, particularly if you contrast such a production with one in the Main House (pp. 27, 77). If, however, you weigh up the effect the choice of space will have on the birth of a new play, you are making a much more fundamental decision. For example, the decision to do *Pentecost* [by David Edgar] in The Other Place (p. 76), as opposed to the Swan, bearing in mind that it is a twenty-actor, thirty-three character piece, is fundamental to the effect the production will have, and hence the birth of the play. The crucial thing about space, and this is exemplified in the *Pentecost* choice, is not necessarily size, but *personality*. Spaces have different personalities. A space that holds only 250 people can feel barn-like. One that feels intimate can to your surprise seat 800. Beyond that, a space can have a distinctive atmosphere. To return to *Pentecost,* our reason for putting that in The Other Place rather than in the Swan (which is a wonderful space) was to do with what I call the Swan feel-good factor. The moment you walk through the door you feel good. The audience sits with, if not a literal, a metaphorical grin on their faces. That would be unhelpful for *Pentecost,* a play that has danger, and an element of the thriller about it. We would have spent a good deal of our production time combating the feel-good factor. In terms of scale, *Pentecost* would fit the Swan. It needs a tall set, so the height of the Swan would have been wonderful. But in terms of the theatre's personality, it would have been all wrong.

The personality of a theatre space is also to do with where it is sited. An audience makes a journey *into* the space. They have a sense of a world round the space. So you are aware, if you are sitting in the Hampstead theatre [a small-scale venue in London], that you are sitting in a pre-fab, and that people are walking past, along the Finchley Road down to Camden Library, past the emergency exit of your theatre. At The Other Place, people are walking through the car park. It's an isolated building. It is not in any sense protected, so when you are asking the audience to respond to people bursting in from the outside, they know that is exactly what they are doing. When someone bangs on the door, they are banging on the door of the theatre. If someone bangs on the door of the Swan, there's the RST Collection, reading rooms, shops etc. outside. There's a sense of being safe, with Stratford's Shakespearean heritage around you. So, for reasons to do with both the interior and the exterior, we came to the conclusion that The Other Place was the better theatre for *Pentecost*. Other factors also of course come into play. For instance the intimacy of the auditorium, where the relationships between characters can be played almost naturalistically. The bigger the space the less naturalistically you can play.

There was another debate when we had to decide which space to bring *Pentecost* into in London.

Michael Attenborough has been since 1990 Executive Producer of the Royal Shakespeare Company. In that period he has directed five productions for the Company, including the award-winning new plays *After Easter* by Anne Devlin and *Pentecost* by David Edgar. He was previously Associate Director of the Leeds Playhouse, the Mercury Theatre Colchester and the Young Vic, and then Artistic Director of the Palace Theatre Watford and Hampstead Theatre. Freelance work includes productions in the West End, on Broadway and for the Royal Court, the Tricycle Theatre and the Abbey Theatre Dublin.

There was initially a choice between the Barbican and the Pit. I was on the side of the Pit, largely because of the nature of the production. If you have pitched a show at a particular level, it can be quite destructive to change it. I felt that all the changes and choices we would have to make to pitch it for the Barbican, to go from a two hundred to an eleven hundred seat auditorium, would be negative ones. Most of the positive changes resulting from going into a big space would have been to do with spectacle, image, scenery – if you like with visual poetry. The visual images in the play are definitely under-resourced in The Other Place. Nobody can step back and look at the picture, as you certainly could in the Barbican. But I felt that in terms of the relationships between people, and the pitch of the acting, it would have been damaging to go into the big space. In fact, we are going into the Young Vic, which is a much bigger theatre than The Other Place, with twice the number of seats, but which retains an intimacy and a 'wrap round' quality (p. 172).

The history of a theatre is also important. People, unless they are coming for the first time, do have a sense of when they were last there and of the kind of work a theatre does. It is all part of the emotional experience of visiting the theatre. The new Other Place hasn't yet acquired its history. It hasn't been roughed up yet. It is still a bit new and squeaky clean. Most people have little sentimentality about the old Other Place (p. 85). They are glad not to have to change in freezing conditions. They don't miss not being able to flush the loo in the middle of the show. Nevertheless the quality one had there, namely that it was a rough space, and a space where the focus was on the actor not on the spectacle – it's fair to say that we retain that in the new building. It now has to acquire a tradition, a history of its own.

So far as directing in large spaces is concerned, there is an historical problem. Generations of directors have been reared in the studio theatre and the televisual or filmic traditions. So the idea of the large space breeds worries in directors' heads to do with (at its most extreme) rhetoric and declaiming and playing out front, not relating to your fellow actor

and losing the truth. I think that behind that is a half truth. All these are dangers. But it doesn't automatically follow that a play's truth is lost through size, particularly in relation to classical work. There is a scale to the language, which if you underpitch, in my view you leave the actor stranded in a no man's land of apparent naturalism, but with words coming out of his or her mouth that are simply not naturalistic. Intimacy of space can often prevent an actor rising to the language. The benefit of a large space is not that you get louder and louder, but that you rise to the scale, richness and stature of the writing. It encourages a poetic leap through the technical challenge. This is not always matched by the director's ambitions, who can think he or she will get truthfulness in a small space. I would argue that this is not necessarily so, and you might actually find the reverse. You might find that a bigger space brings out the truth, if you are genuinely investigating the language.

Adrian [Noble] talks very eloquently about the problem of going into a big space: how you have to energise it. Watching his work, it is fascinating to see the ways in which he does that. A crude example would be his production of The Winter's Tale when on a couple of occasions the whole company entered and walked right round the central cube, so that by the time they got down-stage centre they had created a kind of whirlwind energy. What you can't do in a big space is just walk on and chat. You have to have a relish for the challenge of the big space. This is part and parcel of hitting the level of the language.

In my opinion, there are very few theatres with above six hundred seats which give you an equally good view from everywhere. There is a limit, no matter what configuration the building uses. Beyond that, there will always be first and second class seats. At a certain point, the human scale of a performance is lost. I think the Barbican theatre is excellent (pp. 95, 122). Most directors, designers and actors enjoy working in it. The theatre is of course influenced by the journey there and the atmosphere of the building through which you walk, and it's tarnished

by that. But it is nevertheless a good theatre. Yet if you go and sit on the top level you are a long way away from the stage. You can't avoid that.

I worked for five years at what was the Leeds Playhouse and is now the West Yorkshire Playhouse (p. 75). The Quarry stage at the new West Yorkshire Playhouse is modelled almost exactly on the old Leeds Playhouse stage. Audiences love it, but it brings all the same problems. The upper reaches of the theatre are bad seats. It's a steep rake, you are miles away and you are cut off from the experience. If you sliced the top two hundred seats away, you would lose almost all the bad seats.

I am also rather against semi-thrust stages, for the simple reason that they are neither fish nor fowl. The problem of directing and designing for a semi-thrust stage is that you cannot fully use the diagonals. Not for any length of time. In the Swan, the Young Vic and the Other Place, you *can* use the diagonals. People can come down and turn up. You simply cannot do that for long with a semi-thrust stage, such as that at the West Yorkshire Playhouse. Equally, you are hampered by the sightlines. What you end up with are sets that tend to be wide and flat.

Arts Centres have always faced the problem of establishing any kind of community for theatre. It's not just that there have been colossal architectural errors in designing the Barbican, but that in a building as diverse as this, it is difficult to generate a sense of occasion. Yet the thrill of this place when it works at its best is its diversity and its complexity. There's a great challenge in how you use the Barbican complex, how you stage-manage the forty minutes or so before a performance. When there's a concert in the Concert Hall, and films, and people coming to see the galleries, and both theatres working, it's a very exciting place. It's an easy place to mock, but once you have got here, it's a much more pleasant place to be in than it's often given credit for. However, like any Arts Centre, if it's half full it feels daunting.

The Stratford theatres are often criticised as tourist traps, where people come and go away again, with little sense of participation in a theatrical community. You have to accept that a large proportion of the audience will arrive in Stratford to see the show, rather than come from Stratford. But I think this brings a different kind of atmosphere, and that is a sense of pilgrimage. There's a sense of occasion about theatre-going in Stratford. People have made a pilgrimage to see the work. They might stay the night and see two or three plays. If people drop into the Royal Court or the Duke of York's [both in London], they don't have anything like the same sense of occasion. There's a sense of identity about the Company and Stratford. The place is steeped in Shakespeare associations, whereas London is a great complex of different identities all rubbing shoulders with each other. Stratford has a very singular purpose to it. One of the special thrills of Stratford is the existence of those three different theatre spaces, and that, within that identity, there are contrasting experiences to be had. The policy of the Company is a triangle with Shakespeare at the apex, with the other two strands being the classics (the Greeks, Shakespeare's contemporaries, Chekhov or Ibsen) and contemporary and new work. They are *counterpoints* to the central point of Shakespeare. Two thousand people a night make that conscious, celebrating decision to come and have one of those three experiences. The new work draws some of its energy from being done in conjunction with the work in the Main House, and by using the same company of actors, so that for example, you can see Stella Gonet playing Titania, and then the lead in *After Easter* [by Anne Devlin; at The Other Place] (*see* right). There's a cross-fertilisation of skill for the actor. The actress who has an appetite for conveying the rich language of Titania will bring that same appetite and skill to the more poetic elements of Anne Devlin's writing. Anne Devlin wanted her play about nationhood and identity to be seen in Stratford alongside classical work that was exploring similar timeless themes.

Despite the backstage limitations I have enjoyed working at the Royal Court. You have to go a long way to beat those beautifully intimate proscenium arch theatres. I don't think it is any accident that

Stella Gonet (centre) in Anne Devlin's *After Easter*
(The Other Place, 1995). Directed by Michael Attenborough
(*Photo: Shakespeare Centre Library*)

much of the best new writing of the last twenty five years has emanated from small proscenium arch or end-on theatres.

There was however a danger through the seventies that new writing was being consigned to the black box ghetto, the studio theatre tacked on to the main building. Leicester, Sheffield, Birmingham, Bristol, all the major reps insisted (understandably) that they wanted a smaller experimental studio-sized space. The problem with such places is that it came to be understood that that is where you do new plays. This led the writers to address themselves to small spaces, but in so doing they got nearer and nearer their alternative means of employment, namely film and television. And so a sense of scale, a sense of poetry, a sense of the non-naturalistic has sometimes been lost.

I come back again to the importance of the personality of a space, especially for a new play. You can make or break a new play by that choice. There is as well a scale of audience expectation attached to particular spaces. The scale of expectation attached to the Swan is quite different from that attached to smaller, more domestic spaces. You have to respect that. There's a kind of cosmology attached to the Swan, it's a *public* space. All in all, finding the right theatre in which to give birth to a new play is a delicate and crucial decision.

SPACE AND THE DIRECTOR

Richard Eyre

Richard Eyre CBE has been Artistic Director of the Royal National Theatre since September 1988. Born in Barnstaple in 1943, he directed his first production, *The Knack*, at the Phoenix Theatre, Leicester in 1965. Since then he has been Associate Director and Director of Productions at the Royal Lyceum Theatre, Edinburgh (1967–72) and Artistic Director at Nottingham Playhouse (1973–78), before becoming Associate Director of the National Theatre in 1981.

He joined the BBC as producer of 'Play for Today' (1978) and has directed films including *The Ploughman's Lunch* (1983) and *Laughterhouse* (1984 – Venice Film Festival Award for Best Film) as well as opera (*La Traviata* at the Royal Opera House, 1994). Richard Eyre's productions for the National Theatre include *Guys and Dolls* (1982) *Futurists* (1986) *Richard III* (1990) and the David Hare trilogy, *Racing Demon, Murmuring Judges* and *The Absence of War* (1993).

Based on a conversation with Ronnie Mulryne and Margaret Shewring

I have written something recently about this topic in my book *Utopia and Other Places* (Vintage, 1994). Let me quote a few sentences:

> The Royal Lyceum Theatre in Edinburgh … is one of many theatres designed in the late-nineteenth century that really works: the actors can be seen and heard, the audience feels comfortable with them, the attention is focused, and everyone shares more or less the same viewpoint of the action. I have never understood why architects, or at least those who design theatres, seem so reluctant to draw on the lessons of the past. A theatre, more than any other building save perhaps a public lavatory, must be defined by its function: it's there in order for a few hundred human beings to sit in the dark and watch and listen to a few other human beings on a lighted platform. Yet almost without exception theatres built in the last thirty or forty years provide bad sightlines, poor acoustics, stage proportions that don't relate to the human figure, and self-advertising architectural features that intrude on the audience's attention, so demonstrating an arrogance that in a theatre professional would be simply laughable. (p.147)

The Italian theatre shape is a good one for drama. It has humane proportions. In this country the Royal Court [in London] has many of the features of a good theatre space (though it does not, one has to say, have perfect sightlines). Let me quote again from my book:

> The Royal Court is the ideal size for a playhouse; it seats about 400 people (200 less than in Granville Barker's day), it has perfect acoustics, (if one can ignore the occasional rumble of the Circle Line), its stage has humane proportions, and it's perfectly placed between the (now) ersatz Bohemianism of Chelsea, and the wealthy austerity of Belgravia. (p.141)

The humane proportions of a playhouse and its stage relate to the matter of drama. Its essence is after all the behaviour of human beings: human beings on a stage and human beings in an auditorium. Any auditorium that doesn't take account of that interaction is a failure. I can't believe there is anybody, any practitioner, who doesn't share this view. The audience must have the potential of being unified – offered more or less the same focal point – has to be able to see, and has to be able to hear. The characteristic materials of almost all the Italian theatres are plaster and lathe (or wood), which are sympathetic to the human voice. Concrete, chrome and steel are not sympathetic.

We need to consider the proper relationship between stage and audience in terms of scale, but also in terms of elevation and incline (a slightly raked space may give better contact). Actors instinctively understand space, and where the focal point is. In my view, invariably architects of the twentieth century ignore the lessons of the previous three centuries in these respects. The Lyttleton [the proscenium-arch space at the National] (p. 93) is completely flat. There is no curvature, no attempt to embrace the stage. You are left struggling to focus the action, not embracing it. It's like a cinema, a rectangular room with a stage at one end. The proportions are inhumane; they do not have, to cite a master architect, Le Corbusier's sense of a building echoing human dimensions.

There are problems with the Olivier [the large theatre at the National] in relation to its capricious acoustics (pp. 95, 120). The sound is washing about in a huge space. I recall discussing this with the actor Albert Finney, who knows the Olivier stage as well as any actor. I quoted Peter Brook to him once: 'A theatre should be a musical instrument.' 'Yes', said Albert, 'and who'd make a violin out of fucking concrete?'

The tradition of theatre in this country is a living tradition. We do many plays from the past. We even know in many cases how they were done in the past. We should therefore learn from them how spaces have worked in the past.

The Olivier can be a noble space. One's heart does lift when the theatre is full. You can get a terrific sense of elation, when you feel yourself part of an audience, part of a communal event, an occasion. When the Olivier is less than full and the audience is not 'with' the play, the space can be the coldest place in the universe. It's a hard space to focus, hard to design for, and hard to get the audience working for you. Some actors are very happy in the Olivier: Michael Bryant, Michael Gambon, Judi Dench. Julia Mackenzie when she stepped on to the Olivier stage for the first time to rehearse *Guys and Dolls* said it would be a good cabaret house. Denys Lasdun refers for comparison to Epidauros. But in Epidauros you can hear a pin drop – and the seats there are in a single tier.

Most of today's theatres are too big. It is very difficult to put on the best of new writing in a 1200-seat theatre, although David Hare's trilogy and Tony Harrison's *Trackers* challenged the space. They used this big public space for plays with a big public theme. The Olivier obliges you to do work that uses public address, and acknowledges the existence of the audience.

Inevitably, size and architectural characteristics influence the choice of plays. The Lyttleton has 900 seats. It is very wide and very high. You have to think if a play will fill the space.

Some small theatres are magnificent. The Cottesloe is a wonderful space (p. 166). Iain Mackintosh turned the existing shell into a really good space. The Tricycle is fine (pp. 18, 174). Bury St Edmunds. Five or six West End theatres. Perhaps the West Yorkshire Playhouse. The Swan [Stratford-upon-Avon] is really good, whereas the Barbican spaces are awkward.

Theatre design requires kinetic space, changing space, three dimensional space. Peter Brook says, 'I don't want to monumentalise, I want flexible space'. Some nineteenth century spaces were both three-

dimensional and kinetic: there was joy in transformation, in changing the space, in building into the background.

In the Olivier, the architecture intrudes into the province of the practitioner, with great jaws and gun emplacements on the side. It isn't an amiably responsive space. Yet I often love working in the Olivier. For example, in *The Absence of War* [October 1993], where the design used minimal, emblematic elements, and then, in one scene, there were just two actors – John Thaw and Richard Pasco – and, a very long way up stage, the tail of a plane. This opened the stage into a kinetic, dynamic space. If you just use an empty space throughout, of course, the Olivier can't sustain it. Usually, the Olivier needs open space *plus* scenic elements. Or it needs some form of false proscenium to create a focus. It's a virtue of the space that it discourages the use of a lot of scenery.

For designers, the Olivier can be an exciting space. Designing for the Lyttleton can be thrilling because of the scale. Most designers enjoy it. It encourages the production of a *tour de force*.

I come back to the point that the human figure is the central inalienable fact about theatre performance. In television you can change proportion and perspective, through manipulation of the camera. In theatre you are stuck with the proportions of the human frame. When the lights go down, what you have is people watching people. Too large a space can overwhelm an actor.

Of course there is a sense in which it is positive for a director or actor to test himself in a big space. That challenge has always been there for theatre: the big role, the big space. You can't take out of theatre the aspect of the bull fight. There's an element of blood sport about it. Pulling off a show in the Olivier requires a technical mastery that is formidable. I don't think the technical mastery should be sneered at. A conductor might enjoy working with a chamber orchestra or a small ensemble, but you'd expect him to be able to handle a symphony orchestra too. We have a new generation of practitioners in the theatre who have perhaps forgotten the bloodline.

Previous page:
The Lyttleton Theatre (Denys Lasdun and Partners, 1976).
(*Photo: Courtesy of RNT Archive*)

Left:
The Olivier Theatre (Denys Lasdun and Partners, 1976) under construction.
(*Photo: Courtesy of RNT Archive*)

Left: Main Auditorium,
Barbican Theatre, London.
Chamberlin, Powell and Bon,
1982.
(see also pp. 122–3)
(Photo: Clive Barda)

Below: Olivier Auditorium,
Royal National Theatre, London
Denys Lasdun and Partners,
1976.
(see also pp. 120–1)
(Photo: Richard Einzig, Arcaid)

Above:
Auditorium of the Edinburgh
Festival Theatre. Built 1892 as
the Empire Theatre, rebuilt by
the Law and Dunbar-Nasmith
Partnership, 1994.
(see also pp. 152–3)
(*Photo: Clive Barda*)

Left:
Auditorium of the Royal
Lyceum Theatre, Edinburgh
(*Photo: Ian Grundy*)

DESIGNING FOR SPACES

William Dudley

Based on a conversation with Ronnie Mulryne and Margaret Shewring

The most difficult space I have worked in for a wide diversity of plays is the Olivier (p. 99). I made it my business to find out how it came to be as it is. If you think of the list of theatre talents on the Planning Committee – Peter Brook, John Dexter, Jocelyn Herbert, Kenneth Tynan, Bill Gaskill, Olivier himself – they are a very remarkable group, but they never fully reached agreement. John Dexter's request that you take a square room and put the actors in one corner wasn't followed by the architect. Peter Brook and John Dexter wanted a very informal space, something on the lines of what is now Brook's theatre at the Bouffes du Nord [in Paris]. Olivier wanted a kind of Globe, with a running Juliet balcony all the way round. I must have designed fifteen or more shows in the Olivier by now, and I am working in it currently [with *Under Milk Wood*]. It strikes me again just how unyielding it is as a space. Architects seem to want to leave something to posterity. They are very mindful of the permanence of what they do. Stage design is as impermanent as an actor's performance. My plea to architects is not to make all our decisions for us. The Olivier is cluttered with too much concrete where you want space to adapt for the changing dynamic of different kinds of shows.

A week ago, I opened an opera at the new Bastille opera house in Paris. The architect there has provided a quite remarkable exterior and an extremely well-equipped stage. I doubt if one could find fault with the planning of the stage area. But what I did find was an extremely cold auditorium. The space is lit with a big raft of fluorescent lights, similar to an airport lounge. The main body of upper seating is very far away from the stage. There is no wrap-around seating. I don't see how that can be easily remedied. For the piece I was doing, *Lucia di Lammermoor* by Donizetti, the auditorium suited the austerity of our production. But some lightweight piece, some colourful, friendly, warm, human piece would be damaged. It worries me, generally, that auditoriums impose themselves on the design of shows in that way.

I am not saying that big auditoriums are inherently wrong. But there has to be a better solution for getting a large body of people in. You think in the Olivier that you are in a two-thousand seat theatre. It actually seats eleven hundred. That is not as many as the Aldwych [in London; formerly the base of the Royal Shakespeare Company]. We all know how intimate the Aldwych is. One reason for the RSC moving out was that they needed more repertory space back stage, but have since desired to come back to a warmer, intimate theatre in London.

There is a widespread misconception about what stage designers actually do. The scene designer is part engineer, part dress-maker, part painter, part logician, sometimes part casting-director. You may even as a designer be involved in adapting the text.

Once the Cottesloe got its bare-bones shape, money ran out before adaptability could be built in. This ironically freed it up more. It meant that the early productions, of which I did several, were free to experiment with a shell. It was a wonderfully liberating experience (pp. 101, 166).

In the Cottesloe, we started to explore the forms of theatre, from Shakespeare's time through to contemporary America. We took a particular interest in the court masque. What we found was that the

William Dudley is a designer who has worked for the Royal National Theatre, the Royal Shakespeare Company, the Royal Court, and the Old Vic, as well as in Hamburg, London's West End, and for Glasgow's Cultural Capital of Europe year. He has also designed opera for the Welsh National Opera, the Metropolitan Opera, and for Glyndebourne, the Royal Opera House, Bayreuth and the Salzburg Festival. Recently he has designed *The Big Picnic* at Harland and Wolff, Glasgow, *Lucia di Lammermoor* at the Paris National Opera, *Persuasion* for BBC television, and *Under Milk Wood* and *Wild Oats* for the Royal National Theatre.

development of theatre forms followed the development of easel painting. Sometimes theatre is the avant garde, sometimes it's painting. I would say that currently painting is the leading form. In a period like Shakespeare's, theatre featured as the avant garde. We began to find our research in other visual forms very useful for our work in the Cottesloe. The court paintings of Watteau, for example, consciously inspired our staging of a play about the English Civil War. We took the notion of a royal theatre where the King and Queen sat on a dais, and the play took place down the long body of the room, with assembled courtiers either side. We mixed that with our own most famous meeting place, the Houses of Parliament, which is clearly in some of its aspects a theatre. For a play about the Civil War, necessarily about the birth of the modern parliament, the space was dynamically suited to the play's argument.

You could refine the Cottesloe further. You could make the sightlines slightly better. You could even, as Iain Mackintosh has done at the Wilde theatre in Bracknell, arrange for the stage area to truck back. But I have never found a problem in designing for the Cottesloe as it is. It has always provided the kinds of opportunity I've just described, and it never imposes itself on the play.

In the last five years, I've done some plays outside London, in much bigger spaces, for example in the disused Harland and Wolff Engineering shed in Govan. There we enlarged on the Cottesloe principle [for *The Ship* and *The Big Picnic*] from a seventy foot room to a two hundred and fifty foot room, and this time had our audience mobile. Currently I'm thinking of another production there, for later this year. What is important for me is a bare-bones rectangle, a more flexible space than, for example, a circle. Actors will tell you that if you are not at the point of command in a circle, that is dead centre, the actor can feel dynamically weak. And the circular shape over-dictates design, whereas a rectangle affords you endless possibilities of balance and placement. The Renaissance Spanish theatres were rectangular. In the English Renaissance theatre even if the auditorium was circular, the *stage* wasn't circu-

lar, and therefore the disposition of actors wasn't in a circle. Theo Crosby's talks about the restored Globe (pp. 34–39) showed how the circle and the square were reconciled in these theatres in a true geometry, and it felt very harmonious. (My only contribution to that discussion was to suggest the moving of the pillars supporting the 'heavens' a further two feet up-stage, to allow the area downstage to be a really effective acting area). It seems to me that most of the significant theatres historically (with the exception of the Greek outdoor amphitheatres) have been rectangular in plan.

There was an assumption among the design team for the restored Globe, based on a single line of evidence, that the interior of the auditorium should be gaudily painted. It was argued that the public buildings of the period had garish decoration. Evidence from contemporary painting in the Netherlands suggests this was not so. Some scholars argued that theatre in those days was a 'vulgar' art form and so crude colours and fake marbling would be appropriate. I would comment that a modern fun fair in daylight looks dismal and tawdry. I begged that this wonderful building now going up in natural oak should be left alone to weather for two years at least, before any 'colour scheme' is chosen. Design in that auditorium should be in terms of what the actors are going to wear or carry or fight with, and not be imposed by painting or marbled effects. It's in many ways the same situation as in the Olivier. The architects always want to seal up all the options. I'd beg them not to do so. Theatre is about human activity, how people interact with each other. The architecture of the theatre ought not to inhibit that interaction. The sheer diversity of productions both then and now needs a bare bones structure only.

The Swan in Stratford is interesting in this connection. Terry Hands told me that they had deliberately kept the scene dock in that theatre small, so that designers like me wouldn't be able to overwhelm the appearance of the place. The irony is that I would actually honour that space, and use it as intended. To my chagrin I have not worked in the Swan yet.

The Lyttleton (p. 99) has its problems. It is well-

equipped. But it is an extremely audience–unfriendly auditorium. The main problem is that there is no visual or easy oral contact between the stalls and the circle. You can sit in either one and not be aware of the other (p. 93). In the old Frank Matcham theatres laughter runs around the audience like wildfire because the side boxes conduct it. Those boxes are crucial. The Lyttleton seems, consciously or not, to have been modelled on a cinema auditorium, with no regard for anything to replace the boxes. In fact, the Lyttleton appears to have suffered in the design stage from too little sensitive planning. It became known as the Any Other Business auditorium, as a result of always slipping to the bottom of the agenda, when everything else had been discussed. But nobody ever seemed to have time, and so the Other Business theatre was built. It's such a pity that the horseshoe, and centuries of experience, should have been neglected.

Some alterations to the Olivier have recently improved the space from an audience's and designer's point of view. Timothy O'Brien built out the stage [for *The Merry Wives of Windsor*] over the first two or three rows, and raised it slightly. This was tried first by Jocelyn Herbert for *The Trackers of Oxyrynchus*. It seems to me an improvement, but it can't always be used, for revenue reasons and for technical reasons. I hope, however, that this different configuration is adopted more. Jocelyn has thought about this auditorium for years. She tried unsuccessfully to get the concrete rim around the stage removed, since it contributes to the inflexibility of the space. She wanted in the seventies to take a thermic lance to it. We would do much better if only we could strip the theatre back to its essential shape.

At Stratford, once the Swan opened, the Main House became slightly the poor relation. There was a real devaluation of any scenery in the Main House. To see a play of Shakespeare's unencumbered is a breath of fresh air. But we have this inheritance of big stages, with proscenium arches. These are *scenic* stages, so it is not reasonable to use them as an apology for the Stratford Swan or the Globe. Once again, my plea is for diversity and multiple options.

Set for Middleton and Rowley, *The Changeling* in the Lyttleton auditorium of the Royal National Theatre, London, directed by Richard Eyre, designed by William Dudley, 1988.
(*Photo: John Haynes*)

Set for Ben Jonson's *Bartholomew Fair* in the Olivier auditorium of the Royal National Theatre, London, directed by Richard Eyre, designed by William Dudley, 1988.
(*Photo: John Haynes*)

TOURING AND SPACE

Jason Barnes and Roger Chapman

Jason Barnes has been since 1977 Production Manager of the Royal National Theatre's Cottesloe Theatre. In this capacity he has staged more than two hundred productions for directors and designers such as Sir Peter Hall, Arnold Wesker, Harold Pinter, John Schlesinger and John Bury. He has enjoyed a long association with the Director/Designer team of Bill Bryden and Bill Dudley, including working on the acclaimed production of the York Mystery Plays.

Based on a conversation with Ronnie Mulryne and Margaret Shewring

Roger Chapman: Principally we tour out of two theatres, the Lyttleton and the Cottesloe. The three things that concern us first of all are the depth, width and height of the receiving theatre. Depth is a major concern in the Lyttleton, which has one of the deepest stages in the world. Because it has a full back stage and a full side stage, one of our greatest problems is restraining designers from using these wonderful facilities on a production that has got to tour. The difficulty is to find stages that are compatible, particularly in moving to the United States, where there is no real conception of stage depth. You might have the width and the height, but no depth at all. So you have to squeeze the whole product.

Jason Barnes: If we can't achieve the basic groundplan, in terms of depth and width, and the play is not suitable for cutting down, then we can't do it. If the stage is all right, the next thing is size of auditorium. The restraints there are the income, though we sometimes tour to Festivals where they don't care about income at all, but this is unusual. The next consideration is the quality of the auditorium. Touring from the Cottesloe, which can be laid out in any of a dozen ways (p. 166), if the play is very specifically laid out, we have to try to match that in the receiving theatre. In trying to prepare tours we sometimes have to identify two spaces, one for instance that is capable of staging a play on an end stage, and one that is capable of staging it in the round – this is before the creative team has decided on the staging they want to use in the Cottesloe. There is often a difficulty in the timing of tours. Peter Hall's production of the three Shakespeare Late Plays left the day

after the Press night. The Russian authorities technically required the customs lists in two languages eleven weeks before that, when the plays hadn't even been rehearsed.

One major difficulty is that if we are touring from the end stage of the Cottesloe, the plays are presented for a small auditorium, but on one of the larger stages in the country. The depth in a West End theatre is typically 24 feet or 27 feet; in the Cottesloe we have a minimum of 30 feet, and often 36 feet. Though the stage is large, it has a sympathetic and good-sized auditorium. So we can step on to many touring stages in the country very happily, and plays that have been developed in the Cottesloe almost by definition have the strength to grow into a larger space. This is illustrated by moving very often to the Lyttleton, and even the Olivier.

Iain Mackintosh has explained how the strength a space like the Cottesloe confers is a science and an art [in his *Architecture, Actor and Audience,* Routledge, 1993]. The 'mystery' about the success of the Cottesloe is that it has a very special proportion, and that it is a courtyard theatre. It's an 'embrasive' theatre. The Lyttleton by contrast is two auditoriums, so that the actors are trying to play to two audiences. Wherever you sit you are watching two performances. You are part of one and perhaps excluded from the other. There are problems in a courtyard theatre of looking sideways, but the benefits of the corporate experience are incomparable. This is what Roger and I are principally looking for when we are trying to transfer a Cottesloe production. It is this that gives the plays that initial inbuilt strength.

The productions *do* transfer to bigger theatres. We are clearly not going to take a production to a 2500 seat auditorium. It is just too big. Vocally, al-

Roger Chapman is Head of Touring at the Royal National Theatre, a post he has held since 1988. He was a founder member of the Theatre in Education Company at the Belgrade Theatre, Coventry, and has been Director of Theatre in Education companies at the Octagon Theatre, Bolton and at Leeds Playhouse. He has directed productions in England, Ireland, Hong Kong and Australia, where he has been, among other appointments, the Director of the First Australian International Puppet Festival and Executive Director of the Ninth World ASSITEJ Congress. He has negotiated tours across the world for the National Theatre, is a member of the Drama Panel of the Arts Council of England and has published *Snap Out of It* for Eyre Methuen.

The Cottesloe Theatre under construction, 1977
(*Photo: Courtesey of the RNT archive*)

The new Stephen Joseph Theatre in the round, under construction, 1995
(*Photo: Ian Grundy*)

though in the Cottesloe you have to keep a text up or else it gets lost, it is well heard, and to translate a play conceived in a space like that to a bad acoustic is unacceptable. The next thing that needs attention is the relationship between the front of the acting area and the first row of seats. In the United Kingdom, this is generally all right. Most of the turn-of-the-century theatres now have an orchestra-pit lift which can be dropped and made available to the audience, and this brings them closer. We can usually push through the proscenium and under the safety curtain to close it up from the other side. But what happens when you get abroad is that almost exclusively the Germans have been around, and they have put in great steel gantries that are totally immovable and probably around ten or twelve feet deep, and if you are trying to enter down stage of the proscenium into the space, and you are doing this another ten feet away from the audience, there can be anything up to thirty feet – not three feet – between the front of the action and the first row of the audience. That presents a tremendous difficulty. The ability to make entrances very far down stage is lost, and you cannot bring the actor quickly into the audience's field of view.

Roger: It's usually my place to try to squeeze the productions, to find a compromise, in order to get them to tour. It is often a nightmare to move shows in our repertoire. What we are trying to re-create is the kind of feeling you get in these three houses. There is an acceptable level of compromise, but at some point there's a no. We are all the time moving around that compromise area and I am trying to convince directors that we should do the tour. We are very positive about trying to get things out, but we know there are points where we say, 'The experience that we are going to get is substandard and we'd rather not do it'.

Jason: It's not just a matter, even, of the volume of the theatre space. There are Cottesloe plays that are strong enough to take on a fifteen hundred seat theatre. It's the nature of the floor coverings, for example, that determine the acoustic, and whether it feels like a lively warm acoustic or an echoing acoustic or a completely dead acoustic. Acoustics can now be altered at the touch of a button, as at the Performing Arts Centre in Calgary (to the design of Theatre Projects) (p. 58). I should like every new space to be capable of alteration in that way.

Roger: Another factor is the role of the leading actor. You get actors with a particular attitude towards buildings. Ian McKellen is very keen on touring, and when he was last here at the National he said he would play on tour in any theatre built by Frank Matcham. These are big houses, with anything up to eighteen hundred seats, but, as Ian said, in a Matcham house you can stand centre stage and almost reach out to the whole of the audience, because Matcham has wallpapered the auditorium with people, and you feel at complete ease with the whole of the house. A cantilevered house by contrast is a nightmare. You find you have a split house. Directors are always giving actors notes saying don't forget you have an upstairs to play to. You never get that with a Matcham theatre.

Jason: When we've considered a host theatre in terms of the basics – the size of the stage and the auditorium –the next thing is front-of-house lighting. We tend to take our own lights and place them where they have always been in relation to the stage. But when you get out front you are completely in the hands of the auditorium, given its shape and size. You can even have a catwalk across the whole auditorium, which happens in a lot of modern courtyard theatres. Setting up new rigs costs a lot of money, but if you don't spend it you can't reproduce what happens here at the Cottesloe.

Roger: Once you start hiring lighting to go into theatres, you are into a fortune in costs.

Jason: Many European theatres have fixed-beam lights which you cannot move. The head of sound at Düsseldorf told us after the show there that, whatever the difficulties we had had with lighting, he greatly admired the effects we'd achieved, and it was a great example to German theatres, where lighting was given little concern. Actors in the National company, and in most British companies, get into a state the moment lighting is changed. It's like putting an understudy on. If you have worked on moments between two actors for weeks, it's deeply disconcerting to make a change on tour.

Roger: So far as ideal stages are concerned, I think the Lyttleton is the best stage in the world. I have never come across a stage like the Lyttleton. The opportunities it offers, and as a theatrical box of tricks, it's incomparable. Imaginative directors and designers just adore it. When we go to other theatres we look at wings. The joy of having a side stage, as at the Lyttleton, the joy of being able to truck shows, to move them off, the joy of being able to use that full depth, the joy of being able to use the traps, and being able to fly to the full – you can't do all that anywhere else. When we toured *Sweeney Todd,* we just gave up on the traps, we couldn't find them anywhere. It's a wonderful stage for a spectacular show like the Ninagawa *Suicide for Love* for example [a Japanese production toured into the National].

Jason: Our designers in the Cottesloe give a lot of thought to the stage floors. The seating configuration is of great importance and whether as a member of the audience you are looking down at the stage floor.

Roger: In the Cottesloe, our floors are crucial to our productions. Audiences are aware of their texture, and of everything about them. Whether they are raked or not. These are essential matters. Many times we have wanted to take our own rake on tour.

Jason: In the Cottesloe, the centre of gravity is above the stage. The bulk of the audience is above, looking down. Iain [Mackintosh] conceived originally a very low pit rake, that only came up to stage level. We experimented over the years, trying to reach the level of the middle gallery, and eventually the GLC gave us the money for a system to do this. An actor wants his or her eye line to be above the centre of gravity of the audience. A director wants the audience to be above. That debate goes on and on. For us, the steeper pit rake gives more flexibility.

Roger: In terms of touring in, we can take anything in the Lyttleton. In the case of Peter Stein's *The Hairy Ape or* Ninagawa's *Suicide for Love* we were the only theatre in London which could take them. The Cottesloe does take some tours in, for example Lepage's *Needles and Opium* and an Argentinian company with *Tango.* We are currently presenting *Two Weeks with the Queen,* the first time we have succeeded in setting out the 21 feet by 21 feet Stephen Joseph stage from Scarborough. Transfers from that theatre work very well (p. 101; new theatre).

Jason: A lot of touring work from the Cottesloe over the years has been playing in 'found' spaces, non-theatre spaces, particularly for the promenade work. In the early days we played a factory in Milton Keynes, more recently we took *The Mysteries* to a Cathedral in Cologne. *Machine Wreckers* could well do a lace factory in Nottingham. With *Fuente Ovejuna* we played the Assembly Hall in Edinburgh. Sometimes if the room is large enough, and not unsympathetic, you can create your own space within it. For *The Mysteries* in Cologne, we were inside a 'box' we constructed ourselves. We weren't aware of the Cathedral – except that we had the most extraordinary foyer as the audience came in – a building that had been closed since the war, since it had been smashed up by our aircraft. Acoustically we had to wrap the performance up. An eleven second reverberation time. We have even looked at St Paul's, but the reverb time was hopeless, about fourteen seconds.

Roger: Sometimes we tour outside shows into the Olivier, for example with *Medea*. But there the big question is economics. We couldn't take in anything but a big technical show, with the right kind of financial backing. It's sad but true that so much comes back to the economic basis of touring.

DIRECTING, DESIGNING AND THEATRE SPACE

Declan Donnellan and Nick Ormerod

Based on a conversation with Ronnie Mulryne

Nick: Our favourite spaces are the Cottesloe [the studio theatre at the National] (p. 166) which we've worked in a lot, and the Bouffes du Nord in Paris. The Cottesloe provides two things. One, it provides an intimacy (in terms of the distance between the actor and the audience) and two, it provides an epic dimension as well. It's actually a big stage, and the nature of the space and its flexibility allows you to use the theatre in an epic way, but maintaining an intimacy which we believe theatre absolutely requires.

Declan: An epic space for me is one in which the actor can run across the stage, in which grand gestures are possible. A very restricting space for me would be the Pit [the RSC studio at the Barbican]. Intimacy isn't everything. At the Pit you are so hemmed in, in such a relatively small space. I get very depressed in theatres where the space is too small. It's sad when actors can't run, if they wish to.

Nick: I suppose it comes down to the size of the stage, but also the height. The height of the Cottesloe helps to give it an epic quality. The Pit is too low, as well as having quite a small stage.

Declan: The Royal Court is a stage that can be reasonably epic. For its width it is quite deep, yet the theatre also feels intimate. It's all to do with the ratio between the epic stage and the intimacy of the auditorium. What you need is maximum intimacy with maximum epic quality or scale.

Nick: I suspect there's a magic figure, and that is the distance from any member of the audience to an actor on stage. A theatre architect in Israel told me he reckons this is twenty-one metres. About eighteen rows. And that is probably a maximum. The problem with the Lyttleton [the proscenium arch theatre at the National] is that they have ex-

Declan Donnellan is Artistic Director of Cheek by Jowl theatre company, and Associate Director of the Royal National Theatre. Among his productions for the National are *Peer Gynt, Fuente Ovejuna, Angels in America: Millennium Approaches, Perestroika* and *Sweeney Todd.* He has also directed in Ireland, Finland, Japan and France. He has won Olivier awards for Best Director (1987) and for Outstanding Achievement (1990), and most recently for his production of the all-male *As You Like It,* which in 1995 won two Oliviers.

Nick Ormerod is a stage designer and co-Artistic Director of Cheek by Jowl, which he founded with Declan Donnellan. Trained at Wimbledon School of Art, he has designed for the National Theatre *Peer Gynt, Fuente Ovejuna, Angels in America: Millennium Approaches* (which won the Time Out award for Best Design) *Sweeney Todd, Perestroika* and *As You Like It.* He has also designed *Macbeth* and *Philoctetes* for the Finnish National Theatre. For the English National Opera he has recently designed *The Rise and Fall of the City of Mahagonny.* In 1988 he received an Olivier Award Nomination for Designer of the Year.
(Photo: John Steward)

panded it width-ways, so that if you are sitting to the left of the auditorium, looking at an actor on the right, you might as well be in the Albert Hall. In a theatre seating only eight hundred people it's unbelievable.

Declan: It's fair to say that this isn't an exact science. Certain buildings have a mysterious atmosphere of their own. However much one tries to analyse it, we are dealing with something that is human, and because it is theatre it has a sacramental quality. There will always be mystery about it, something magic or at least transforming. You are not going to design a great theatre just with a computer.

Nick: There are some elements you *can* put your finger on. One is an awareness on the part of one member of the audience of other audience members. The relationship of one person to the person sitting next to them is important, and also their relationship to other members of the audience sitting at a distance, whom they should be able to see, because it's essential that they feel they are *in* an audience. One of the problems with the Lyttleton is that there is no connection between the circle and the stalls, and there's no curve in the stalls, so you don't get a sense of being in a community.

Declan: One of the worst theatres we have seen was one in Aachen, originally a rather nice Victorian theatre but where they had put in air-plane seats, so that you couldn't see even the top of the head of the person in front. The seating arrangement in that theatre was as if watching videos was what theatre was aspiring to, and if only we could sit in a comfortable armchair on our own, that would be an improvement. It's very interesting that in time of war people close the theatres in case you get colds and flu and various epidemics. I think it's rather important that you *can* get an epidemic of some-

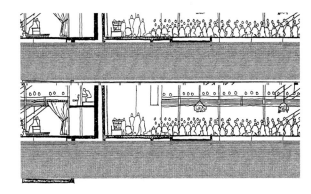

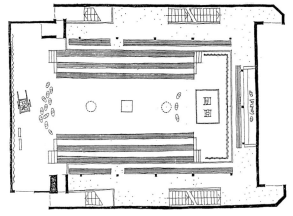

Above: Cottesloe Theatre: stage plans for the traverse production of Lope de Vega's *Fuente Ovejuna,* directed by Declan Donnellan, designed by Nick Ormerod, 1989. (*Courtesy of RNT Archive*)

Right: Performance of Lope de Vega's *Fuente Ovejuna* in the Cottesloe Theatre, 1989. (*Photo: Robert Workman*)

thing in the theatre. If you look at it positively, it's rather important that you can catch cold in the theatre.

It is possible for the seats to be a fraction too comfortable. It's not good that people should fall all the way back into their seats. It's quite important, and something that's becoming lost in our culture, that the audience should be invited to lean forward and make the piece of theatre work for them. The audience and the actors should share a communal imagination. There's a huge difference between leaning forward into an event and sitting back and watching it happen. Large armchair seats and masses of scenery are for us part of the same equation. You are having things done for you. It's a problem for me that modern theatre frequently imposes a pas-

sivity on people that is quite difficult to overcome. It's de-eventing theatre.

Nick: We enjoy courtyard theatres like the Cottesloe and the Tricycle (pp. 18, 174) partly because in a sense they are related to Victorian theatres. You get a kind of wrap around feeling, a sense of being enveloped by the audience, with people looking down on to the stage from the balconies. And also that height.

Declan: Height is curiously important, isn't it? There are exceptions to that rule, like the Khan in Jerusalem, where even a low building can have an energy from its past, its roughness.

Nick: As a designer, I'm not particularly interested in providing a perfect picture for each member of the audience, even if in the courtyard theatre it were possible to do so. Theatre is a much more three-dimensional form. Like sculpture it should be able to survive from different angles. I'm more interested in what the actor is doing. The audience needs to be close in – on top of the actor – to witness this. The intention of the Olivier space [at the National]

is three-dimensional, but they've copped out on it. It works better as a proscenium.

Declan: The great classic plays which many of us spend our lives going to see or performing in were performed originally in relatively small theatres. This is true going back through Ibsen and Strindberg. The Moscow Art Theatre, though now enlarged, initially seated about four or five hundred, and so did the Abbey for O'Casey. The evidence from the Elizabethan Rose theatre shows how small it was, more like the Donmar Warehouse. Many, many people were crammed into it, but those were the spatial sizes. Once you start trying to put *Hedda Gabler* on at the Olivier, or *The Way of the World* into the Lyttleton, I'm not saying that it won't work, but it's as much of a directorial imposition as setting the play in an abbatoir in Frankfurt. There are many many plays you can't do in the Olivier or the Lyttleton unless you allow the space to impose a huge inner change on the plays themselves. I think it's rather unfortunate that when the Lyttleton and the Olivier were being built people presumably didn't ask themselves what plays were going to be

performed in them. One thing about the Olivier is that you can't hold a conversation on stage, because the profiles don't work. You can do Ancient Greek plays on it, you can do soliloquies in Shakespeare, you can do musicals, but you can't really do conversation, and that rather limits your choice of play.

Nick: Actors tend to get the blame, because the critics say, 'Where are the actors who can fill these great spaces?' The point is that they never have. Only once or twice in a generation do you get an actor whose voice is big enough to do it. But why should they?

Declan: Young actors frequently have to prove themselves at the Royal Shakespeare Theatre or in the Olivier or the Lyttleton. Any actor can be *heard* in a two thousand seat theatre. But the more you increase volume, and the cubic metres of space the actor has to energise, the more you risk increasing the blandness of their performance. That is what is so terrible. Judi Dench can do it. But Judi Dench comes along once in a generation, once in two generations, and she doesn't like playing in these vast spaces either. This has destroyed so many young actors. In casting conversations you hear, 'Has he proved himself on a large stage?' Those spaces often force young actors into giving performances of sufficient blandness and crudity that they will carry, whereas something smaller but more subtle *won't* necessarily carry. Directors too feel that have to do their *Hamlet* on a huge stage, in order to prove themselves. But this is a modern *invention*.

Nick: Architects think the Olivier is beautiful. And it is (p. 95). You will also get actors who say they like it. Standing in the middle of that stage they feel fantastic. It's wonderful because it feels intimate. But the actor plays to the stalls, the expensive seats, and forgets three quarters of the theatre.

Declan: The people on the sides seem to be there to make those in the centre feel more secure. What's so elusive about it is that nobody quite knows why they are not having a good time. As Ian McKellen said, the amount of space the actor has to energise before he hits the first audience is immense. A huge void. It's a theatre trying to entertain too many people in too great comfort.

Nick: The word on the play in the rehearsal room is often 'fantastic'. It's electric on the last run through. And when they get on stage everybody wonders why it doesn't happen.

Declan: The Barbican is more contained than the big spaces at the National, but it is still a bit too big. Ultimately, you don't really feel connected to people in the audience.

Nick: At the time there was a general cultural pressure to build these auditoriums on one bank. There was a resentment that a particular class of person went to the Circle, another to the Pit, and so on. Put them all on one bank and they'll feel better. All it means is that people at the back of the auditorium have a more miserable time than they would have had in the Gods. If Epidaurus had not been built outdoors they would not have built it on one bank. They couldn't after all build balconies in the open air!

Declan: Both the Lyttleton and the Barbican have a terribly wintry feel about them. Ultimately it's very difficult to make people laugh in them. And this is very serious.

Nick: There are some nineteenth century theatres we feel very much at home in. Like the Albery [in London's West End]. It seats eight or nine hundred, but at the back of the Circle or the Stalls, you feel really *there,* really included. Why can't current architects do the same? We also like the Theatre Royal in Bury St Edmunds, though that is very small. That's a wonderful space. The Swan [Stratford-on-Avon] (p. 168). That's fantastic. The architect had a small space and he had to build high. A brilliant space.

Declan: The concept of courtyard theatre is not really theatre at all. The Cottesloe wasn't meant to be a theatre, it was a void in the plans. And along came Iain Mackintosh and made it into something wonderful. It's using an *ad hoc* space. The Spanish *corrales* of the Renaissance, such as the one at Almagro, used the existing space between buildings.

Nick: The English Renaissance theatres, the Globe or the Rose, grew out of courtyard theatres.

Declan: I do think a theatre has to be treated with a certain disrespect. We went to see a perfectly good modern play in the Duke of York's theatre, set behind this incredibly ornate proscenium arch, and the arch made such a statement that it overwhelmed the play.

Nick: The bliss of the Swan is that the actor is bang there in the middle (p. 26). Any set is really redundant. In our theatre-work, we always light the audience, because it's very good for our actors to see the audience – as indeed was the case in the Shakespearean theatre.

Declan: These large airy spaces are a very modern thing. There's no historical precedent for them at all, or no convincing precedent. We work on a stage as large as Shakespeare, Ibsen, O'Casey. There's another thing worth mentioning as a parallel. The Renaissance theatres were deeply temporary. Henslowe's original agreement for financing the Rose was for eight years only. Going to a modern institutional theatre is intrinsically different from that deep temporariness that was part of the original impetus behind Renaissance writing. And that is why Shakespeare works so well in temporary type settings. Permanence is a rather untheatrical thing, and if a building *looks* permanent, it is difficult to make a convincing theatrical occasion within it. Manchester Royal Exchange (pp. 17, 160) has the intimacy, the height *and* the sense of temporariness you need. Or the Young Vic (p. 172). Temporariness is theatrical. As a touring Company, we are temporarily wherever we are. Something very significant goes out of the heart of a theatrical experience, for audiences as well, when they go into a space that has that sense of institutional presence about it. You have a very alienated, Kafkaesque experience, because you don't quite know what you're not getting, and so you take the guilt on yourself. Those institutional buildings militate against the rawness which is part of theatrical life. The smell of permanence about a theatre can be a killer!

SPACE AND THE ACTOR
Simon Russell Beale

Simon Russell Beale as Oswald *in Henrik Ibsen's* Ghosts, The Pit, 1994
(Photo: Ivan Kyncl)

Simon Russell Beale is an Associate Artist of the Royal Shakespeare Company, who began his theatre career at the Traverse in Edinburgh before going on to play Osric in the Edinburgh Royal Lyceum *Hamlet* and the Ward in William Gaskill's *Women Beware Women* at the Royal Court. His roles for the RSC have included Thersites in Sam Mendes' production of *Troilus and Cressida*, the title role in Marlowe's *Edward II*, directed by Gerard Murphy, Konstantin in *The Seagull* and the King of Navarre in *Love's Labour's Lost* (both directed by Terry Hands) as well as leading roles in the Restoration season at the Swan. His performance of the title role in *Richard III*, directed by Sam Mendes, received outstanding praise, as did his performances of Edgar in *King Lear*, Oswald in *Ghosts* and Ariel in *The Tempest*, for which he was nominated for an Olivier award.

Based on a conversation with Ronnie Mulryne and Margaret Shewring

My experience of theatre space has been mainly with the Royal Shakespeare Company, in Stratford, in London and on tour. The Swan theatre [in Stratford-on-Avon] is really my great love (p. 168). I think that's the most beautiful space in England. I thought it was going to be rather a treacherous space, but in fact it proved to be exactly the opposite. When we did Chekhov's *The Seagull* in the Swan, we wondered if it would be too 'light' for the play, but in fact it worked better there than in the Barbican. You can take a play right down – that's the joy of the place – so that while it does work fantastically well for a light-hearted piece, it can take a serious piece too. It's an incredibly intimate theatre. The presence of the audience, with the first row only a few inches away, is immensely important.

I enjoy the Barbican too. The theatre is easier to play in than the Main House at Stratford. It's to do with the shape of the auditorium, that curve around that embraces the stage (p. 95). The worry about the Barbican's location is probably justified, though it must be said that we continue to get good audiences.

The old Other Place in Stratford was marvellous for the one play I've done there (p. 85). It was a fantastic place. I used to love watching the audiences going to get their takeaway cups of coffee. It was almost like camping out – a shared experience under fairly primitive conditions. The new Other Place has become a little more formalised (p. 27). You don't now have to go out into the snow to get your coffee. But the actors still use the same entrance as the audience, as we did in *Ghosts* and *Richard III*. I love all the informal things that happen. You have to wait for your entrance in the secretary's office. And the sense of sharing is very strong. I've never before done a promenade production, but *Julius Caesar* worked wonderfully in the Other Place.

Simon Russell-Beale as Ariel, Alec McCowen as Prospero in Shakespeare's *The Tempest*, RSC at Stratford (1993-4) and The Barbican (1994-5)
(Photo: Shakespeare Centre Library)

Theatre is of course ephemeral. It takes place and exists in the moment of its performance. I felt that particularly when I was heckled at the Barbican [as Ariel in *The Tempest*] (p. 107). Some people made it very clear what they felt about my performance. It's good that if people disagree with a performance they do still heckle. At the time my stomach went into my boots. Of course, you just want to be loved. But in retrospect it seems actually quite good. And the fact that it happened in the Barbican I find extraordinary and quite encouraging.

Touring *Richard III* was quite instructive about theatre space. The Royal Shakespeare Company do this remarkable thing of taking the whole stage and auditorium with them. In each place you get identical theatre space to work in. The big difference is acoustics. Sometimes the sound doesn't go at all where you expect it. I remember at Belfast a very large hall, in which you had to adjust the performance up. I like the security of a familiar space, but I do see the argument for needing to adjust to new audiences and new places, instead of operating the notion of an RSC *product* which you are taking around.

Working at Greenwich [with Juliet Stevenson on *The Duchess of Malfi*] is a quite different experience. The whole operation is tiny. I don't mean the auditorium, but the financial backing, the administration, the whole back-up area. It will be very interesting to see how the production changes when it goes into Wyndhams in the West End. Wyndham's is a delicate theatre, and the play is a thumping great piece – it doesn't pull its punches linguistically or in the plot line. The space will undoubtedly modify what we do and how we do it.

Juliet Stevenson

Juliet Stevenson has worked extensively for the Royal Shakespeare Company and the Royal National Theatre. Her RSC appearances include Mme de Tourvel in *Les Liaisons Dangereuses*, Rosalind in *As You Like It*, Cressida in *Troilus and Cressida*, and Isabella in *Measure for Measure*. Her National Theatre appearances include Hedda in *Hedda Gabler* and the title role in *Yerma*. She also played in *Trackers of Oxyrhynchus* both at the National and in the arena at Delphi. Her performance in *Death of a Maiden* at the Royal Court and subsequently at the Duke of York's won her an Olivier award. She played the lead role in Howard Barker's *Scenes from an Execution* at the Mark Taper Forum in Los Angeles, and is currently playing the title role in *The Duchess of Malfi* at Greenwich and Wyndhams. Her films include *Truly Madly Deeply*, for which she won a number of awards and *Drowning by Numbers* directed by Peter Greenaway.

Based on a conversation with Ronnie Mulryne

A fair amount of the work I've done has been in enormous spaces like the Royal Shakespeare Theatre in Stratford, seating about twelve hundred. I spent the first eight years of my professional career working between there and the Barbican and the Pit. Subsequently I've worked at, for example, the Theatre Upstairs at the Royal Court (p. 87), which only seats seventy – like having people in your sitting room.

The Main House at Stratford was terrifying to start with (p. 77). It seemed so vast and made you feel so diminutive. You felt quite intimidated and humbled by the space, which is not necessarily conducive to good acting. I was twenty-one, and just beginning. I was doing very small roles, so that I had no time to get used to the space, and the relationship with the audience, some of whom felt miles away.

The first time I really understood how the space could work *for* you was doing Titania and Hippolyta in *A Midsummer Night's Dream*. I played Titania not as a gauze-winged fairy but as a quite robust and energetic spirit. There was something absolutely releasing about that space, being able to delve right into it. I began to understand what Cicely Berry the voice teacher at Stratford was showing us, how to commit to the language. Absolutely having to commit to the language, send it ringing around that huge auditorium, actually teaches you a great deal. *Placing* your energy in a very committed way in order to be heard gives you back something as well. You begin to understand a great deal more about the play because you *have* to be very bold in your choices. I found it very releasing doing the *Dream,* and thereafter I got used to the space when playing some of the larger roles, like Isabella in *Measure for Measure*. I really got to love it.

Always the very difficult thing about large spaces is moving from the rehearsal room, where you have been doing the play in a small community, all very much within four walls. You create a world within those four walls, living it. And then you move to a very large space where one of those walls has been removed. It's as though the side of your house has been taken away and the whole world can see into your bathroom.

Later on at the National Theatre I did *Hedda Gabler* in the Olivier. I remember pleading with Richard Eyre to do it in the Cottesloe, but he felt that at that moment in time great plays should be performed in great spaces. I see his point, but many great plays, including *Hedda Gabler,* consist essentially of two-handed conversations. It's very difficult to do that play in the Olivier. Hedda is consumed with a kind of pathological claustrophobia, and when you are playing in a vast airy light-filled arena it's very difficult to convey a sense of being pressed in on all sides, and to create that sense in yourself.

There's an acoustic problem with some large spaces that is also an acting problem. When you *have* to be heard a long way away in the most intimate scenes, it does affect the choices you make. It's very much more difficult to play ambiguity, or to think one thing and say another. In large houses, it's a bit like those very small architectural drawings that by a mathematical adjustment can be enormously enlarged. You have to take the choices you made in rehearsal and blow them up. The great thing about small spaces is that you can use the work as you have explored it in rehearsal, and there is no transition required.

You *can* get that intimacy in large spaces. It's extraordinary standing on an enormous stage, on your own, and doing a soliloquy to twelve hundred people. There's an extraordinary intimacy about it. It all depends on how you relate to the space.

We did *Death of a Maiden*, which opened upstairs at the Royal Court in a very tiny closed room, very hot and sweaty (p. 87). The people who came had a feeling of being invited into someone's front room. I think they felt privileged to be there because there

Juliet Stevenson and Alan Rickman in *Les Liaisons Dangereuses*,
Royal Shakespeare Company 1986
(*Photo: Shakespeare Centre Library*)

were so few of them and they were so close. When we moved downstairs to the Royal Court Theatre, and then into the West End, into an even bigger theatre, each of those stages felt like a bereavement, because something was being lost in the move. Of course in the long run, you don't lose because you find something different. Yet in a small space I love the sense that we're all in it together, that nothing separates the audience from the performer. The space feels right. What I *don't* enjoy are those proscenium theatres where you are on a raised stage and the audience is very separated from you. My joy in theatre is that we are all part of the same event.

It has been very interesting doing *The Duchess of Malfi* at Greenwich. The danger of doing a Jacobean play is that there tends to be a very fine line between the melodramatic, the absurd and the truly tragic. If you wring the material out like a cloth, and pound it, it moves towards the absurd. So to work in a huge auditorium (which Greenwich is not, and Wyndhams is not) where you have to send the language flying out would be very alarming, because *The Duchess* is in the end a fragile beast, even if a powerful one. The challenge of doing the play is to help the audience identify with the characters, rather than feel that they are watching creatures from another planet. That is harder to do in a large space.

I've always liked the Pit. The main Barbican house is very difficult, very alien (p. 95). The Pit wasn't built as a theatre. At the last moment it was rethought and adapted. Something about the fact that it wasn't built as a theatre actually makes it work. I've always preferred spaces not purpose-built as theatres: the Tramway in Glasgow, for example (p. 57).

Yet, having said that, the most exciting place I've ever played is the ancient Arena at Delphi, with *Trackers of Oxyrhynchus*. That is a wonderful theatre space. Everything depends on the relationship the actor establishes with the space and with the audience.

Sir Derek Jacobi

Sir Derek Jacobi began acting while still at school, and at Cambridge reading history he kept on acting. After Cambridge he spent two and a half years at the Birmingham Repertory Theatre, then in 1963 joined Sir Laurence Olivier's company at Chichester, which subsequently became the National Theatre at the Old Vic, where Sir Derek remained for eight years. For most of the seventies, Sir Derek worked with the Prospect Theatre Company, before joining the Royal Shakespeare Company in 1982, where he played Prospero, Peer Gynt and in *Much Ado About Nothing* and *Cyrano de Bergerac*, both of which transferred to Broadway. Among many West End roles, he has played Richard II and Richard III, the title part in *Kean* and in Hugh Whitemore's *Breaking the Code*. He has played Macbeth for the Royal Shakespeare Company and most recently in *Hadrian VII* for the Chichester Festival Theatre, of which he is Artistic Director for 1995.

Based on a conversation with Ronnie Mulryne and Margaret Shewring

I've worked in a very wide variety of theatre spaces, the smallest, probably, a gymnasium in Ludlow and the largest the outdoor Herodus Atticus in Athens. The size of an auditorium is very influential on an actor's work, especially in terms of voice. British actors learn to use their voices in all kinds of spaces.

The trend nowadays is towards smaller spaces. Actors feel free to use their emotions and imaginations to the full in intimate spaces. You don't have to worry about the technical difficulties. I think Shakespeare probably works best in a small space. His work can be wonderfully enriching and stimulating when you don't have to worry about vocal strain. Yet some large spaces can be made to *seem* intimate. For example, Chekhov's *Uncle Vanya* at Chichester – a large space – was excellent, because the actors' personalities made it seem intimate.

I like Chichester (p. 156), even though you have got to work much harder to energise the space. Many actors find Chichester a difficult house to play, preferring the smaller space, the Minerva. You can trace such a preference to the actors' experience of working on television, a medium in which you have got to be more intimately real on screen. There is a great difference between acting on the stage and on screen. If you are principally a camera actor, you are used to all the safety nets that surround you in a studio. The camera angle can be changed, the microphone can be brought nearer to you, you can do a sequence again to get it right. A stage actor, by contrast, is engaged in a continuous creative process, with the adrenalin flowing at an incredible rate. There is the inspiration that comes from the excitement and expectation of the moment. This sort of inspiration is 'edited out' on camera, in favour of other processes. Theatre has to live and gel in a specific space at a specific moment; it has to be real *in the present*.

Some theatres have acquired a personality of their own. They have become their own critics. You very soon know if the theatre is approving of you, and you respond to that. You get a feeling when you walk out on to a bare stage, a gut feeling about the space, about whether your work there is going to be successful.

The physical structure of a theatre can affect spectators and players alike. If your journey to a theatre ends up with you arriving somewhere that looks like a bunker, that militates against the special experience that theatre-going should be. There is sometimes a sense of bare utility about modern theatres. They can lack the flair that should beckon performer and spectator.

Theatre is not complete until you have an audience. The audience is the one thing you lack in television or film, so that the process becomes totally self-absorbed. There is no sounding-board other than the cameramen and technicians. The great joy of theatre is that you do a play over and over again to different sets of people. Each show is a journey to be made with different companions. I am in rehearsal now, for *Hadrian VII* for Chichester, but we are almost at our limit: we need to put it on stage before an audience to give it a kick start. That is the magic of actors and audience in the theatre space.

Sir Derek Jacobi as Cyrano and Alice Krige as Roxane in *Cyrano de Bergerac*. Royal Shakespeare Company (*Photo: Shakespeare Centre Library*)

THE THEATRES

STEERING COMMITTEE

Professor Derek Sugden	*Arup Acoustics (Chairman)*
Colin Amery	*Prince of Wales Institute of Architecture*
Dr Peter Brinson	*Dance Consultant*
Professor James Dunbar-Nasmith	*Law and Dunbar-Nasmith*
John Earl	*The Theatres Trust*
Tim Foster	*Tim Foster Architects*
Roderick Ham	*Roderick Ham and Partners*
Elaine Harwood	*English Heritage*
Peter Longman	*Museums and Galleries Commission*
Iain Mackintosh	*Theatre Projects Consultants*
Ann Minors	*Theatre Projects Consultants*
Professor Ronnie Mulryne	*University of Warwick*
Michael Reardon	*Michael Reardon and Associates*
Francis Reid	*Lighting Designer*
James Sargant	*The Royal Shakespeare Company*
Dr Margaret Shewring	*University of Warwick*
Michael Wilford	*Michael Wilford and Partners*
Frank Woods	*Austin-Smith: Lord*

EXHIBITION CREDITS

Exhibition devised, researched and edited by Iain Mackintosh
Produced by the British Council Exhibitions and Audio-Visual Unit, Arts Division

David Elliott	*Project Management*
Marsha Lebon	*Design*
Clive Barda	*Photographic Editor*
Mark Stroomer	*Parallel Plans*
Kentish Graphics	*Graphic and Stand Production*
Falcon Electronic Imaging	*Typesetting*
John Tydeman	*Sound Track*
Jan Piechowicz	*Audio Visual Editor*
Ladbroke	*Audio Production*

MAKING SPACE FOR THEATRE

Forty Years of British Theatre Architecture

Thirty theatres have been chosen by a Steering Committee to represent the hundred or more built or restored in Britain since 1958.

Generally British theatres are less technically complex than those of Germany and other European countries. They are smaller than most American theatres. The thirty have been chosen because they succeed in bringing together audience with actor, singer or dancer in a vital way which distinguishes live theatre from cinema and all other mechanical art forms.

For four hundred years the British theatre had been wholly commercial: carpenters, builders and specialist theatre architects built for owners and actor managers who had to succeed at the box office to survive. There were no kings, princes, presidents or municipalities to pay for monuments. In the whole of the nineteenth century only one pure opera house was built, the Royal Italian Opera House, Covent Garden, in 1858. Elsewhere opera was performed in multi-purpose lyric theatres. Hence a workmanlike pragmatism has always been at the centre of the best of British theatre architecture. But the introduction over the past forty years of public money for housing the performing arts should lead to a cautious coming together of the arts of theatre and of architecture with the aim of creating buildings which both work as theatres and please as architecture. This exhibition is part of the much needed dialogue between architecture and the theatre.

The thirty chosen theatres are in two groups. The first eighteen are mostly conventional proscenium arch theatres with a few open stages. The second group are twelve newer drama spaces: thrust stages and in-the-round; courtyard theatres, and the simpler and low-cost spaces which are so often the setting for the best theatrical experiences. Each theatre has been re-drawn in plan for the exhibition and reproduced here at 1:500. The plans show stage and auditorium only, with the whole building indicated by a dotted line.

The third section is a section illustrating the contribution of British architects, engineers and consultants to theatre architecture across the world.

Iain Mackintosh

CONTENTS

The Theatres

PART I

MAINSTREAM THEATRE
Proscenium Arch and Open Stage

The theatres designed in the 50s and 60s solved problems conventionally with good sight lines, good acoustics, uniformly good seating and well tried technology. In contrast the open stages of the Olivier and Barbican, designed in the second half of the 60s, represent new solutions to old problems. They were designed at a time when old theatres were scarcely appreciated. Significantly it was theatre people rather than architects – Sir Laurence Olivier, Peter Hall and committees of leading directors and designers – who first insisted on the abolition of the proscenium arch and the introduction of wider open stages.

But Billingham and Inverness, with their wrap round walls papered with people, together with the restoration to full theatre use of theatres serving temporarily as television studios, cinemas or bingo halls, pointed the way to a new understanding of the prime purpose of theatre architecture. This is the channelling of energy from actor to audience and back again. The new Glyndebourne epitomises this new approach at the larger scale while the newer spaces of Act II explore this theme in many different ways.

Iain Mackintosh

Larger (over 850 seats)
1958 Belgrade Theatre, Coventry
1976 The Olivier, Royal National Theatre
1982 Barbican Theatre, Royal Shakespeare Company
1982 Theatre Royal, Plymouth
1983 Derngate Theatre, Northampton
1994 Glyndebourne Festival Opera

Medium (400–850 seats)
1963 Nottingham Playhouse
1967 Forum Theatre, Billingham
1969 Thorndike Theatre, Leatherhead
1976 Eden Court Theatre, Inverness
1979 Wolsey Theatre, Ipswich
1981 Pitlochry Festival Theatre

Restorations
1963 Georgian Theatre, Richmond, Yorkshire
1975 Theatre Royal, Glasgow
1980 Grand Opera House, Belfast
1990 Lyceum Theatre, Sheffield
1993 Prince Edward Theatre, London
1994 Edinburgh Festival Theatre

BELGRADE THEATRE, COVENTRY

Belgrade Square, Coventry CB1 1ES

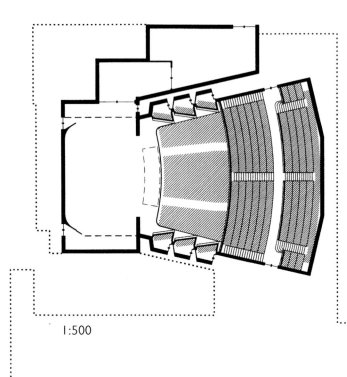

1:500

Design Intent

This is the first new theatre to be built in Great Britain since the end of the war. This theatre, designed to seat an audience of 910, is sited in the central area of the City with one frontage on to a new square which will be laid out with grass, trees and a small pool. The foyers and bars will overlook the square and the ground floor foyer will open on to a terrace alongside.

The auditorium and stage have been designed for the presentation of drama in an atmosphere of intimacy and comfort. Boxes are arranged in two tiers on either side of the auditorium and also line the rear of the stalls. There is one balcony with entrances from either side and this is divided into a circle and dress circle. The orchestra pit can be covered over to provide a forestage when required and is so designed that it gives a visual link with the boxes on either side with the object of creating a very close relationship between the actor and his audience.

A control room at the rear of the stalls accommodates the remote control for lighting and sound and enables the stage director to have a view of the stage and be in touch by telephone with the stage and dressing rooms. The theatre has been wired to take the equipment for television broadcasts.

Alongside the main entrance to the theatre are six shops and twenty-one single roomed flats, some of which are to be reserved for the Belgrade Theatre Trust for letting to the actors and actresses.

The theatre is now under construction and is programmed to be completed in March, 1958.

Arthur Ling, *Architect, January 1958*

Users' Verdict

The Belgrade auditorium, with its traditional elements of boxes and balcony, has proved remarkably well suited to the later development of regional producing theatre. It encloses and groups the audience well, puts them in a good relationship with the stage, has excellent sight lines and first-rate acoustics for the spoken word. It is a sufficiently large space to be receptive to the large-scale musical, while not making a small-scene play seem out of place.

Its stage facilities, however, now seem inadequate. The lack of wing space, depth, and full height fly tower are severely limiting. The inflexibility of the apron stage, pit and proscenium areas, the emphasis of width rather than height, and inappropriate lighting positions, give a theatrically dated quality. The absence of modern backstage facilities is unacceptable and a second auditorium is much needed.

As the Belgrade approaches its fortieth anniversary, a complete revamp is now being planned, taking the auditorium as its heart, and building around it a modern theatre which will perhaps adopt a less institutional and more dramatic architectural style to reflect the vitality of theatre use.

Robert Hamlin, *Director and Chief Executive since 1980*

Playhouse
Civic theatre built for new regional theatre company presenting mainly own productions with occasional tours

First performance
27 March 1958

Auditorium
Stalls, single balcony and side boxes
Capacity / 867
Volume / $3900m^3$ ($4.5m^3$ per person)
Furthest seat / 23m
Stage edge to facing tier / 10.2m

Orchestra Pit
Area / $27.5m^3$
Formed by removing traps in permanent forestage

Stage
Proscenium width / 10.85m
Depth of stage / 11.6m (*including forestage*)
Width of stage / 18.25m
Flying height / 12.5m

Designers and Builders
Client / *City of Coventry*
Architect / *Arthur Ling, city architect*
    Douglas Beaton, principal architect
Acoustic consultant / *Building Research Station*
Structural and services engineers /
    Granville Berry, city engineer
Cost consultant / *Bellamy and Wareham*
Main contractor / *George Wimpey and Co Ltd*

Building Cost
£0.25m (1958)

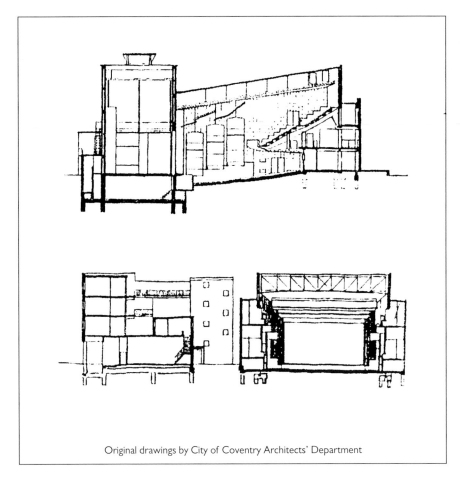

Original drawings by City of Coventry Architects' Department

THE OLIVIER

South Bank, London SE1 9PX
Royal National Theatre

Design Intent

We searched for a single room embodying stage and auditorium whose spatial configuration, above all else, would promote a dynamic and emotional relationship between audience and actor – between a fixed architectonic geometry of vision, acoustics and concentration and the chance irregular demands of dramatic performance. We searched for an open relationship that looked back to the Greeks and Elizabethans and, at the same time, looked forward to a contemporary view of society in which all could have a fair chance to see, hear and share the collective experience of exploring human truths. The room thus offers many possibilities and certain contradictions.

Sir Denys Lasdun, *Architect*

Users' Verdicts

The relationship between actor and audience is not confrontation – as in the conventional proscenium stage; it is rather participation – where the spectator is made to consider and evaluate the arguments of the actor. The Olivier is therefore a great epic theatre, good for Shakespeare, Shaw, Brecht or the dialectic of David Hare.

It is less good for Chekhov or Ibsen: it does not communicate understatement. But as a space for debate which keeps the theatre a living force, it is unrivalled and takes us all the way back to the Greeks, like most very modern things.

Sir Peter Hall, *Director 1973–88*

The Olivier theatre possesses most of the characteristics of the actor whose name it bears: grand, grandiose, bold, ambitious, difficult, exasperating, but often thrilling and occasionally unique. When it works – a full house for a successful production – there is no auditorium in the world that is as intoxicating, and when it is less than full, or the audience are less than totally engaged, it's a space that is ungenerous both to actor and spectator. It's a hard stage on which to focus attention, hard to design for, and hard to animate. Its monumental scale militates against intimacy, its architectural features intrude on the province of the director and designer, and its enormous volume gives rise to lamentably capricious acoustics.

Nevertheless, for all its maddening drawbacks, for all its lack of easy amiability, there are few theatres in the world that lift the heart and challenge the spirit in quite the way that the Olivier does – either as a practitioner or as a member of the public.

Richard Eyre, *Director since 1988*

Playhouse

Open stage theatre contrasting with adjacent proscenium stage theatre, the Lyttleton, and experimental studio, the Cottesloe
The three theatres, together with facilities for the public and for rehearsal and production, are home to Britain's Royal National Theatre founded in 1963 at the Old Vic by Sir Laurence Olivier after whom the largest theatre is named
The whole building has been listed Grade II Star by Act of Parliament as 'a building of special architectural or historical interest'.

First performance

At the Olivier 16 September 1976

Auditorium and Stage

90° arc on three levels, comprising centre seats, raised side seats and unbroken circle
Capacity / 1160
Volume / (*auditorium*) 13,500m³ (11.6m³ per person)
Furthest seat / 21m
Width between end of side walls / 17.7m
No orchestra pit
Stage raised 0.32m in 1980

Designers and Builders

Client / *The South Bank Theatre Board*
Architect / *Denys Lasdun and Partners*
Theatre consultant / *Theatre Projects Consultants*
Acoustic consultants / *Hugh Humphries* and
    Sound Research Laboratories
Structural and services engineer / *Flint and Neill*
Cost consultant / *Davis Belfield and Everest*
Main contractor / *Sir Robert McAlpine and Sons Ltd*

Building Cost

£16.6m for whole three theatre complex (1976)

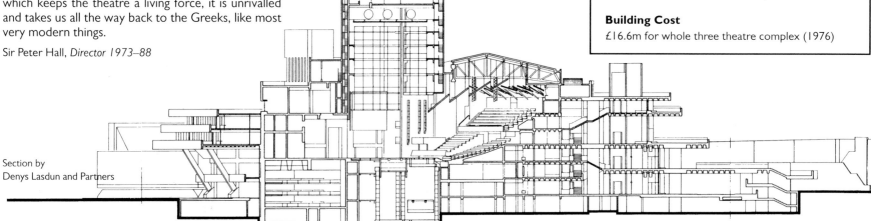

Section by
Denys Lasdun and Partners

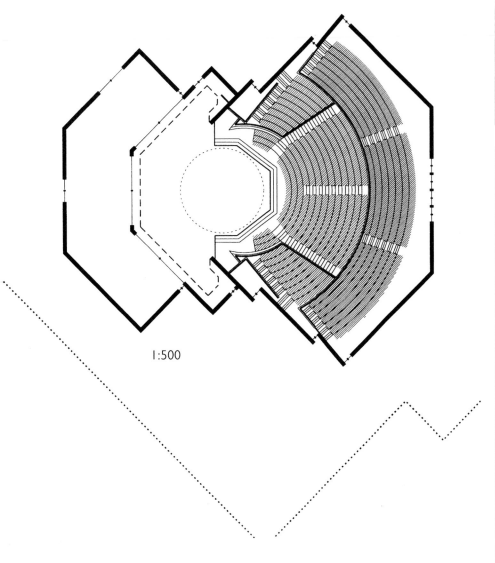

1:500

BARBICAN THEATRE

The Barbican Centre, London EC2Y 8DS
Royal Shakespeare Company

Design Intent

In basic conception the theatre is the oldest part of the design. The original brief for the theatre, drawn up by Richard Southern was that the auditorium should be fan-shaped or a modified horseshoe. These recommendations produced the basic shape of the auditorium, with the balconies, each thrusting forward one over the other, creating a unique auditorium. Each seat row leads to its own individual door, held open before the show and during intervals by an electromagnet. During the design development we worked in close collaboration with Peter Hall, John Bury and Patrick Donnell to develop the auditorium and stage concepts.

Frank Woods, *Architect for Chamberlin, Powell and Bon*

Peter Hall, then director of the RSC, Peter Chamberlin, Architect, and I, then Head of Design for the RSC, designed the large auditorium and the stage for the Barbican Theatre in 1965. This antedates the planning of the National Theatre's Olivier Auditorium by several years, although the Barbican Theatre was not to be unveiled to the public, through the vicissitudes of the British building industry, until several years after the Olivier opened.

So we were breaking very new territory. A large auditorium – 1150 seats, but a one room theatre, with no proscenium arch – heady stuff in those days, particularly in view of the fact that this was to be a *Theatre For Shakespeare*.

Now Shakespeare means soliloquies and to Peter Hall that means actors talking to – yes talking to, not talking at, their audience. And talking intimately – face-to-face – and an arc of command no greater than can be encompassed in a gesture, or, as Sir Laurence put it, the audience had to see both his eyes.

So this was going to be very different from the then prevailing Guthrie open stages where the unfortunate actor had to keep on the trot, rationing out his words and gestures to the various seating areas. 'I cannot make all the audience laugh at the same time' said a despairing Olivier at the Chichester Festival Theatre! Our stage, of course, had a very rigid geometry, defining a point of command from where all the prerequisites functioned. But did not that also apply to the Globe? It applies to all good theatres – one knows exactly where Hamlet has to stand!

John Bury, *Theatre Design Consultant*

Users' Verdict

The Barbican Theatre was designed principally to serve the needs of a major classical theatre company, performing the works of Shakespeare in repertoire. The characteristics of the Elizabethan canon, requiring a battle scene one minute and an intimate monologue the next, were the principal challenges facing the architects. The proportions and facilities are generous and the stage is the perfect focus of an 1100 seat auditorium, ingeniously designed so that the circles and balcony curve back in towards the stage.

Adrian Noble, *Director since 1991*

Playhouse

Open end stage theatre designed in late 1960s for the RSC to replace the Aldwych Theatre as its London home
Part of a large complex also comprising a concert hall, cinema, school for music and drama and small second theatre for RSC

First performance
9 June 1982

Auditorium

Central single block of aisle-less seats with doors for each row
Three shallow balconies facing stage and steeply raked at sides
Capacity / 1162
Volume / 4150m^3 (3.6m^3 per person)
Furthest seat / 21m
Stage edge to closest tier / 15m

Stage

Variable raked stage / *generally 1:15*
Proscenium width / *21.59m*
Cranked safety curtain following line of semi-thrust stage
Depth of stage / *15m*
Width of stage / *38.2m (at front)*
Flying height / *30m*
Orchestra Pit / *None*

Designers and Builders

Client / *The City of London*
Architect / *Chamberlin, Powell and Bon*
Theatre design consultant / *John Bury*
Theatre equipment consultant / *Theatre Projects Consultants*
Acoustic consultant / *Hugh Creighton*
Structural engineer / *Ove Arup and Partners*
Services engineer / *E.H. Buckle*
Cost consultant / *Davis, Langdon and Everest*
Main contractor / *Laings*

Building Cost

£163m (1982) for whole of Barbican Arts Centre

Section by
Chamberlin, Powell and Bon

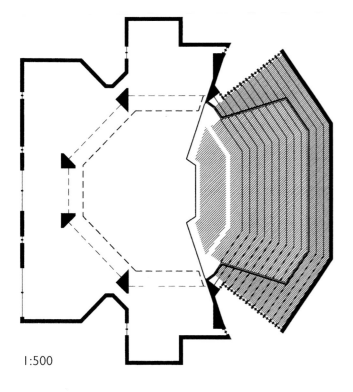

1:500

THEATRE ROYAL, PLYMOUTH

Royal Parade, Plymouth PL1 2TR

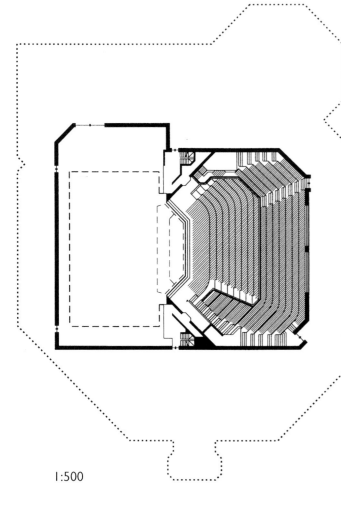

1:500

Design Intent

Without compromising its prime function, the new theatre had to be suitable as a concert hall and conference centre. Assisted resonance allows the reverberation time to be adjusted for speech or music.

The city council was divided as to what sort of theatre should be provided. Some favoured a small intimate theatre of about 700 seats, others a much larger theatre for touring productions such as music hall, ballet and opera with an audience of over 1200 seats. To resolve the impasse a moving ceiling has been installed, which when lowered cuts off the gallery and varies the seating capacity from 1296 to 768.

One of the major design aims was to create a proscenium theatre which, through the interlocking geometry of all elements, removes the physical division between auditorium and stage normally associated with this form. The stage riser is stepped and the fire curtain, when lowered, is formed to the geometry of the forestage.

Peter Moro, *Architect*

Users' Verdict

I have had the pleasure of directing very many productions in both the Theatre Royal and the studio theatre over the last ten years and I have found them exciting and agreeable spaces to use.

The Theatre Royal, despite its large audience capacity and big stage, has a friendly and warm actor/audience relationship with good acoustics and sight lines. It works well for large scale musicals, ballet and opera as well as for smaller and medium scale drama. My only regret is that at the time of design the city council did not include workshop and rehearsal facilities in its brief to the architects.

Roger Redfarn, *Director 1984 to 1994*

Touring Theatre

New theatre with adjacent studio theatre presenting mixed programme of national drama, opera and dance companies and own productions including major revivals of musicals and annual pantomimes

First performance

5 May 1982

Auditorium

Asymmetric with adjustable ceiling
Capacity / 1296 with ceiling raised
768 with ceiling lowered, cutting off second balcony
Maximum volume / (ceiling raised) 5050 m³ (3.9m³ per person)
Furthest seat / 22.5m
Stage edge to first tier / 10m

Orchestra Pit

Safety curtain falls on fixed orchestra rail
Two pit/forestage elevators
Maximum / 69m² (40 m² in open)

Stage

Proscenium width / 12.55m
Proscenium height / 8.5m ceiling raised
  6m ceiling lowered
Depth of stage / 16.9m
Width of stage / 29m
Flying height / 25m

Designers and Builders

Client / *The Council of the City of Plymouth*
Architect / *Peter Moro Partnership*
Theatre consultant / *Carr and Angier*
Acoustic consultant / *Sound Research Laboratories*
Structural and services engineers / *Ove Arup and Partners*
Cost consultant / *Davis, Belfield and Everest*
Main contractor / *Costain Construction Ltd*

Building Cost

£4.9m (1978)

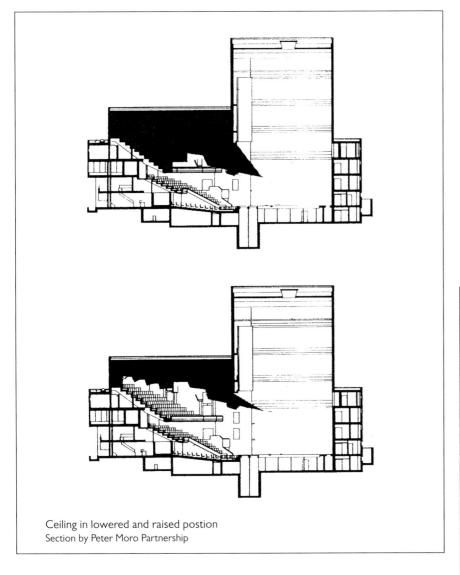

Ceiling in lowered and raised postion
Section by Peter Moro Partnership

DERNGATE THEATRE, NORTHAMPTON

19–21 Guildhall, Northampton NN1 1DP

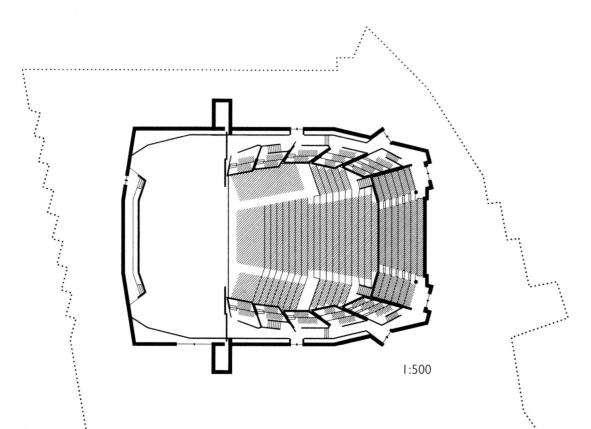

1:500

Multi-purpose and Multi-form Theatre
New theatre adjacent to smaller Royal Theatre of 1884
Multi-form design allows diverse programme including symphony concerts, touring opera and dance, snooker and other activities which use an arena format as well as exhibitions and banquets using flat floor

First performance
4 April 1983

Auditorium and Stage
Adjustable auditorium achieves fixed appearance in each format
Two large elevators in stalls area receive air castored seating blocks while five audience box towers on each side also move on air castors to vary shape of Auditorium
Capacities / 1472 to 1550 concert
     1172 end stage without pit
     1088 end stage with pit
     1483 arena
Flat floor / 648m^2
Volume of auditorium in end stage / 8800m^3 (7.5m^3 per person)
Furthest seat / 30m
Proscenium width / 14m
Proscenium height / 11.4m
Depth of stage / 12.6m
Width of stage / 28m
Flying height / 21.5m

Orchestra Pit
One of the elevators provides pit, seating or flat floor alternatives / 49m^2 (all in open)

Designers and Builders
Client / *Northampton Borough Council*
Architect / *Renton Howard Wood Levin Partnership*
Theatre consultant / *Theatre Projects Consultants*
Acoustic consultant / *Artec Consultants*
Structural and services engineer / *Ove Arup and Partners*
Cost consultant / *Gardiner and Theobald*
Main contractor / *Taylor Woodrow Construction (Midlands) Ltd*

Building Cost
£8.5m (1983)

Design Intent

The brief demanded a building that would accommodate the widest range of art and entertainment events. Our innovative design of the auditorium, developed with Theatre Projects Consultants, allows events as diverse as televised snooker, symphony concerts, opera, ballet, rock, exhibitions, balls and banquets to be mounted in rapid succession.

The 'no compromise' multi-form approach to staging and seating draws heavily on the best features of the traditional theatre design, with the walls of boxes ensuring a successful audience/performer relationship, and is complemented by acoustical adjustability, ease of access and rigging plus the attractions of dramatic foyers and excellent backstage facilities.

Nick Thompson, *Architect*

Users' Verdict

Derngate is a joy to manage. The flexibility of the auditorium design gives room for both creativity and commercial edge whichever is needed at a given time. The design is reliable, effective, well liked by the people of the town and a cause for civic pride.

The wide proscenium, easy stage access, and street level dressing rooms all combine to give a positive advantage to performance presentation.

More stage depth and 25% increase in capacity would have been helpful if space or funds had been available.

Howard Raynor, *General Manager since 1993*

GLYNDEBOURNE FESTIVAL OPERA

Near Lewes, East Sussex BN8 5UU

Design Intent

How to respond to our clients' seemingly conflicting requirements – inserting a larger theatre while still retaining the familiar scale?

We built on the existing site, using the surrounding buildings to mediate between new and old, but we turned the new theatre around, bringing the foyers to the garden side, enabling us to bury the huge backstage areas naturally in the slope of the site, minimising their impact.

We chose materials for their aesthetic and acoustic qualities. We built in solid load bearing brickwork, using a warm red brick similar to the house and covered the wide new roofscape with lead.

The accommodation is grouped so that the large fixed elements – the stage, side stages and backstage – are surrounded by peopled spaces – dressing rooms, offices and workshops – giving views out and a domestic scale to the exterior. We adopted a horseshoe shape for the auditorium for intimacy.

We formed the acoustically prescribed 'music box' interior with reclaimed pitch pine, to avoid the feel of a plush city house.

Sir Michael and Lady Hopkins, *Architects*

Users' Verdict

Glyndebourne feels critically happy with its new theatre which has officially received wide acclaim from the architectural and construction professions. Even the media have been warm and benign in their response.

We have now had a Festival in the new theatre and the stage and backstage areas have worked to very good effect. Inevitably there have been minor teething problems – nothing which the hygienist cannot deal with.

We have also been very happy with the auditorium and front-of-house facilities. The acoustics – an aspect which is not predictable in the planning stages – have turned out to be a significant success as far as concerns both performers and audiences.

Sir George Christie, *Chairman since 1962*

Opera House

New theatre replacing original of 1934 which held 830
Presenting own opera productions in repertoire
Festival season late May to late August
Short pre-touring season October/November

First performance

28 May 1994

Auditorium

Stalls and three tiers in semi circular horseshoe form
Capacity / 1342 (*comprising public seating 1182, standing 42, private and staff boxes*)
Volume / 8300m³ (*6.2m³ per person*)
Furthest seat / 29m
Stage edge to closest tier / 18m

Orchestra Pit

Fixed orchestra rail, one pit elevator
Area / 111m² (*52m² in open*)

Stage

Proscenium width / 11.6m
Depth of stage / 17.4m
Width of stage / 37.2m
Flying height / 20.6m

Designers and Builders

Client / *Glyndebourne Festival Theatre Ltd (Chairman: Sir George Christie)*
Architect / *Michael Hopkins and Partners*
Theatre consultant / *Theatre Projects Consultants*
Acoustic consultant / *Arup Acoustics*
Structural and services engineers / *Ove Arup and Partners*
Cost consultant / *Gardiner and Theobald*
Project manager / *Eric Gabriel*
Theatre adviser / *John Bury*
Construction manager / *Bovis Construction Limited*
Construction advisor / *Stanhope Properties plc*

Building Cost

£23m (1994 prices)

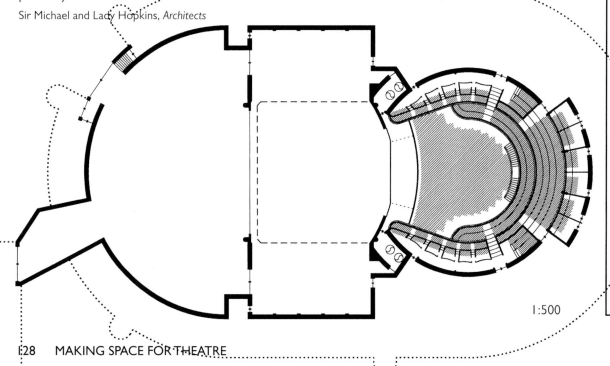

1:500

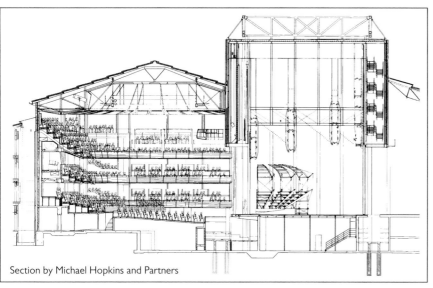

Section by Michael Hopkins and Partners

NOTTINGHAM PLAYHOUSE

Wellington Circus, Nottingham NE1 5AF

Design Intent

In the design of this theatre we have attempted to combine in one building two seemingly incompatible forms of theatre; open and proscenium stage. So called adaptable theatres had been attempted at the time but with little success.

In Nottingham the auditorium is cylindrical and instead of the traditional framed hole in the wall, the proscenium is just a gap in the surrounding wall. In addition this gap can be closed by continuing the auditorium wall treatment or by other scenic devices and the action transferred into the auditorium by the provision of a large mechanically raised thrust stage.

This at least was our design intention and although the theatre has been used a few times in this 'open stage' form, it is the proscenium form which is now preferred.

In recent years insensitive alterations have marred the integrity of the building, culminating in the installation of a lift shaft in the centre of the foyer of this Grade II listed theatre.

Peter Moro, *Architect*

Users' Verdict

The foyer shows the influence of the Royal Festival Hall's open foyer on Peter Moro's thinking and provides an exciting space for late night performances, talks, installations, exhibitions. The auditorium is his greatest achievement and has an unusually intimate feel, with an immediacy between artist and audience, and a flexibility of stage/auditorium relationship which help our artists to reinvent the space and the art.

In summer, with the outdoor cafe space outside the theatre full of people, the building looks as if it has always been in the midst of the Victorian buildings round the circus and it looks as beautiful and enticing as Peter Moro could have hoped for.

Ruth Mackenzie, *Executive Director since 1990*

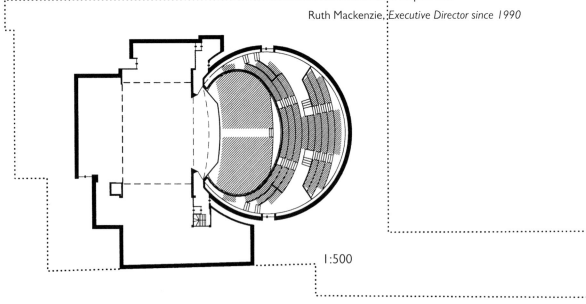

1:500

Playhouse

New proscenium theatre replacing old smaller repertory theatre
Presenting own productions and occasional tours
The whole building has been listed Grade II Star by Act of Parliament as 'a building of special architectural or historic interest'.

First performance

11 December 1963

Auditorium

Drum shaped auditorium with single balcony
Capacity / 756 (*reducing to 675 with large forestage or orchestra*)
Volume / 4,500m^3 (5.9m^3 per person)
Furthest seat / 22m
Stage edge to balcony / 13.2m

Orchestra Pit

Maximum / 70m^3 (*of which 46m^3 in open*)
Formed by using both elevators which also provide for seating or a forestage

Stage

Proscenium width / 9.75m
Depth of stage / 12.3m
Width of stage / 25.75m
Flying height / 18m

Designers and Builders

Client / *Nottingham Theatre Trust*
   (Artistic director *Val May*)
Architect / *Peter Moro and Partners*
Stage consultant / *Richard Southern*
Structural engineer / *Clarke, Nicholls and Marcel*
Services engineer / *Steensen, Varming and Mulcahy*
Cost consultant / *Davis, Belfield and Everest*
Main contractor / *W.J. Simms, Sons and Cooke Ltd*

Building Cost

£0.33m (1961)

FORUM THEATRE, BILLINGHAM

Town Centre, Billingham TS23 2LJ

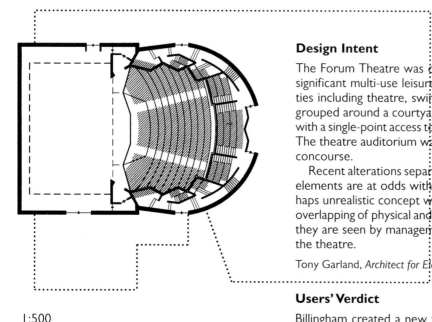

1:500

Design Intent

The Forum Theatre was one element within the first significant multi-use leisure building in the UK. Activities including theatre, swimming and ice skating were grouped around a courtyard and first floor concourse with a single-point access to the building at ground level. The theatre auditorium was entered directly from the concourse.

Recent alterations separating the theatre from other elements are at odds with the original brave but perhaps unrealistic concept which placed emphasis on an overlapping of physical and cultural activities. However, they are seen by management as raising the profile of the theatre.

Tony Garland, *Architect for Elder Lester Associates*

Users' Verdict

Billingham created a new town centre to be the one stop centre for administration, shopping, leisure and culture. By making it a traffic free precinct the Council hoped to encourage the free mingling of its community. The Forum was the leisure building which was to house activities across the sport and cultural divide in the hope that cross fertilisation would take place. The mixed programme and the auditorium worked well but the other mixture of sweaty badminton players with theatre-goers did not produce that special feeling of occasion a visit to the theatre should generate. Changes have now been made to separate the theatre audience from the sports element of the complex and good facilities for disabled people have been added to extensively refurbished bar and refreshment areas. The original vision has been successfully modified.

Councillor Harry L. Davies, *Chairman of the Development Committee*

Touring Theatre

Theatre which forms part of sports and recreation complex
Mixed programme theatre with some own productions

First performance

16th August 1967

Auditorium

Fan shaped stalls in three blocks; surrounded by three shallow tiers and side stepped boxes
Capacity / *631*
Volume / *3500m³ (5.5m³ per person)*
Furthest seat / *18.28mm*
Stage edge to closest tier / *14.2m*

Orchestra Pit

Formed by removing forestage / *34.2m²*

Stage

Proscenium width / *13.4m*
Depth of stage / *11.73m*
Width of stage / *19.5m*
Flying height / *16.4m*

Designers and Builders

Client / *Billingham Urban District Council*
Architect / *Elder and Lester*
Theatre consultant / *Michael Warre*
Acoustic consultant / *Elder and Lester*
Structural and services engineers / *Blyth and Blyth*
Cost consultant / *Turner and Townsend*
Main contractor / *Shepherd Construction*

Building Cost

£1m (1968) for whole leisure complex

THORNDIKE THEATRE, LEATHERHEAD

Church Street, Leatherhead, Surrey KT22 8DF

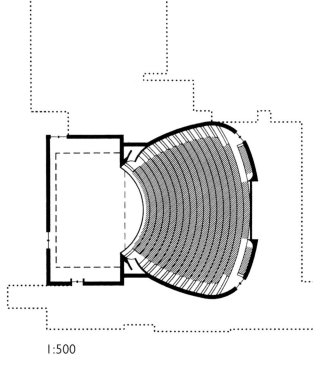

1:500

Design Intent

The stage and auditorium, at the heart of the project, are in the proscenium form with all the scenic advantages of a flying system but without emphasis on the proscenium arch. The lighting slots merge into the walls, the lighting bridges are moulded into the ceiling and flow into a single space embracing the acting area. The sculptured eyeball shape of the auditorium is revealed in the three adjacent levels of foyer. A series of spaces giving architectural expression to the theatrical purpose of the building prepare the theatre-goer for the excitement and emotion of a dramatic performance.

Roderick Ham, *Architect*

Users' Verdict

During eighteen years in our ageing but beloved old theatre we had pioneered a policy which had succeeded in filling the theatre to overflowing. Roderick Ham was in complete accord with our need for a building designed to be an arts centre, a social centre and a vital part of the life of the community. So with this beautiful and practical building we have presented plays, films, concerts and art exhibitions, worked with young people and educational projects and provided good food for all around the clock.

Achieving high standards and serving the community has been rewarding and over it all Dame Sybil Thorndike seems to be casting her approving gaze.

Hazel Vincent-Wallace, *Director 1969 to 1981*

Playhouse
New theatre replacing smaller Playhouse
Repertory theatre presenting own productions

First performance
17 September 1969

Auditorium
Single block of raked seats
Capacity / 526
Volume / 1450m^3 (2.75m^3 per person)
Furthest seat / 19m

Orchestra Pit
19m^2 (all in open)
Formed by orchestra pit lift in forestage

Stage
Proscenium width / 11m
Depth of stage / 9m (plus 3m of forestage)
Width of stage / 18.6m
Flying height / 14m

Designers and Builders
Client / *Leatherhead Repertory Theatre*
    (Director *Hazel Vincent Wallace*)
Architect / *Roderick Ham and Partners*
Theatre consultant / *Theatre Projects Consultants*
Acoustical consultant / *Roderick Ham and Partners*
Structural and services engineers / *Edwards and Blackie*
Cost consultants / *Young and Brown*
Main contractor / *W.E. Chivers and Sons Ltd*

Building Cost
£0.25m (1967)

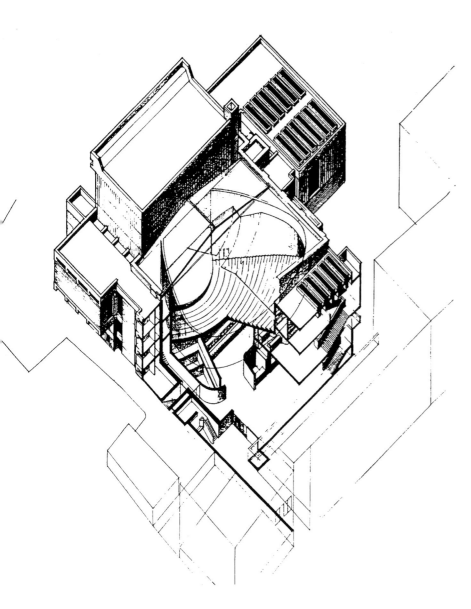

Axonometric by Roderick Ham and Partners

EDEN COURT THEATRE, INVERNESS

Bishop's Road, Inverness, Scotland IV3 5SA

Design Intent

A proscenium opening and fly tower are mandatory in a touring theatre of this size but the designers reacted against the customary modern single-tier fan shaped auditorium in favour of a multi-tier horseshoe arrangement as frequently advocated by Iain Mackintosh, by virtue of which he was asked to advise the Design Team on this aspect of the scheme. So at Eden Court the walls are papered with people, each member of the audience is conscious of being part of that audience, the theatre can look nearly full when it is in fact half empty and it is accepted that there are good seats and bad seats and that which are which varies according to the type of production. We hope that the result is a more intense and exciting theatrical experience.

Graham Law, *Architect*

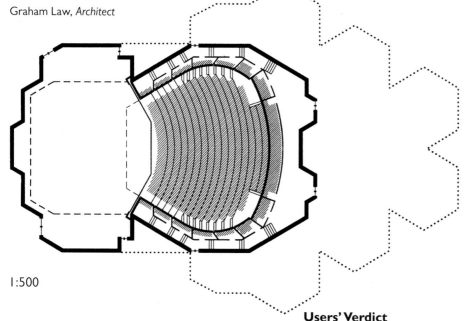

1:500

Users' Verdict

Eden Court is user-friendly. At all levels the audience enters the auditorium from the rear and attention is focused immediately on the stage. One hardly notices that decoratively the building is quite austere. Seats are comfortable, with unusually generous legroom. Lighting, sound reproduction, sight lines and acoustics are all good. Headphones, if required, are available on free loan. The programme caters for a wide range of tastes and audiences are of all ages and socio-economic groups.

James Shaw-Grant, *Vice Chairman of Governors*

Touring Theatre

New theatre attached to old Bishop's Palace which provides dressing rooms and other facilities
The only major theatre in the Highland Region
Presenting drama, opera, ballet, symphony music and popular entertainment

First performance

15 April 1976

Auditorium

Stalls and three stepped tiers in horseshoe form
Capacity / *814*
Volume / *5050m^3 (6.2m^3 per person)*
Furthest seat / *19.2m*
Stage edge to closest tier / *17.4m*

Orchestra Pit

Safety curtain falls on fixed orchestra rail
Whole stage slides giving variable pit size
Maximum / *70m^2*

Stage

Proscenium width / *12.3m*
Depth of stage / *(from forestage) 17.4m*
Width of stage / *27m*
Flying height / *17.9m*

Designers and Builders

Client / *Inverness Town Council*
   (Protagonist *Baillie Douglas Baxter*)
Architect / *Law & Dunbar-Nasmith*
Theatre consultant / *John Wyckham*
Acoustic consultant / *Frank Fahy*
Structural engineer / *W.H. Aubrey*
Services engineer / *John C.R. Pearce*
Cost consultant / *Soutar and Jaffrey*
Main contractor / *Crudens*

Project Cost

£2m (1976)

Currently being renovated
Architect / *Law & Dunbar-Nasmith International Partnership*

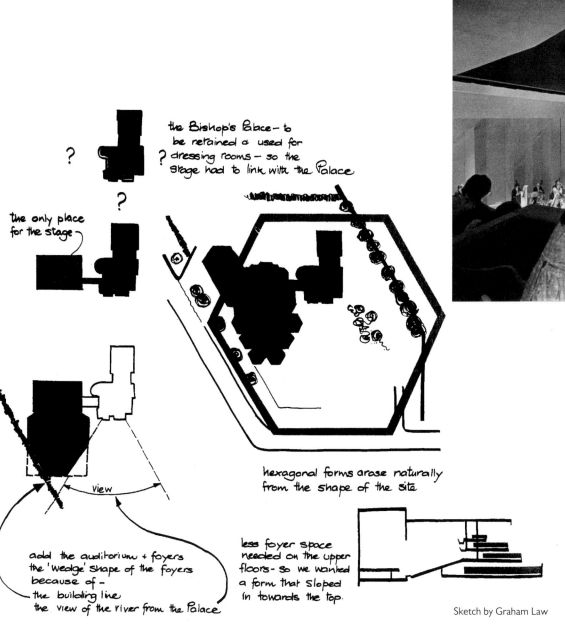

? ? the Bishop's Palace - to be retained & used for dressing rooms - so the stage had to link with the Palace

?

the only place for the stage

view

add the auditorium + foyers the 'wedge' shape of the foyers because of - the building line the view of the river from the Palace

hexagonal forms arose naturally from the shape of the site

less foyer space needed on the upper floors - so we wanted a form that sloped in towards the top.

Sketch by Graham Law

WOLSEY THEATRE, IPSWICH

Civic Drive, Ipswich IP2 2AS

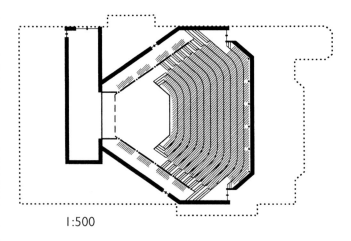

1:500

Design Intent

The audience and the performance are in the same space with steeply stepped seating focused on the acting area. The close relation is emphasised by the galleries running into and behind the stage. Budget restrictions were accepted and a kind of drama has been extracted from the exposure to view of all the structure and services. The walls, the roof, the columns, ventilation ducting, lighting galleries are all visible and are designed to contribute to the theatrical atmosphere. A similar character of simple self finish materials pervades the foyers. The building is designed to be literally a 'playhouse'.

Roderick Ham, *Architect*

Users' Verdict

In some ways Wolsey is an unlikely building for a catholic policy. The thrust stage and the galleries that narrow behind it, the deep inner stage, would seem to indicate a 'beautiful carpets and handsome dresses' style production. In fact, it has proved extraordinarily versatile and although every set has to be made to lock into the building it has meant that every production has somehow achieved a feeling of newness. Clearly, even a thrust stage theatre lacking elaborate flying facilities works at some disadvantage, although we have never allowed this to influence our choice of play.

In essence the Wolsey is the ideal audience and actors in the same room building. The architectural balance between the auditorium and the stage is so perfect that even raising the stage by the necessary 250mm to place our revolve on it or building a small orchestra pit at the front is a noticeable intrusion upon the space. Although with the passing of the years we have felt a pressing need for more space, the intimacy of the building and the feeling that the auditorium is at its heart has made it a good building for personal communication. The control room area high above the back of the auditorium is as good as any in Britain. It is an elegant and successful building and though on occasions another 50 seats would be valuable, the architect definitely used the limited space at his disposal to the best possible advantage.

Antony Tuckey, *Director since 1980*

Playhouse
Regional theatre presenting own productions
Open stage fan shaped theatre with side galleries

First performance
19 September 1979

Auditorium and Stage
Single block of raked seating with side audience galleries wrapping around open stage
Volume / 2000m³ (5m³ per person)
Furthest seat / 11m
Stage / 10m wide between galleries at side of thrust
Thrust edge to cyclorama (if required) / 12.2m
Flying height / 8.5m

Orchestra Pit
No pit but modular stage removable

Designers and Builders
Client / *The Ipswich and Suffolk New Theatre Trust* (Director *John Southworth*)
Architect / *Roderick Ham and Partners*
Theatre consultant / *Carr and Angier*
Acoustic consultant / *Roderick Ham and Partners*
Structural and services engineers / *Edwards and Blackie*
Cost consultant / *Davis, Belfield and Everest*
Main contractor / *Haymills (Contractors) Ltd*

Cost
£0.75m (1979)

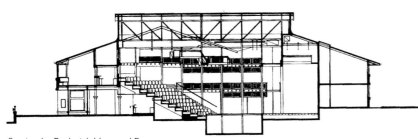

Section by Roderick Ham and Partners

PITLOCHRY FESTIVAL THEATRE

Pitlochry, Perthshire, PH16 5DR

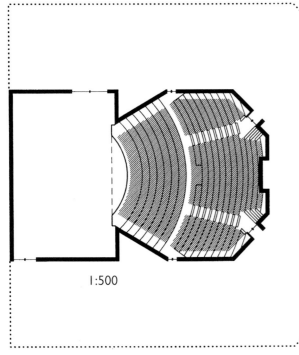

1:500

Design Intent

Pitlochry: A small Victorian tourist town, in the very Heart of the Highlands, with cast-iron and glass shopping arcades for the sale of whisky, tartan and tweeds, surrounded by the most beautiful scenery in the world, with trains direct from London.

Festival: A summer season of entertainment – stay six days and see six plays in Scotland's Theatre in the Hills – the theatre born in a tent, nearly half a century ago, the obsessive dream of one man, John Stewart.

Theatre: For me, the most exciting of all building types to design: in this case, a house for drama, with strong emphasis on comfort and provision for the disabled, above all a building that will be a worthy permanent expression of John Stewart's dream.

Graham Law, *Architect*

Users' Verdicts

The permanent building fulfilled the management's brief for all-year-round working conditions, while audiences were delighted with its amenities and inspiring location.

Limited finance prevented certain desirable installations – flytower, studio theatre, workshop administration block – though the last two have since been added.

Truly, Founder John Stewart's vision has been amply vindicated.

Kenneth Ireland, *Director 1957 to 1983*

With continued audience support, it has been possible to maintain what is now virtually unique in Britain, namely a permanent repertory company of twenty-four actors performing seven plays in repertoire in a season from Easter to the second week of October. In addition to the theatre, opened in 1981, the new production workshops and administrative and technical offices have been completed and plans are in hand to build a second studio and concert arena, and redesign and improve the front of house and restaurant facilities.

With a newly commissioned play added to the company's programme each year, it is now possible to stay six days and see seven plays at the height of the season.

Clive Perry, *Director since 1987*

Playhouse

Replacing original tent theatre opened in 1951
Summer festival theatre
'Stay six days and see six plays'

First performance

19 May 1981

Auditorium

Single rake of seats with cross aisle
Capacity / 544
Volume / 2150m³ (3.9m³ per person)
Furthest seat / 21.7m

Orchestra Pit

38m² created by removing traps in forestage

Stage

Proscenium width / 10.47m
Stage depth / 13.1m
Width of stage / 21m
Flying height / 9.15m
(Fly tower can be added)

Designers and Builders

Client / *Pitlochry Festival Society*
    (Director 1957–83 *Kenneth Ireland*)
Architect / *Law and Dunbar-Nasmith*
Theatre consultant / *John Wyckham*
Acoustic consultant / *Frank Fahy*
Structural engineer / *Ove Arup*
Services engineer / *John C.R. Pearce*
Cost consultant / *Gibson and Simpson*
Main contractor / *J. Fraser Construction*

Project Cost

£2m (1981)

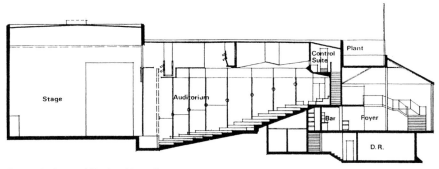

Section by Law and Dunbar-Nasmith

GEORGIAN THEATRE, RICHMOND

Victoria Road, Richmond, North Yorkshire DL10 4DW

Design Intent, 1963

The actor-manager, Samuel Butler, built and opened this theatre in Friars Wynd on 2 September 1788 with a production which started by his reading a prologue and was followed by a comedy and a comic opera which had been performed in London only a few months before. The theatre was in regular use till 1830 but then performances became less frequent and in 1848 it was let as an auction room. The auditorium was floored over flush with the stage, and the pit turned into wine vaults.

In 1960 the Trust was formed, an appeal launched and restoration began. The original paybox and pit, boxes, gallery and forestage have survived neglect and escaped demolition; now restored they keep alive an important period of our English theatre tradition. No other playhouse can give the authentic atmosphere of an old piece written for such a stage, or enable a more intimate appreciation of a new one. Actors and audience are in the closest company in the enchantment of a performance with a recreation of the original candlelight.

Nancy Crathorne, 1962

Users' Verdict

The theatre today is a hive of activity and as a living theatre is dedicated to productions of the highest quality. Its season runs from April to December with touring presentations of drama and music, both classical and modern.

The Georgian Youth Theatre has been successfully established and there are plans to form a company specialising in Restoration and Georgian works. The company will tour schools and colleges in the area and beyond, increasing the involvement of the theatre with local education establishments and enabling it to play a leading role in the cultivation of local drama and music.

Bill Sellars, Manager since 1992

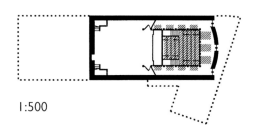

1:500

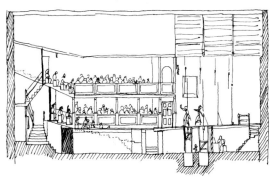

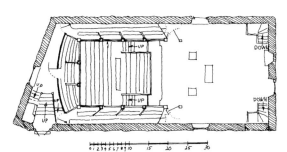

Playhouse

Restoration completed in 1963 of theatre built in 1788, known as the Theatre Royal Richmond and closed in 1846
Britain's only Georgian playhouse has been listed Grade I by Act of Parliament as 'a building of special architectural or historical interest'
Varied programme with an emphasis on classic plays

First performance

Of a play after restoration 1 July 1963

Auditorium

Typical 18th century pit (stalls) rectangular in form with boxes on three sides and small gallery above
Capacity / 220 seated on benches except for chairs in boxes (1788 c. 400)
Volume / 840 m^3 (3.8m^3 per person)
Furthest seat / 10.7m
Stage edge to facing box / 7.6m

Stage

Proscenium width / 4.72m
Depth of stage / 6.4m (to back wall)
Orchestra pit / 5m^2

Designers and Builders for the restoration

Client / The Georgian Theatre (Richmond) Trust Limited (Chairman Lady Crathorne)
Progenitors / Richard Southern, Scholar David Brooks, Town Clerk
Architectural adviser / Richard Leacroft

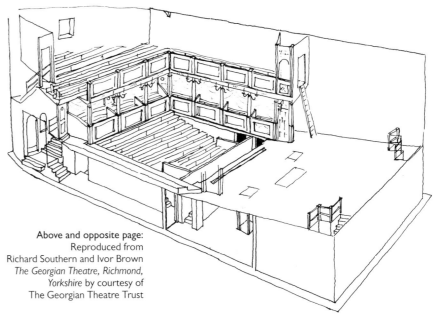

Above and opposite page:
Reproduced from
Richard Southern and Ivor Brown
*The Georgian Theatre, Richmond,
Yorkshire* by courtesy of
The Georgian Theatre Trust

THEATRE ROYAL, GLASGOW

Hope Street, Glasgow, Scotland G2 3QA
Scottish Opera

Design Intent, 1975

The last Theatre Royal Glasgow was opened in 1895. Scottish Television bought the theatre in 1956 and virtually destroyed its elegant interiors apart from the main elements of the auditorium. Following a feasibility study undertaken in 1972, Arup Associates were appointed in April 1974 to produce design and contract documents for a contract to ensure the re-opening in October 1975!

The aim of our design was to realise the essential qualities of Phipps' Victorian French Renaissance interior, to reduce the number of seats to between 1500 and 1600 and to achieve the best possible acoustic for opera in a lyric theatre of a very limited volume per seat. In addition, the whole of the stage equipment and mechanical and electrical services had to be renewed, including the theatre, production and house lighting. All had to be introduced without destroying the restored interior. One of the most important decisions taken in agreement with the client was to maintain the original position of the orchestra rail and provide a semi-covered pit to house 85 players, to ensure that elusive balance between stage and pit sound.

Derek Sugden, Head of the design team

Users' Verdict

The acquisition in 1974 and rapid conversion of the Theatre Royal into a working opera house was a milestone in Scottish Opera's history, which enabled it to develop into a full-time company with a permanent home. The theatre has also served as a home for The Scottish Ballet and as a regular venue for major touring drama companies. It has proved a popular focus for high quality entertainment in Glasgow.

Since 1974 opera productions have tended to become heavier and more complex. This has highlighted the restrictions in storage space backstage. The orchestra pit is now reckoned to be set too far back under the stage, producing a dampened sound and poor playing conditions for the musicians. Public expectations of the front of house space have changed and the cramped foyers, bars and staircases, which were extended in 1975 only as far as a tight budget would allow, are no longer acceptable. Accordingly a further remodelling, retaining the best of the existing elegant auditorium but also taking in adjacent sites, is presently under consideration.

Richard Jarman, Director since 1991

Opera House

Restoration in 1975 of 1895 theatre rebuilt from a theatre of 1880
Listed category A by Act of Parliament as 'a building of special architectural or historic interest'
Home of Scottish Opera who also present Scottish Ballet and touring drama

First performance

After restoration 14 October 1975

Auditorium

Renaissance auditorium by C.J. Phipps
Stalls and three circles with side boxes
Capacity / 1566 (in 1956, 1950)
Volume / 5050m³ (3.3m³ per person)
Furthest seat / 27m
Stage edge to facing gallery / 11.5m

Orchestra Pit

Formed by elevator with alternatives of pit/forestage
Area / 104m² (41m² in open)

Stage

Proscenium width / 10.36m
Depth of stage / 12.2m (scene dock beyond)
Width of stage / 16.5m
Flying height / 17.1m

Designers and Builders for the restoration

Client / *Scottish Opera*
  (Directors *Alexander Gibson* and *Peter Hemmings*)
Architect / *Arup Associates*
Theatre consultant / *John Wyckham*
Acoustic consultant / *Arup Associates*
Structural and service engineers / *Arup Associates*
Cost consultant / *Arup Associates*

Building Cost

£2.2m (1975)

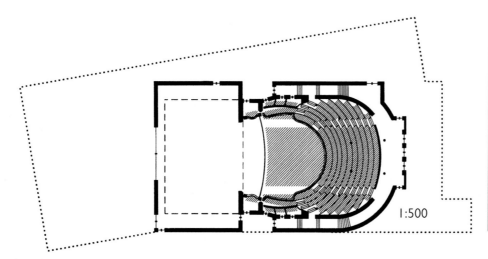

1:500

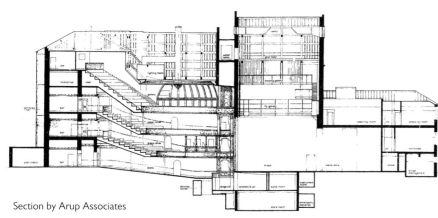

Section by Arup Associates

GRAND OPERA HOUSE, BELFAST

Great Victoria Street, Belfast, Northern Ireland BT2 7HR

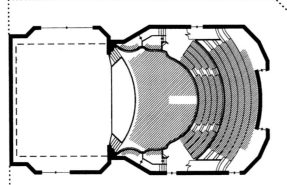

1:500

Design Intent, 1980

Central to the work was Matcham's superb auditorium miraculously intact. Here, restoration was minimal and the comprehensive refurbishment included a more generous seating layout. The original front of house foyers and bars ruined by the 1960s cinema conversion were stripped out and redesigned along with a new conservatory-like bar pinned to the front facade. Detailing here is in a modern thirties-inspired style not pastiche Matcham. Back stage the restricted site meant that all upgrading had to take place within existing perimeter walls; a tall mansard roof masks the higher fly-tower.

Robert McKinstry, *Architect*

Users' Verdict

The 1980 restoration has preserved Matcham's genius for combining in one theatre, a lyric and a dramatic house, which still performs superbly in both roles. It has given today's theatregoers the only Number One house in Northern Ireland, with ample leg room, and a theatre interior which is a fine combination of the arts of Victorian architects and craftsmen. The addition of the over-street bar at circle level has helped to satisfy the need for refreshment and for revenue, but only a more radical approach could improve the very restricted front-of-house facilities. The seating capacity of 1000 makes it unrealistic to present productions on a very large scale – which is arguably a function of a Theatre in this unique position. Of course Matcham built for 2500 people, though seated in conditions we would find unacceptable.

Derek Nicholls, *Director since 1994*

Touring Theatre

Restoration in 1980 of 1895 theatre
Northern Ireland's major theatre presenting opera, dance and popular entertainment
The theatre has been listed Grade II Star by Act of Parliament as 'a building of special architectural or historic interest'

First performance

After restoration 15 September 1980

Auditorium

Exuberant auditorium by Frank Matcham in Anglo-Indian style with stalls, two circles and side boxes
Capacity / 1,001 (in 1895 c. 2,500)
Volume / 5750m³ (5.74m³ per person)
Furthest seat / 24.4m
Stage to first circle / 13.7m

Orchestra Pit

Single elevator provides alternative of pit or 4m deep forestage
Area / 87m² (of which 60m² under stage)

Stage

Raked / 1:20
Proscenium width / 12.1m
Depth of stage / 12.8m
Width of stage / 21.9m
Flying height / 18m

Designers and Builders for the restoration

Client / *Arts Council of Northern Ireland*
Architect / *Robert McKinstry and Melvyn Brown*
Theatre consultant / *John Wyckham Associates*
Acoustic consultant / *Frank Fahey*
Structural engineer / *Kirk McClure and Martin*
Services engineer / *Williams and Shaw*
Cost consultant / *Hastings and Baird*
Main contractor / *H. and J. Martin Ltd*

Building Cost

£3.1m (1980)

Reinstatements and Improvements carried out in 1992 and 1994
Architect / *Robinson and McIlwaine*

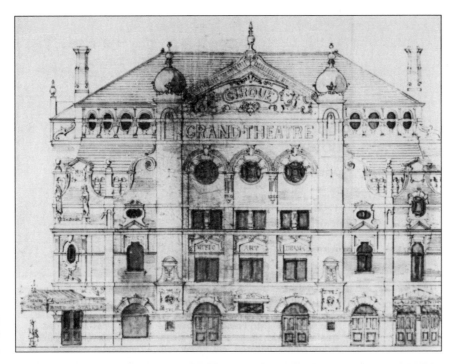

Right: Sketch of proposed Grand Opera House, 1894, for Frank Matcham and Co.

LYCEUM THEATRE, SHEFFIELD

Norfolk Street, Sheffield S1 1DA

Design Intent, 1990

It was our intent that the superbly refurbished Lyceum Theatre would act as a cata-lyst for the transformation of Tudor Square into the heart of arts and tourism within the city. The proximity of the Lyceum to the Crucible and the very differing styles of the two theatres make a unique combination. The fine auditorium with its delicate rococo plasterwork has been painstakingly restored. We meticulously researched and collected samples of plaster, paint and gold leaf from the original to inform our redecoration in shades of cream and gold set in burgundy surround with highlights in gold leaf. The existing foyers were expanded and linked by the striking new stain-less steel and glass staircase which sweeps up through all public areas and is crowned by a stunning modern chandelier. Backstage a new stagehouse and new dressing rooms equipped with the latest facilities attract the very best touring companies.

Nick Thompson, *Architect*

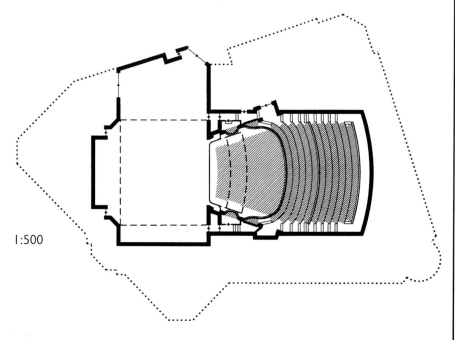

1:500

Users' Verdict

One of Sprague's finest interiors is reborn in Sheffield and the city has once again a major touring venue. The public have flocked to see a wide range of excellent productions and except for the very largest, Sheffield can now see the very best touring productions avail-able.

Stephen Barry, *Director since 1990*

Touring Theatre

Restoration in 1990 of 1893 theatre extensively rebuilt in 1897 which has been listed Grade II Star by Act of Parliament as 'a building of special architec-tural or historic interest'
Mixed programme theatre with drama, opera, dance, musicals and popular entertainment operated in conjunction with adjacent Crucible Theatre

First performance

After restoration 18 December 1990

Auditorium

Lavishly decorated by architect W.G.R. Sprague
Stalls two circles and three tiers of side boxes
Capacity / 1129 (in 1897 c. 2,500)
                 1051 *with Orchestra Pit*
Volume / $3650m^3$ ($3.2m^3$ *per person*)
Furthest seat / 27.5m
Stage edge to facing circle / 11.5m

Orchestra Pit

Formed by elevator providing pit/seating/forestage
Area / $63.75m^2$ ($47m^2$ *in open*)

Stage

Raked / 1:30
Proscenium width / 8.6m
Depth of stage / 11.8m
Width of stage / 17m
Flying height / 18m

Designers and Builders for the restoration

Client / *Lyceum Theatre Trust*
Architect / *RHWL Partnership*
Theatre equipment consultant / *Technical Planning International*
Acoustic consultant / *RHWL Partnership*
Structural and services engineers / *Ove Arup and Partners*
Cost consultant / *Bucknall Austin*
Main contractor / *Bovis Construction Ltd*

Building Cost

£8.7m (1990)

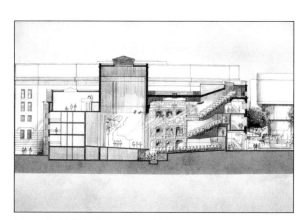

Section by R H W L Partnership 1990

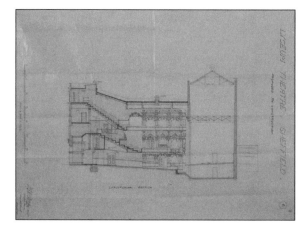

Section for W.G.R. Sprague c.1893

PRINCE EDWARD THEATRE

Old Compton Street, London W1V 6HS

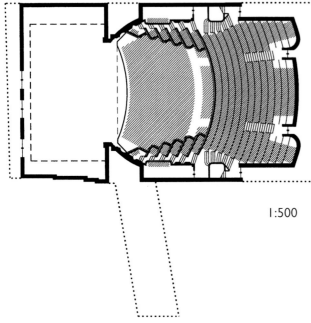

1:500

Design Intent, 1993

Our comprehensive proposals to recreate the glamour of the 1930s resulted in restoring many of the original exterior features long hidden by advertising hoardings and introducing key elements such as new bronze entrance doors, a decorative canopy and poster panels together with a new flood lighting scheme.

In the auditorium the problems were complex. There was a sense about it appearing to be two rooms, with large expanses of wall treated with only small scale low relief decoration. The auditorium also had a poor acoustic for amplified sound demanded by today's musicals.

Our solutions included the introduction of additional boxes, loges and side galleries continuing the lines of decoration and breaking down the scale of the blank sidewalls. Fret-work screens and low frequency absorption panels help the acoustic and reduce the apparent width of the stalls.

The interior design is unified by a new colour scheme including carpets, drapes and seat fabric, as well as the painting conceived together with the lighting to take full advantage of original features.

Nick Thompson, *Architect*

Users' Verdict, 1994

The scheme has successfully brought warmth and intimacy to the theatre and greatly improved seating configuration, sightlines and public areas. The new box, circle slip positions and the re-raked grand circle give a greater focus to the stage, most particularly for circle patrons. This has also provided the opportunity for badly needed modelling, colour detailing and restoration of the original decorative plaster work to the auditorium walls. The stalls aisle screens create a soft and more intimate decorative finish to what was a large blank space and together with the redesigned foyer and bar areas, improves audience access and circulation.

Martin McCallum *for Delfont Mackintosh Theatres Ltd*

West End Theatre
Restoration and remodelling in 1993 of 1930 theatre
Presenting long run musicals

First performance
After remodelling 3 March 1993

Auditorium
Original art deco auditorium by Marc-Henri and Laverdet within building by Edward Stone which had since been heavily altered
Stalls, two circles and two tiers of boxes
Capacity / 1643
Volume / 9500m^3 (5.8m^3 per person)
Furthest seat / 33.5m
Stage edge to facing circle / 15.2m

Orchestra Pit
Fixed
Area / 46.8m^2 (area depends on scenery)

Stage
Proscenium width / 13.4m
Depth of stage / 11.7m
Width of stage / 21.4m
Flying height / 19.6m

Designers and Builders for the remodelling
Client / *Delfont Mackintosh Theatres Ltd*
Architect / *RHWL Partnership*
Acoustic consultant / *Arup Acoustics*
Technical lighting consultant / *Howard Eaton*
Technical sound consultant / *Autograph Sound*
Structural engineer / *John Mason and Partners*
Lighting consultant / *Lighting Design Partnership*
Cost consultant / *Frost Bevan Partnership*
Main contractor / *W.F.C. Ltd*

Building Cost
£2.7m (1993)

Above: Drawing of the London Casino, Soho (the former name of The Prince Edward Theatre) from *Architecture Illustrated*, May 1936

1930

1993

EDINBURGH FESTIVAL THEATRE

13–29 Nicholson Street, Edinburgh, Scotland EH8 9BE

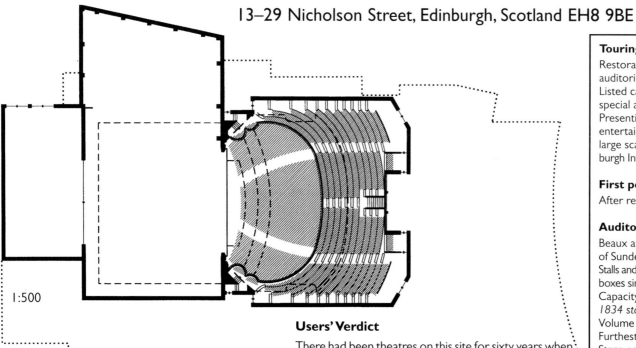

1:500

Touring Theatre

Restoration of 1928 theatre retaining only the original auditorium
Listed category B by Act of Parliament as 'a building of special architectural or historical interest'
Presenting opera, ballet, musicals, drama and popular entertainment as well as being the principal theatre for large scale productions at the annual three week Edinburgh International Festival in August and early September

First performance

After remodelling 18 June 1994

Auditorium

Beaux arts style by W. & T.R. Milburn, architects of Sunderland
Stalls and two flattened circles close to the stage and stepped boxes similar to North American theatres of the period
Capacity / 1913 no orchestra pit: 1889 small pit: 1834 standard pit: 1769 largest pit
Volume / 8850m^3 (4.7m^3 per person)
Furthest seat / 28.4m
Stage edge to first circle / 13.5m

Orchestra Pit

Three alternative pit sizes formed by three elevators
Areas / largest pit 151m^2 (of which 57m^2 under stage)
        standard pit 114m^2 (of which 57m^2 under stage)
        small pit 80m^2 (of which 57m^2 under stage)

Stage

Proscenium width / 13.4m
Depth of stage / 17m (with scene dock beyond)
Width of stage / 31.25m
Flying height / 23m

Designers and Builders for the rebuilding

Client / Edinburgh Festival Theatre Trust
   (Chairman Lord Younger of Prestwick)
Architect / The Law and Dunbar-Nasmith Partnership
Theatre consultant / Theatre Projects Consultants
Acoustic consultant / Sandy Brown Associates
Auditorium decoration consultant / David Hannivan
Structural and services engineers / Blyth and Blyth
Cost consultant / Doig and Smith
Main contractor / Bovis Construction (Scotland) Ltd

Building Cost

£15.5m (1994)

Design Intent, 1994

Edinburgh asked of us a touring lyric theatre of international standard, a principal home for opera and dance for the Edinburgh International Festival after 47 years of inadequate provision, a theatre requiring no revenue funding and a symbol for the City of architectural and artistic renewal.

That these ambitions have been achieved using the auditorium of a 1928 variety theatre used as a bingo hall since 1963 reflects the inherent qualities of the original space and that of its site to accommodate change. A new stage house and support facilities meet the needs of touring companies. The auditorium has been given a very flexible orchestra pit and new production lighting positions without detriment to the historic auditorium. New glass enclosed foyers offer a stimulating welcome where seeing and being seen is celebrated as part of the dramatic occasion.

Colin Ross, *Architect*

Users' Verdict

There had been theatres on this site for sixty years when Frank Matcham built the first Empire in 1892. This was replaced in 1928 by the Milburns' larger palace of varieties. Our present theatre retains only the auditorium of the second Empire to which has been added the biggest stage in Britain and the best front-of-house. The former allows us to book the world's leading dance and opera companies, as well as provide Scottish Opera and Scottish Ballet with an Edinburgh home, plus musicals, large scale drama, popular entertainment and supporting concerts. The latter's glass fronted bars and street cafe are welcoming and make money. The acoustics of the auditorium, previously thought unremarkable, have been universally acclaimed and a capacity of nearly 2000, plus an intimacy enhanced by the clever improvements and decorations of present day designers, allow us to provide a broader programme of excellence than that of any other touring theatre.

However, problems persist; a tight construction budget, due in part to over optimism as to what an international theatre should cost, led to economies backstage which must be corrected (the site is now available) while balancing the books even with a near full theatre remains problematic in a city where the competition is either subsidised or else has more seats.

Paul Iles, *Manager since 1992*

1928

1994

1994

PART II

NEWER SPACES
Different Forms and Found Space

First of these new different forms to be built was the thrust stage with audience on three sides. This form originated with Tyrone Guthrie's conversion of the Assembly Hall for the Edinburgh International Festival in 1948. Chichester (1963) was the first new thrust stage theatre built in Britain although not judged as successful as the Crucible, Sheffield (1971), in the design of which Guthrie's collaborator Tanya Moiseiwitsch was closely involved

There are only four significant in-the-round theatres in Britain. The Orange Tree of 1991 is the smallest and the latest. The second example chosen is the Royal Exchange, Manchester of 1976 which was conceived by director Michael Elliott (1931–84). This is a confident high-tech late 20th century version of a 16th century Shakespearean playhouse which has been set lightly down in the found space of a 19th century commercial basilica. The theatre its creator thought of as ephemeral may yet turn out to be more enduring and influential than contemporary concrete constructions also exhibited here.

'Courtyard theatre' was a phrase re-coined for the opening of the Cottelsoe in 1977: a description with non-specific connotations of both form and tradition. But the arts centre at Christ's Hospital School had anticipated the Cottesloe by two years and became a strong influence on the designers of Stratford's Swan. The Lawrence Batley, which owed much to the earlier Wilde Theatre, Bracknell is the latest courtyard and, like so many theatres in this second part, is a conversion of found space.

Three of the simple and low-cost theatres which complete this review of British theatre architecture are London 'fringe' theatres. The Young Vic was a temporary industrial addition in 1970 to a disused butcher's shop. The Tricycle is a scaffolding structure within a 20s dance hall, rebuilt in 1989 after a fire. The Almeida has been gradually converted and improved within a 19th century lecture hall. The fourth theatre, the conversion of a gymnasium at Winchester College, is a further representative of many attractively straightforward new school theatres in Britain.

Iain Mackintosh

Thrust and In-the-Round
1963	Chichester Festival Theatre
1971	Crucible Theatre, Sheffield
1976	Royal Exchange Theatre, Manchester
1991	Orange Tree Theatre, Richmond, Surrey

Courtyard Theatres
1975	Christ's Hospital Theatre, Horsham
1977	The Cottesloe, Royal National Theatre
1986	Swan Theatre, Stratford-upon-Avon
1994	Lawrence Batley Theatre, Huddersfield

Simple and Low Cost
1970	Young Vic, London
1980/9	Tricycle Theatre, London
1982	Queen Elizabeth II Theatre, Winchester College
1984	Almeida Theatre, London

Postscript
1959/1982	The Mermaid Theatre, London

CHICHESTER FESTIVAL THEATRE

Oaklands Park, Chichester, West Sussex PO19 4AP

Design Intent

The concept of festival drama and a current movement seeking a return to the character of Elizabethan theatre combined to inspire this building. Expressed in practical terms, the brief sought an open stage theatre, seating approximately 1400 people dispersed on three sides of a performance area having two acting levels, and all contained within as economical a structure as possible.

In response, the design offers an uncompromisingly modern architectural statement of these needs, clearly and dramatically expressing, both internally and externally, function, structure, form and materials in a finely balanced composition.

The hexagonal shaped auditorium maximises the practical advantages, is acoustically efficient and, together with a light roof structure, allows a compact, column free, optimum seating arrangement with clear uninterrupted views and sight lines for all.

Sir Philip Powell, *Architect*

Users' Verdict

Chichester is famous for its renowned Festival Season of Plays in the summer. It is also a main receiving house during the winter and spring. Despite its limitations – there can be no flying and there is no orchestra pit – it is well equipped technically. Be it straight theatre, musicals, chamber or symphony concerts, recitals, jazz, ballet, modern dance, opera or circus the excitement of its thrust stage creates a unique awareness, intimacy, magic and realism.

Paul Rogerson, *General Manager since 1974*

Thrust Stage Playhouse

Open stage summer theatre inspired by Tyrone Guthrie's creation of the Festival Theatre, Stratford, Ontario in 1953
First season directed by Sir Laurence Olivier of 10 weeks
1995 season directed by Sir Derek Jacobi of 23 weeks
Winter season of touring shows and concerts from 1981

First performance

3 July 1963

Auditorium and Stage

Audience on three sides of open stage within hexagonal space
Capacity / 1374
Stage on a long axis / 9.34m wide, area 82m^2
Volume / 6585 m^3 (4.8m^3 per person)
Furthest seat / 19.2m

Designers and Builders

Client / *Chichester Festival Theatre Trust*
  (Chairman *Leslie Evershed Martin*)
Architect / *Powell and Moya Partnership*
Structural engineer / *Charles Weiss and Partners*
Electrical and mechanical engineers / *Peter Jay and Partners* in association with *David Kut and Partners*
Cost consultant / *Davis, Belfield and Everest*
Main contractor / *Sir Robert McAlpine and Sons*

Building Cost

£0.95m (1962)

1:500

1971

1994

CRUCIBLE THEATRE, SHEFFIELD

Norfolk Street, Sheffield, South Yorkshire S1 1DA

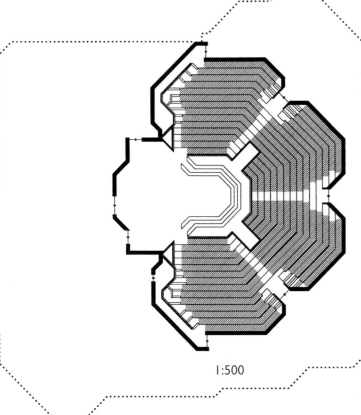

1:500

Design Intent

For the design of the Crucible we worked closely with Tanya Moiseiwitsch, Tyrone Guthrie's designer, to develop an intimate actor audience relationship of great intimacy but permitting three dimensional staging using narrow promontory stage with step, moat and diagonal vomitory entrances. The Grecian concept of emphasis on performance and costume rather than scenery influenced the architecture with the enclosing octagon developing into a scenic wall whilst above tiny lights give a sense of an open sky.

The public areas are conceived as a street bringing people into the building throughout the day and leading them up to a broad spacious foyer where the interplay of levels and voids creates places for people to see and be seen.

Nick Thompson, *Architect*

Users' Verdict

Simply one of the most challenging and engaging large-scale theatre spaces in the UK. A surprising intimacy is achieved.

Stephen Barry, *Director since 1990*

Thrust Stage Playhouse

Open stage theatre replacing company's earlier proscenium theatre
Presenting own productions and annual snooker tournament
Operated in conjunction with adjacent Lyceum Theatre since 1990

First performance

6 November 1971

Auditorium and Stage

Audience evenly arranged on three sides of thrust stage
Design in direct succession to other theatres conceived by Tyrone Guthrie and
Tanya Moiseiwitsch at Stratford, Ontario
(tent 1953, building 1957) and Minneapolis (1963)
Capacity / 1013
Volume / 7120m³ (7m³ per person)
Furthest seat / 16m
Stage / 10.2m x 10.2m
Original encircling steps and moat are generally filled in today to produce larger acting area

Designers and Builders

Client / *Sheffield Playhouse Company*
  (Director *Colin George*)
Architect / *Renton Howard Wood Associates*
Theatre design consultant / *Tanya Moiseiwitsch*
Stage lighting and equipment consultant / *Theatre Projects Consultants*
Acoustic consultant / *Hugh Creighton*
Structural engineer / *Ove Arup and Partners*
Mechanical engineer / *Dale and Benham*
Cost consultant / *Gleeds*

Building Cost

£0.88m (1971)

1971

ROYAL EXCHANGE THEATRE, MANCHESTER

St. Ann's Square, Manchester M1 6FT

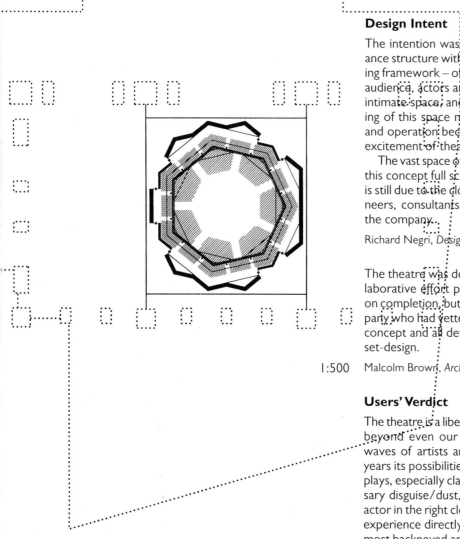

1:500

Design Intent

The intention was to design a free-standing performance structure within a building, a transparent supporting framework – of medium seating capacity – in which audience, actors and operational crew share the same intimate space, and can enter from all sides. The sharing of this space means that all equipment, its access and operation becomes open to view and part of the excitement of theatrical performance.

The vast space of the Royal Exchange building allowed this concept full scope, and the success of the venture is still due to the close collaboration of architects, engineers, consultants, specialists and many members of the company.

Richard Negri, *Designer*

The theatre was designed over a long period. The collaborative effort produced a building which surprised on completion but was anticipated by the theatre company who had vetted, contributed to and approved the concept and all details just as they would have done a set-design.

Malcolm Brown, *Architect*

Users' Verdict

The theatre is a liberating, demanding and creative space beyond even our high expectations. It has inspired waves of artists and technicians. Even after eighteen years its possibilities seem endless. The effect it has on plays, especially classics, is to strip them of all unnecessary disguise/dust, and because its emphasis is on an actor in the right clothes in a light, sharing an emotional experience directly with the audience, it brings up the most hackneyed and proscenium arch classic as a fresh piece. The challenge of the space is the single greatest factor in the success of the Company.

Braham Murray, *Director since 1970*

In-the-Round Playhouse

A free standing structure within Royal Exchange of 1874 and 1921 which is a building listed Grade II by Act of Parliament as 'a building of special architectural or historic interest'
Present theatre followed temporary theatre created in 1973
Theatre presents exclusively its own productions

First performance

8 September 1976

Auditorium and Stage

Auditorium on three levels surrounding 10m diameter stage
Capacity / 740
Volume / $2917m^3$ ($4m^3$ per person)
Furthest seat / 6m at stage floor level
Flying height / 7.6m

Designers and Builders

Client / *The Royal Exchange Theatre Company* (Director *Michael Elliott*)
Architect / *Levitt Bernstein Associates*
Theatre design consultant / *Richard Negri*
Theatre equipment consultant / *Theatre Projects Consultants*
Acoustic consultant / *D.K. Jones, University of Nottingham*
Structural engineer / *Ove Arup and Partners*
Services engineer / *Max Fordham Associates*
Cost consultants / *M.D.A.*
Main contractor / *J. Jarvis and Sons Ltd*

Building Cost

£1.2m (1976)

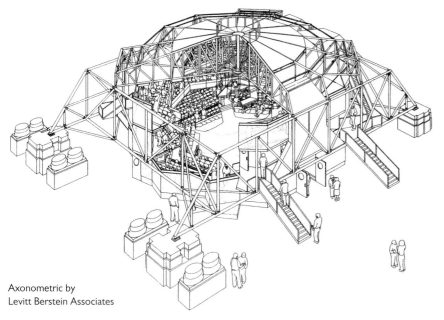

Axonometric by
Levitt Berstein Associates

ORANGE TREE THEATRE

1 Clarence Street, Richmond, Surrey TW9 2SA

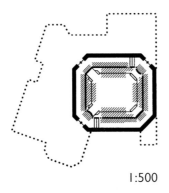

1:500

Design Intent

Sam Walters, director of the company he founded in 1970 to play in the room-over-the-pub, always considered his audience to be guests in his sitting room rather than conventional theatregoers. He continued to want an unusually small acting area and also required that the new theatre feel as intimate as the original pub theatre holding only 80. The solution was no more than three rows of shallow raked seating at stage level and an irregular and timber clad gallery above of only one row, under which actors circulate on two sides to reach entrances at all four corners. Foyers and dressing rooms are in the rebuilt house of the headmaster of a long closed school while the theatre itself is new build where once were the assembly hall and part of the playground.

Iain Mackintosh, *Head of Design Team*

Users' Verdict

The Orange Tree Theatre is a tremendous success. The new space, a truly purpose-built theatre-in-the-round, has delighted audiences, actors, directors, designers and theatre critics alike. With a maximum of three rows on any side, the essential intimacy was created but at the same time doubling the audience capacity from the old pub theatre. Another fulfilled aim was to produce real comfort whilst maintaining informality and, hugely important, to provide the best possible facilities for disabled people.

Any fears that the special atmosphere of the Orange Tree Theatre would be lost when we crossed the road from the pub to the new building were totally unfounded and the art and the audiences go from strength to strength in the new theatre.

Sam Walters, *Director since 1970*

In-the-Round Fringe Playhouse
New theatre to succeed a room-over-the-pub across the street
Theatre presents exclusively its own productions

First performance
14 February 1991

Auditorium and Stage
Room with single row stepped gallery on all four sides
Capacity / *163*
Acting area generally / *5.3m x 4.5m*
Flying height / *4.85m*
Furthest seat from acting area / *5m*

Designers and Builders
Client / *Orange Tree Theatre Ltd*
  (Director *Sam Walters*)
Architect and theatre consultant / *Theatre Projects Consultants*
Acoustic consultant / *Arup Acoustics*
Structural engineer / *Ove Arup and Partners*
Services engineer / *Max Fordham Associates*
Cost consultant / *Michael French Associates*
Main contractor / *Holloway Building Services Ltd*

Building Cost
£1.3m (1991) including value of shell

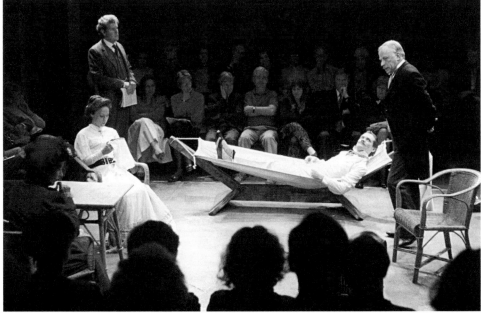

CHRIST'S HOSPITAL THEATRE

Christ's Hospital School, Horsham, West Sussex RH13 7LW

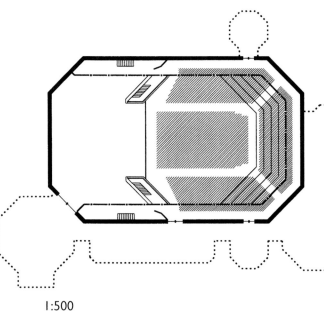

1:500

Design Intent

Our intention was to design an auditorium which had an intimate and unique presence and was adaptable so that it could be transformed from a complete court-yard with a thrust stage to a proscenium arch with end stage configuration. The auditorium had to be suitable for both regional public performances and for school use as a teaching space. The galleries, stall seating and ceiling forming the enclosure of the auditorium were designed in timber stained a deep red colour and this was intended to be a main ingredient contributing to the very special atmosphere of the theatre space.

John Partridge, *Architect and partner of late Bill Howell*

Users' Verdict

The theatre welcomes and excites, its coolly modern exterior sharply contrasting with a traditional inn-court-yard interior that echoes Elizabethan, Georgian and Victorian theatres, yet still provides a modern multi-directional space for innovative experiment and per-formance. The theatre hums with constant activity and its friendly atmosphere encourages young actors to conquer its size and distance. Recent legislation has tethered its towers and limited its flexibility for the moment, but its timeless design remains a perfect frame for our extensive programme of educational and pro-fessional work.

Duncan Noel-Paton, *Head of Drama since 1972*

Courtyard Theatre

School theatre and part of school arts centre comprising theatre, music school, library and classrooms
Wide range of school productions of drama and opera with casts of up to 200 plus professional programme of concerts and touring productions and commercial lettings during vacations

First performance

July 1975

Auditorium and Stage

Conceived with two primary forms: complete courtyard with thrust stage (*capacity 450*), end stage with end towers removed (*capacity 580*)
Volume / 4233m³ (*7.3m³ per person*)
Thrust stage/ 6m wide and 11m deep
Proscenium width / 15.22m
End stage depth / 11m
Flying height / 10m

Designers and Builders

Client / *Christ's Hospital School*
 (Director of drama *Duncan Noel-Paton*)
Architect / *Howell, Killick, Partridge and Amis*
Theatre consultant / *Theatre Projects Consultants*
Structural engineer / *Harris and Sutherland*
Mechanical and electrical engineers / *Edwards and Blackie*
Cost consultant / *David Vevers Partnership*
Main contractor / *Bovis*

Building Cost

£0.6m (estimate of theatre element, 1974)

THE COTTESLOE

South Bank, London SE1 9PX
Royal National Theatre

Design Intent

There should be room in this great theatrical sanctuary for acorns as well as oaks. Here new play-wrights, new directors, new techniques of presentation will be given the chance to prove their worth, testing themselves in a laboratory atmosphere instead of being plunged into the full glare of the two larger auditoria. The National Theatre is not only the custodian of past tradition and present practice: it has a responsibility to the future. Like any other developing organisation, it needs a research department; and this essential service, at a very low cost, is what the experimental studio would supply.

Kenneth Tynan, *Literary Manager 1963 to 1973*

The Cottesloe can be organised inside the space defined by the three walls of galleries in a variety of ways – scenic end stage; theatre in the round; one room end stage and, by raising the auditorium in the central space to stage height and removing the lowest of the three tier fronts, a flat floor over the whole space.

Sir Denys Lasdun, *Architect*

In 1973 Peter Hall, recently appointed Director of the National, called for proposals to complete the abandoned third theatre, doubling its capacity in a vast empty void under the Olivier. The preferred solution was for a courtyard with audience on fixed galleries around a flexible central area modelled on those 17th and 18th century theatres which were used for balls, pony races and circus events as well as for plays. The audience of up to 400 were to enter at middle level from the already built foyer and move up or down to their places which might vary depending on the director's choice of playing area.

Iain Mackintosh, *Author of Design Study*

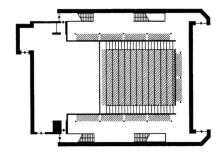

1:500

Users' Verdict

It is beyond argument that, for the practitioner, the Cottesloe is the most successful space of the NT's three auditoria. It combines the characteristics most sought by actors and directors: intimacy, good acoustics, lack of pretension, and flexibility of staging. Everything about the space is in proportion to the human scale. Nothing distracts, and everything allows the imagination to breathe: a black box made for magic. It came about through an exemplary collaboration between a theatre consultant – Iain Mackintosh, the theatre's architect, and John Bury – the National's Head of Design.

Richard Eyre, *Director since 1988*

Experimental Courtyard Theatre

Third theatre of the National alongside the Olivier open stage and the Lyttelton proscenium theatre. The three theatres, together with facilities for public and for production, are home to Britain's Royal National Theatre
The whole building has been listed Grade II Star by Act of Parliament as 'a building of special architectural or historical interest'.

First performance

At the Cottesloe 5 March 1977

Auditorium and Stage

Flexible rectangular space / 9.9m between galleries
Capacity / 200 to 400 depending on layouts which include end stage with or without proscenium, in-the-round, traverse stage on long or short axis and promenade flat floor
Volume / 2100m³ (5m³ per person)
Furthest seat to end stage / 12m
End stage to facing gallery / 9.9m
Length of space / 22m
Width of stage / 14m
Flying height / 7.5m

Designers and Builders

Client / The South Bank Theatre Board
   (Set up by *Government* and *Greater London Council*)
Architect / *Denys Lasdun and Partners*
Theatre consultant / *Theatre Projects Consultants*
Acoustic consultant / *Sound Research Laboratories*
Structural and services engineers / *Flint and Neill*
Cost consultant / *Davies, Belfield and Everest*
Main contractor / *Sir Robert McAlpine and Sons Ltd*

Building Cost

£16.6m for the whole three theatre complex (1976)

Four of many possible
arrangements of the
Cottesloe Theatre

Candleford ('79) Design: William Dudley

Half Life ('77) Design: Jane Martin

Voysey Inheritance ('89) Design: William Dudley

Fuente Ovejuna ('88) Design: Nick Ormerod

SWAN THEATRE

Stratford-upon-Avon, Warwickshire CV37 6BB

Design Intent

Our intention was to create a space for the performance of Elizabethan and Jacobean plays, not a facsimile of any playhouse of that period but one which would recapture their essential qualities. Within the shell of the destroyed Victorian theatre, we therefore set out to build a wooden O, to be at once the scaffolding of the Play and a Microcosm, encompassing Audience and Actor. It was, above all, to be space for the Theatre of the World in which visual illusion would play a secondary role.

Michael Reardon, *Architect*

Users' Verdicts

In the Swan Theatre one is more aware of the audience than in any other theatre I know. It is a place of congregation – no accident that it was carved out of the shell of a rehearsal space known as 'the conference room'. The actor's presence seems to be in perfect balance with that of the audience. All successful productions acknowledge this easy relationship. The space humanises the epic; makes public the private; and enables a secret grief or joy to be shared honestly.

Adrian Noble, *Director since 1991*

Conceived as the venue for the presentation of a trove of neglected Elizabethan, Jacobean and Restoration plays, the building celebrates the seventeenth century actor/audience relationship, with spectators crammed at three levels around a protruding tongue of stage.

Trevor Nunn, *Director 1968–91*

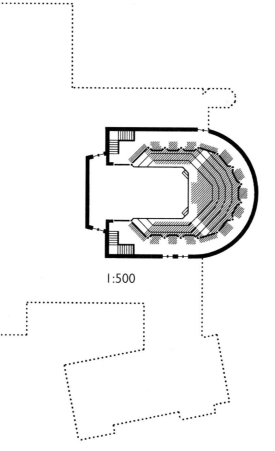

1:500

Courtyard Theatre

Third theatre of the RSC after the Memorial Theatre (1932) and the first Other Place (1974), created within the shell of the auditorium of the first Memorial theatre (1879)
The whole building is listed Grade I by Act of Parliament as 'a building of special architectural or historic interest'
RSC presents its own productions April to January with visiting shows in late winter

First performance

26 April 1986

Auditorium and Stage

Narrow thrust stage with audience on three sides and three levels
Capacity / 460
Volume / 2500m^3 (5.43m^3 per person)
Furthest seat from stage / 10m
Thrust stage / 5.8m wide and 13.1m long

Designers and Builders

Client / *Royal Shakespeare Company*
  (Director Trevor Nunn)
Architect / *Michael Reardon and Associates*
Theatre consultants / *James Sargant and technical staff*
  of the RSC
Structural engineer / *Gifford and Partners*
Services engineer / *Peter Jay and Partners*
Cost consultant / *Gordon Cain*
Main contractor / *William Weaver plc*

Building Cost

£1.4m (1986)

Above: Conception sketch of the Swan by Tim Furby, Michael Reardon and Associates 1978

LAWRENCE BATLEY THEATRE, HUDDERSFIELD

Queen's Square, Huddersfield, Yorkshire HD1 2SP

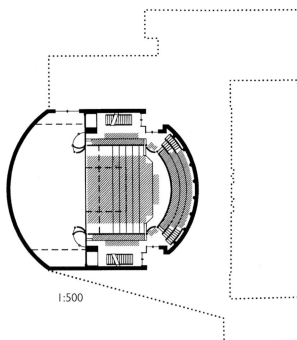

1:500

Joseph Kaye, the original builder, set out the chapel, the courtyard and the wing buildings to a rigorous geometry. We recognised the power of this and took the centre of his chapel as the centre for a galleried theatre: the arc of the facing tier echoes the arc of the east wall. The central area is mechanised so as to provide a convincing thrust stage alternative to end stage. The encircling galleries step up around the corner boxes. This enables a minimal floor to floor dimension to be achieved at the sides, where emptiness is to be avoided in courtyard theatres, contrasting with a wider gap at the end for three rows of the best seats at lower and middle level and, at the top level, a good sized control room behind a single row. The result is the most focused and most densely packed of recent courtyards.

Iain Mackintosh, *Stage and Auditorium Designer*

Design Intent

Built in 1819, Queen Street Mission had ceased to be a place of worship by 1970 and was later gutted and filled with squash courts. The choice of this fine building as a location for a new theatre afforded a superb opportunity to re-establish it as a focal point for the community, this time for secular purposes. The emphasis on community use provided the design theme for the interior. Architectural treatment has been kept low key so as to interpose the minimum of physical and visual barriers between actors and audience. This approach is particularly well suited to the flexible courtyard form which has the audience seated on three tiers and three sides, providing a sense of intimacy and involvement.

Rodney Atkinson, *Architect*

Users' Verdict

The staff of the Lawrence Batley Theatre have been delighted with the audiences' appreciation of the sympathetic conversion of the Georgian Chapel into a theatre. The flexibility of the stage configuration offers exciting artistic possibilities, and the curved back wall of the stage with the original Chapel window looks beautiful when lit. The auditorium seats are comfortable, and there is plenty of leg-room. The acoustics of the Lawrence Batley Theatre are excellent, and it makes a wonderful home for mid-scale touring drama, dance and opera.

Ron McAllister, *Director since 1992*

Courtyard Theatre
Conversion of 1819 Methodist Chapel which is a building listed Grade II by Act of Parliament as 'a building of special architectural or historic interest' Community theatre with mixed programme of opera, drama, music and dance by both professional and amateur companies

First performance
13 September 1994

Auditorium and Stage
Central flexible area with seating on three levels on three sides
Arc of chapel's east wall exposed on fourth side at rear of stage
Four elevators in central area allow easy conversion to thrust stage 5.6m by 5.6m with audience on three sides
Capacity / 474 *without orchestra pit or forestage*
          441 *with orchestra pit or forestage*
          423 *with thrust Stage*
'Flipper' boxes on stage narrow stage opening / *from 11.4m to 9m*
Volume / 2850m³ (6m³ *per person*)
End stage to furthest seat / *14m*
End stage to facing gallery / *11.8m*

Designers and Builders, 1994
Client / *Kirklees Theatre Trust*
   (Chairman *Councillor John Mernagh*)
Architect / *The Design Practice, Kirklees Metropolitan Council*
Theatre consultant / *Theatre Projects Consultants*
Acoustic consultant / *Arup Acoustics*
Structural and services engineers / *The Design Practice*
Cost consultant / *The Design Practice*
Main contractor / *Laings*

Building Cost
£5.3m (1994)

YOUNG VIC THEATRE

66 The Cut, London SE1 8LZ

Fringe Theatre Space
Built as a temporary theatre on a modest budget in 1970
Created for the National Theatre, which was then at the Old Vic, with an emphasis on youth
Independent since 1974

First performance
10 September 1970

Auditorium and Stage
Flexible square space with single gallery on three sides
Used now either in-the-round (*capacity 480*) or with thrust stage (*capacity 400*)
Volume / 4,000m³ (*8m³ per person*)
Stage in-the-round / 8.5m x 8m
Thrust stage / 7m wide 8m deep with further stage to rear
Furthest seat / 6m
Stage edge to gallery / 5m

Designers and Builders
Client / *National Theatre Board*
   (Young Vic Director *Frank Dunlop*)
Architect / *Howell, Killick, Partridge and Amis*
Theatre equipment consultant / *Theatre Projects Lighting*
Structural engineer / *Felix J. Samuels and Partners*
Services engineer / *Drake and Soull*
Cost consultant / *David Vevers Partnership*
Main contractor / *William Mercer, Liverpool*

Building Cost
£0.2m (1970)

Refurbished in 1993
Architects and theatre consultant / *Theatre Futures*

Design Intent

The Young Vic was built on a very modest budget as a temporary theatre for the National Theatre Board and intended to have a six year life only. It consists of a main auditorium with a tongue stage, around which the audience sits on three sides. There is a single gallery and the total seating accommodation is approximately 450. The theatre, which has its emphasis on youth, has been highly successful and the temporary licence for the building has been extended several times during its life. Foyer spaces and offices have been formed in an old butcher's shop, while the main theatre, studio space, coffee bar, dressing rooms and wardrobe accommodation have been provided in new buildings. The building is constructed of concrete blocks and the main auditorium has an exposed steel structure on the outside to avoid the necessity of fire proofing.

The whole project demonstrates how on a very small building budget the changing and adaptable demands of theatre and community can be met. HKPA have modified, extended and refurbished the building several times during its 24 year life by additions and alterations aimed at keeping it in tune with the times.

John Partridge, *Architect and partner of the late Bill Howell*

Users' Verdicts

When I became Administrator of the National it was agreed that I could build a young people's theatre: unconventional, classless, open and welcoming to the theatre's lost generation. We had only £60,000 to build a temporary structure quite the opposite of the concrete monolith on the South Bank. We asked for a cross between the Elizabethan Fortune Theatre, Guthrie's Assembly Hall, and a circus. A genius of an architect, Bill Howell, listened to all the people who were going to work in it. The Young Vic, funded to last five years, is just celebrating its twenty-fifth birthday.

Frank Dunlop, *Director 1970–78 and 1980–83*

The ideal modern auditorium; intimate enough for detail and understatement, open enough for the influence of dance, music and physical theatre. It is informal and yet its shape creates great focus. It is a place of action and sensation.

Tim Supple, *Director since 1993*

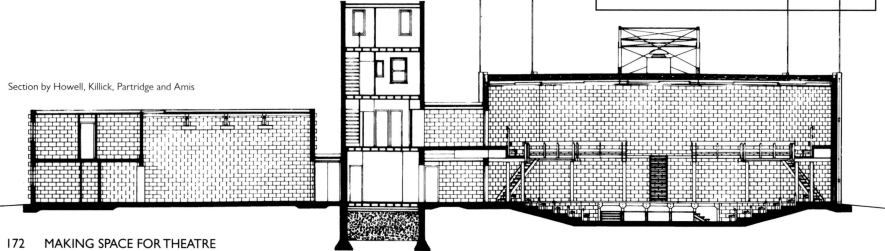

Section by Howell, Killick, Partridge and Amis

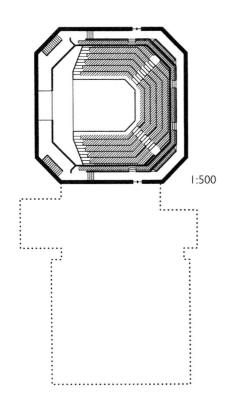

1:500

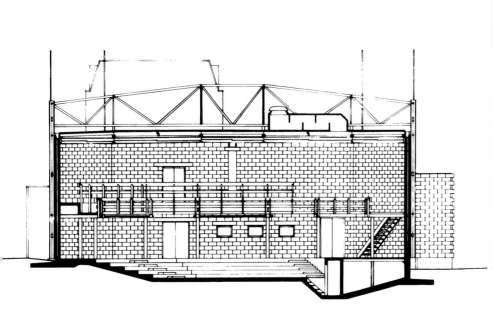

TRICYCLE THEATRE

269 Kilburn High Road, London NW6 7JR

Design Intent

To meet the limited budget and timescale in 1980, the auditorium was conceived as a free-standing scaffolding structure. Its dimensions and form are closely modelled on the Georgian Theatre in Richmond, Yorkshire, providing a very intimate courtyard theatre. The scaffolding aesthetic is extended to include integral stairs and lighting trusses and is completed with timber floors and canvas balustrade panels.

The 1987 fire gave us a unique opportunity to re-examine the design after seven years of use. The original auditorium was restored, with only minor technical improvements, together with a major remodelling of the front of house, office and backstage areas.

Tim Foster, *Architect*

Users' Verdict

In 1987 a fire destroyed most of the auditorium, but although this provided a unique opportunity to re-examine the design after seven years of use, we decided to recreate the original design with only minor modifications. The design is widely admired by both audiences and performers – it combines an intimate atmosphere with the possibility of large-scale 'presentational' performance. The informality of the auditorium is particularly suited to new work and challenging re-interpretations of classic plays.

Nicolas Kent, *Director since 1985*

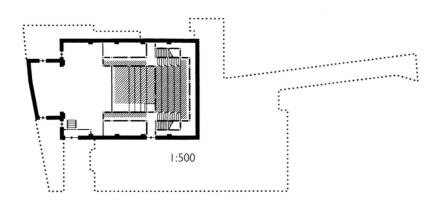

1:500

Fringe Playhouse

Conversion of 20s dance hall
Mixed programme of own productions and touring shows
Also regular programmes for children and schools
Extended after fire in 1987 and reopened 21st September 1989

First performance

16 September 1980

Auditorium

Scaffolding structure with central stalls and two encircling tiers
Capacity / (*since 1989*) 225
Volume / 1,730m^2 (7.6m^2 *per person*)
Furthest seat / 12m
Stage edge to facing tier / 6.1m

Orchestra Pit

None

Stage

Proscenium width (when used) / 6m
Depth of stage / 7m (*plus inner stage*)
Flying height / 4.5m (*clear*)

Designers and Builders 1980 and 1989

Client / *The Tricycle Theatre Ltd*
    (Supported by The London Borough of Brent)
Architect / *Tim Foster Architects*
Theatre and electrical consultants / *Theatre Projects*
    Consultants
Acoustic consultant / *Paul Gillieron*
Structural engineer / (*1980*) *Edwards and Blackie*
    (*Alex Jones*)
Structural engineer / (*1989*) *Alex Jones and Associates*
Mechanical engineer / *Edwards and Blackie*
Cost consultant / *Michael French Associates*
Main contractor / (*1980*) *J.T. Luton and Sons Ltd*
Main contractor / (*1989*) *Brent Building Division*

Project Cost

£0.15m (1980); £1m (1989)

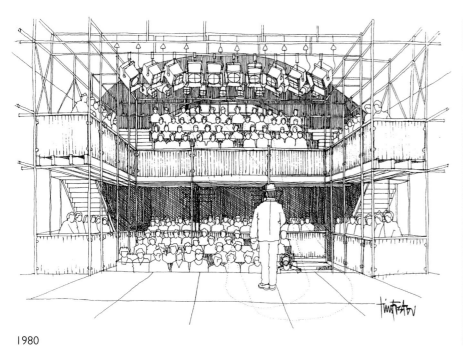

1980

1980

QUEEN ELIZABETH II THEATRE, WINCHESTER

Kingsgate Street, Winchester, Hampshire SO23 9NA

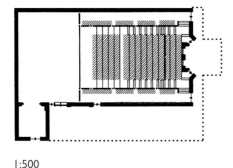

1:500

Design Intent

The Victorian gym at Winchester was useless for modern training purposes. The only place for theatre was a large flat floored modern concert hall. So the gym became a theatre. It was given a new front porch in its gable end, with a balcony in it for entre-acts, trumpets and so on. The porch opens onto a new forecourt for the arts. The pit can be used for an orchestra, for a forward extension of the seating, or for both; it is waterproofed so that it can be flooded for theatrical effect, and it can be partly or wholly covered. There is a full lighting and projection grid.

Edward Cullinan, *Architect*

Users' Verdict, 1994

Packed houses. Fifteen productions annually, range from first year Festival to visits by professional companies. Ideal intimacy for young voices and intense dramas. Though small, QEII has twice recently housed casts of 65. Used for films and talks too. Raked 275 seat auditorium, with 'Cottesloe' side-galleries and cross-aisles, is regularly invaded by actors and musicians. Seats are removed for set extensions. Gable rafters allow for hangings, if not 'flying'. There have been no subsequent structural alterations to this excellent conversion.

Simon Taylor, *Head of English/Theatre since 1990*

Flexible School Theatre

Conversion of nineteenth century gymnasium into school theatre

First performance

8th July 1982

Auditorium and Stage

Single gallery on three sides with part of central seating fixed
Flexible zone in front of this available for additional seating orchestra pit or thrust stage or in-the-round arrangement
Capacity with no orchestra / 275
Proscenium width and width between galleries / 8.4m
Length of space / 21.6m
Stage edge to facing gallery / 10m

Designers and Builders

Client / *Winchester College*
Architect / *Edward Cullinan Architects*
Theatre consultant / *Tim Foster*
Structural engineer / *Felix J. Samuels and Partners*
Cost consultant / *Stem and Woodford*
Main contractor / *Mason and Co (Winchester) Ltd*

Building Cost

£0.15m (1982)

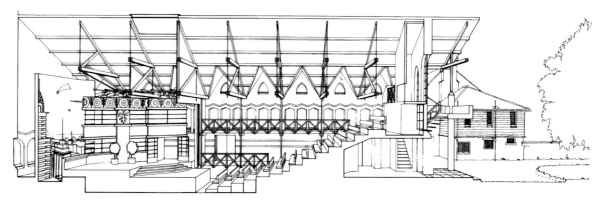

Section by Edward Cullinan Architects

ALMEIDA THEATRE

Almeida Street, Islington, London N1 1TA

Design Intent

The original building, constructed in 1873, was a Literary and Scientific Institute consisting principally of an amphitheatre lecture space and a library at the front of the building. It was substantially altered at the turn of the century when it was converted into a Salvation Army Citadel. Internally, little remains of the original building, but the curved rear wall and its intimate proportions contribute to the basic 'found' quality of the space.

Externally, the facade was restored as far as possible to its original design. The extremely poor condition of the building meant that much of the interior had to be stripped out, including the gallery which was rebuilt to provide a control room, improved sightlines and structural stability. Much care was taken to maintain the intimate relationship between audience and performer, while great sensitivity was employed to enhance the warm, textured quality of the space through the use of lighting, colour and materials, even in the smallest details.

Mark Foley, *Architect*

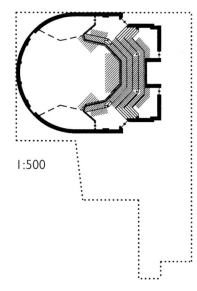

1:500

Users' Verdict

The Almeida Theatre is one of the most charismatic and sought after performance spaces in London. The 300 seats are efficiently arranged in stalls and circle. The performance space is a similar size to the auditorium and the relationship between the two is such that it allows 'epic theatre in an intimate space'. The theatre also has a high reputation amongst artists as a sympathetic space in which to perform.

Jonathan Kent and Iain McDiarmid, *Joint Artistic Directors since 1989*

Fringe Theatre Space

Conversion in phases from 1981 to 1986 of 1837 lecture theatre which is a building listed Grade II by Act of Parliament 'as a building of special architectural or historic interest'
Mostly drama, some opera, mainly theatre's own productions

First performance

4 April 1984

Auditorium and Stage

Open end stage theatre fixed format
Capacity / *300*
Raked lower level in centre and angled side blocks
Volume / *1600m³ (5.3m³ per person)*
Furthest seat / *9m*
Edge of acting area to gallery / *5m*
Acting area / *9m x 9m approx (curved back wall)*
Flying height / *9.45m*

Designers and Builders

Client / *Almeida Theatre Company*
    (Director *Pierre Audi*)
Architect / *Burrell Foley Fischer*
Structural engineer / *Alan Conisbee Associates*
Services engineer / *Max Fordham Associates*
Cost consultant / *Brack Meeking Partners*
Main contractors / *Walter Lawrence (City)*

Building Cost

£0.34m (1983–86)

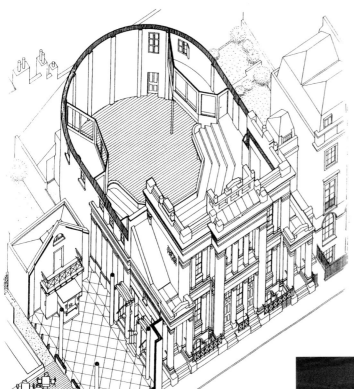

Axonometric by Burrell Foley Fischer

THE MERMAID THEATRE

Puddle Dock, City of London EC4V 3DB

The present Mermaid differs greatly from the original which played such a major role in British theatre for nearly twenty years from 1959 to 1978. The present theatre is the consequence of the incorporation of the original Mermaid, which had been brilliantly converted from a romantic derelict Thames-side warehouse by architect Elidir Davies, within a massive commercial development designed by Seifert and Partners and surrounded by characterless dual carriageways and express slip-roads.

Unfortunately these external alterations, which removed so much (remember those four cast-iron Doric columns which were not original but seemed so?) were accompanied by internal 'improvements' which were equally damaging. In the interests of a small increase in capacity, from 500 to 600, 'ears' were added to each side of the auditorium. Hitherto the parallel and ancient stone walls of the warehouse flanked audience and actor, uniting both in a single theatrically-charged space however elongated. In 1981 the side walls were fanned outwards in banal brick like any dull campus auditorium.

The impression of a proscenium arch is given, which the creator of the original Mermaid had been at pains to avoid, although the stage of the new Mermaid is for the most part no wider than that of the old – 14.7m or 48ft. On the plus side the stage is deeper and the backstage more rationally planned. On the negative side the low arc of the old roof which always lacked lighting bridges has been retained.

Everywhere the magic has evaporated from the truncated foyer once so busy at lunch time till late after the second 'twice-nightly' performance, to the restaurant which no longer juts over the river. The 'improvements' were all paid for by the developer and cost the Mermaid management nothing but its existence. The original not-for-profit company collapsed soon after the reopening and a succession of commercial managements have found it progressively more difficult to fill the Mermaid as memories of its former glory fade. Only a season of RSC productions from the Swan in 1987/8, for which temporary side galleries were installed, have recaptured the power and focus of the old Mermaid.

It is sad that the Mermaid's founder, the mercurial actor-manager Bernard Miles, created Knight in 1969 and Britain's second life peer (after Lord Olivier) in 1978, should have connived at these fatal 'improvements' to the theatre he loved so much. But it must always be remembered first that from 1959 to 1978 Miles wrote a glorious chapter in British theatre history at the Mermaid, second that without his achievement the Barbican would never have been built for the RSC in another part of the City of London and third that the original Mermaid open stage and auditorium was an inspiration to a whole generation of British theatre architects and designers throughout the 60s and 70s.

It is this story that resulted in the Mermaid's exclusion from the thirty selected theatres in this exhibition.

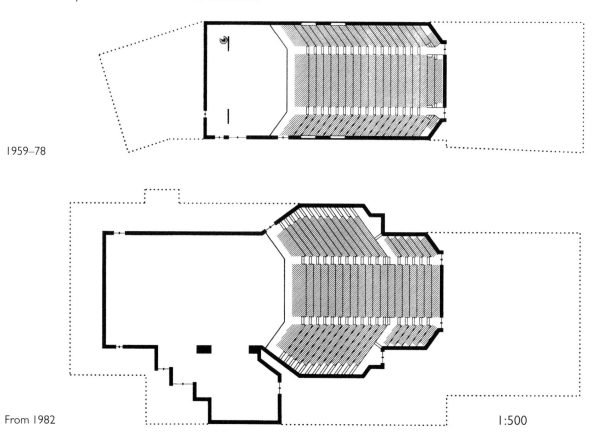

1959–78

From 1982

1:500

First Performance
28 May 1959
First performance after remodelling
7 July 1982

1959

PART III

OVERSEAS THEATRES

The contribution of British architects, engineers and consultants to the creation of new theatres across the world 1973 to 1995.

ARGENTINA
Teatro Colon, Buenos Aires
1991

Theatre Projects Consultants of Britain (American office) were appointed to advise on the installation of a power flying system as part of a long term renovation programme for this famous grand opera house built in 1908.

AUSTRALIA
The Sydney Opera House, New South Wales
1973

The evolution of the Sydney Opera House roof exemplifies successful collaboration between engineer and architect, reconciling the conflict between the free form of the competition entry and the disciplines of structural feasibility, construction, economics and modular cladding. Ove Arup and Partners of Britain were appointed consulting engineers in 1957 and by 1962 thirteen structural schemes had been developed, from Utzon's original concept of concrete shells deriving strength from their shape, through various combinations of steel and concrete shells, arches and space frames, before eventually reaching the precast post-tensioned concrete arch and rib solution which was built. Structural mechanics and geometry were inextricably related; the undefined (but strongly-sculptural) shapes of the competition scheme became combinations of circular arcs, parabolic and elliptical curves and, finally, segments of a spherical surface, giving a simple and consistent geometrical relationship between all components of structure and cladding.

Right: Final scheme for roofs of The Sydney Opera House
Below: The Sydney Opera House

BARBADOS
Central Bank Auditorium
1986

This 400 seat auditorium, facing an open stage in the corner of a square space, was built by the Central Bank as part of a planning arrangement for their new multi-storey headquarters. Theatre consultant Michael Holden and Associates of Britain advised architect Mervyn Arum Associates on the design and technical installation of this busy theatre which is used for indigenous musical dance drama as well as for concerts and plays.

CAYMAN ISLANDS, BRITISH WEST INDIES
F.J. Harquail Theatre
1986

Theatre Projects Consultants of Britain, advised by Ove Arup and Partners, conceived and had built in Britain a steel galleried structure to seat 308 which, together with lighting and sound systems, were shipped to Grand Cayman and erected within an architectural envelope. Architects: Onions, Bouchard and McCulloch.

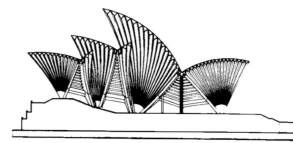

CANADA
School Theatre, the National Ballet School of Canada, Toronto, Ontario
1988

The National Ballet School had occupied inadequate premises until architects A J Diamond and Partners, together with Theatre Projects Consultants of Britain, were commissioned to create a fully equipped ballet theatre. The main stage is full size while the auditorium is equipped with retractable seating which, when withdrawn, reveals a second large dance studio.

CANADA
The Martha Cohen Theatre, Calgary Centre for Performing Arts, Alberta
1985

In 1978 Theatre Projects Consultants of Britain were invited to write the brief and help choose the architects for the down-town Calgary Centre for Performing Arts. This includes the 1800 seat Jack Singer Concert Hall and the 750 seat Max Bell Theatre. The design team was headed by Calgary architects Raines, Finlayson, Barrett and Partners. The Martha Cohen seats 400 in three semicircular wooden clad tiers. These are set off from the brick walls as a structure within space. There is a full fly tower but the seats in the centre are removable, as in the Cottesloe, to make central and environmental staging possible, as for the memorable *Candide* of 1990 directed by Michael Dobbin. (*See also* p. 58)

Below: The Martha Cohen Theatre

CANADA
Max Bell Theatre, Calgary Centre for Performing Arts, Alberta
1985

The 750 seat Max Bell was built for Theatre Calgary alongside the smaller Martha Cohen for Alberta Theatre Project, each Calgary company having its own space. Theatre Projects Consultants of Britain originated the design of the Max Bell which has stepped side balconies not unlike the Eden Court Theatre, Inverness, plus caliper side boxes to vary the opening. Architects: Raines, Finlayson, Barrett and Christie.

CANADA
Jubilee Auditorium, Calgary and Jubilee Auditorium, Edmonton, Alberta
1985

The huge Jubilee auditoriums originally opened in 1955 to celebrate the 75th anniversary of the Province of Alberta. The two auditoriums, in Calgary and Edmonton, are identical. In 1985 Theatre Projects Consultants of Britain advised on the conversion of a function room within each building into an intimate thrust stage theatre.

CANADA
Maclab Theatre, Edmonton Centre for Performing Arts, Alberta
1984

This thrust stage theatre, inspired by those at Stratford, Ontario and Minneapolis, was designed by Theatre Projects Consultants of Britain, working with architects Chandler Kennedy. The capacity is 708 and the theatre is the second space of one of Canada's leading drama companies, the Citadel.

CANADA
Bluma Appel Theatre, St Lawrence Centre, Toronto, Ontario
1983

The 1970 brutalist St Lawrence Centre contained an 830 seat stadium-like open stage theatre with full flytower, modelled on the slightly less disastrous Vivian Beaumont Theatre, New York, of 1965. Oxford educated director Eddie Gilbert called in Theatre Projects Consultants of Britain and architect Ron Thom, responsible for the successful Shaw Theatre at Niagara-on-the-Lake, to replace the old auditorium and foyers with new-build, leaving facade and flytower untouched. The resulting 890 seat theatre occupies only two thirds of the footprint of the original smaller capacity theatre and has a balcony and stepped boxes at the sides. Stage lighting is provided from side slots and stepped central bridges which also form a chandelier.

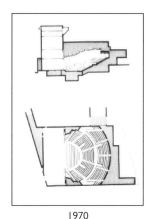
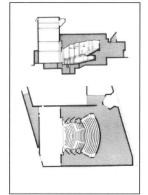

1970   1983

Above: Bluma Appel Theatre, St Lawrence Centre

Espace Jeu de Paume, Albert

The fortunes of the resident drama company, Toronto's senior, improved markedly on the reopening of the theatre in 1983 and a hitherto unsuccessful theatre has gone from strength to strength.

COLOMBIA
William Shakespeare Cultural Centre, Colegio Anglo-Columbiano, Bogota
1994

John Wyckham Associates of Britain wrote the brief for this multi-purpose college/community theatre with retractable seating and fully equipped stage. They then supervised all the planning and equipping of the building with architects Pizano Pradilla Caro y Restrepo (Andres Posada) together with Juan Gozala Botero. The theatre holds 520 for theatre use which includes opera, ballet, concerts and drama and a range of flat floor events. 700 are accommodated for graduation ceremonies. The British Ambassador is ex-officio governor of the college. This project was backed by the British Council in Bogota.

FRANCE
Espace Jeu de Paume, Albert, Pas de Calais
1993

Ian Ritchie Architects of Britain won a limited competition in November 1990 to design a Cultural and Sports Centre in Albert, Northern France having been the only non-French team invited to compete. The winning team also included Ove Arup and Partners engineers and Theatre Projects Consultants. The centre includes a 600 seat theatre, which is also capable of being adapted to receive exhibitions and banquets, a small conference centre, an exhibition gallery and a gymnasium. The linear building is inspired by the evolution of the town from agricultural origins to its present involvement with aeronautical engineering. The centre, which is adjacent to the turreted town hall and the School of Music, faces the town square.

GERMANY
Musik Theater Stuttgart, Baden-Württemberg
1994

This 1800 seat theatre (architect Schwarz und Schwarz) was halfway through construction when British producer Cameron Mackintosh made an arrangement with the theatre owner to bring in his own British architect, Renton Howard Wood Levin Partnership, together with Lighting Design Partnership and his own production staff, to complete the project. Stepped boxes were added to the sides, in essence not unlike those at the Cologne and West Berlin open houses, but with a vigour that is fresh and flamboyant. An otherwise large auditorium is rendered intimate for modern musical theatre.

HONG KONG
Hong Kong Cultural Centre, Tsim Sha Tsui
1989

The Hong Kong Government Architectural and Mechanical Services Department were advised by British consultants: Theatre Projects Consultants for the brief, John Wyckham Associates for detailed design of technical theatre installations and their commissioning, Buro Happold and Partners as structural engineers and J. Roger Preston and Partners as electrical engineers. There is a 1750 seat lyric theatre, a 2100 seat concert hall and a 300/350 seat studio theatre.

HONG KONG
The Academy for Performing Arts, Victoria Island
1985

The Royal Hong Kong Jockey Club was the client for these extensive teaching facilities. The public areas include a 1200 seat lyric theatre, 400 seat drama theatre, studio theatre and recital hall. Architects Michael Heard and Andrzej Blonski of the Peter Moro Partnership had worked on the Theatre Royal Plymouth, and for the lyric theatre centrepiece at the Academy developed further the concept of a moving ceiling and rear wall to reduce the size of audience from 1200 to 700. Other British consultants included

Bickerdike, Allen and Partners as acousticians, and Carr and Angier as theatre consultants in a team led by Hong Kong architect Simon Kwan Associates. A difficult site on reclaimed land over the Mass Transit Railway system did not prevent the project opening on time and on budget.

HONG KONG
Hong Kong Arts Centre, Victoria Island
1977

This centre, the first of the post war Hong Kong theatres, comprises a 450 seat theatre, 200 seat recital room and 100 seat studio all of which were financed by commercial development. Theatre Projects Consultants of Britain conceived the auditoriums with Architect Dr Tao Ho and provided technical consultancy.

ICELAND
City Theatre, Reykjavik
1989

Theatre Projects Consultants of Britain were chosen to advise the country's leading drama company on stage lighting, sound and power flying systems for both the 536 seat main theatre and the studio theatre and on the design of the studio. Due to inflation and the inclement weather in Iceland for a large part of the year, this project took ten years to complete from conception. Architects were Gadm Kv Gudmundson and OlaFur Sigurdsson, FAI.

IRAN
City Theatre, Tehran
1977

The City Theatre in Tehran is a circular building with a wide open stage theatre within. Theatre Projects Consultants in joint venture with the RHWL Partnership of Britain advised on the renovation and re-equipping of the theatre.

IRAN
Gorgon Theatre
1977

Located close to Iran's north eastern border with Russia, Gorgon is a small market town. The theatre design was developed by the RHWL Partnership in joint venture with Theatre Projects Consultants of Britain, who also designed and specified all of the theatre equipment.

ISRAEL
Opera House, Tel Aviv Performing Arts Centre
1994

This new opera house is home to the new Israeli Opera and Ballet Companies. The seating capacity is 1750 and there is an adjustable ceiling which reduces both capacity and

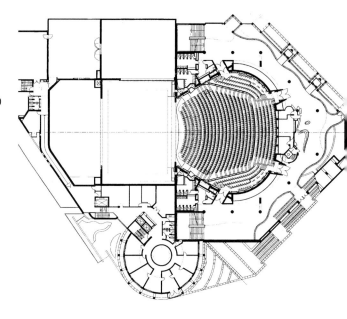

Opera House, Tel Aviv (plan and photo)

Lyric Theatre, Hong Kong, Academy for Performing Arts

acoustic volume when required. An Israeli design team led by Yacov Rechter Architects were advised by John Wyckham Associates of Britain on the technical planning of the building and on the stage engineering, stage lighting and sound and communications systems. Phase Two will follow shortly: this includes a 950 seat drama theatre, a studio theatre and a concert hall for 1100.

KUWAIT
Bayan Palace Conference Centre
1987

This 1800 seat conference centre converts in four hours into a 1200 seat national theatre with proscenium arch and fully equipped stage. Architects were Pan Arab Consulting Engineers of Kuwait, advised by John Wyckham Associates of Britain. The centre was rebuilt after the Gulf War.

LEBANON
New Sidon School Auditorium
1990

At the height of the war in the Lebanon this attractive 500 seat theatre was designed by Nabal Azar, architect of Design Consultants of Beirut, advised by Theatre Projects Consultants of Britain. A highly efficient technical installation was achieved, even though it was not possible for the theatre consultant to visit until two years after the opening.

MALAWI
Kamuzu Institute Theatre, Lilongwe
1978

This 1,000 seat theatre for a tertiary education institute was designed by ministry architects of the Israeli government as part of an aid package. British theatre consultant Michael Holden Associates co-ordinated technical advice and the supply of theatre equipment.

MALAYSIA
Shah Alam Theatre, Selangor
1988

A 1500 seat proscenium theatre with fly tower serving the new town of Shah Alam. Theatre Projects Consultants of Britain provided technical consultancy services. Architects were Jurubena Bertiga International (Team 3).

MEXICO
Teatro San Rafael, Mexico City
1978

This low cost theatre seating 1400 was built as a commercial theatre for the country's leading actor manager. It is a proscenium arch theatre with two balconies, and was

De Maagd, Bergen-op-Zoom

designed by architect Carlos Herrera advised by Theatre Projects Consultants of Britain.

THE NETHERLANDS
De Flint, Amersfoort
1994

De Flint, built in 1970, consists of theatre, concert and multi-purpose hall, creativity centre, restaurant and exhibition spaces linked by internal streets. A fire in 1970, confined to the theatre, allowed architect Onno Greiner Martien van Goor to reconsider this centrepiece. Theatre Projects Consultants of Britain advised on sightlines and seating for Greiner's new larger theatre holding 800 on three levels with two semi-circular galleries.

THE NETHERLANDS
Theatre aan de Parade, 's-Hertogenbosch
1976 and 1994

This typical multi-purpose theatre seats 852 and serves a medium sized Dutch town. It opened in 1976 having been designed by Kraivanger Architects of Amsterdam advised by Michael Holden Associates of Britain. Opera, ballet, drama and light entertainment are presented, usually for one performance only. In 1994 the same team took the opportunity to install a new flying system and refurbish the main auditorium. There is a second studio theatre, the Pleinzaal, which is used generally for cabaret.

THE NETHERLANDS
De Maagd, Bergen-op-Zoom
1991

The imaginative and anglophile Mayor of Bergen-op-Zoom invited the town's Roman Catholics to acquire the medieval Protestant Church, because the Protestants had chosen to move elsewhere. This left the Catholic De Maagd, a neo classical church of 1829 with a long nave, available for conversion into a town theatre. Architects Onno Greiner Martien van Goor, advised by Theatre Projects Consultants of Britain, removed only one pair of the twelve giant Ionic columns for the stage, and slung stepped side boxes and two facing balconies between others. The theatre holds 650, intimate enough for drama as well as having a superb acoustic for music. High open side aisles and an open stair culminating in an informal performance space give the public areas a unique architectural character. (See also p. 38)

THE NETHERLANDS
Twentse Schouwburg, Enschede
1985

A 900 seat cinema-shaped theatre built in 1954 had been rendered worse in the 1960s by the application of glitzy finishes. Architect Onno Greiner of Amsterdam, advised by Theatre Projects Consultants in Britain, stripped out the auditorium leaving only the structure of a single balcony for cost reasons. Stepped boxes were brought down the sides to a reshaped proscenium zone. The ceiling was raised for acoustic reasons (the theatre was also home to the Netherlands' second opera company). Generous stage lighting positions were provided on a two level central crown, which also acts as a huge chandelier, and on stalactites at the side, as at the Olivier Theatre. Front-of-house was animated with a bistro and a bookshop and the adjoining town's original mid-19th century small playhouse restored as a flexible space. The main stage and flytower were unaltered.

THE NETHERLANDS
Stadsschouwburg, Groningen
1980

An 18th century theatre rebuilt in the mid-19th century was renovated in 1980. John Wyckham Associates of Britain wrote the brief and advised architect Jan Kramer of Duintjer BV on the restoration of the auditorium, the replanning of the whole theatre and the design of the technical installation. The theatre holds 750 and presents opera, dance, drama and popular entertainment.

Right: Small theatre, Enschede
Below: Twentse Schouwburg, Enschede

NORWAY
Olavshallen, Trondheim
1989

This 1200 seat rectangular concert hall has a full fly tower and stage facilities enabling major musical, dance and opera to be staged as well as full symphony and choral works. When in concert mode the proscenium is withdrawn and full width ceiling panels in the same style as the auditorium ceiling are lowered from the fly tower. Technical Planning International of Britain advised architect Per Knudsen Arkitektkontor AS on stage and backstage planning, sightlines and the specification of stage engineering, stage lighting, sound and communications installations.

PORTUGAL
Centre Cultural de Belém, Lisbon
1993

The Portuguese government engaged Carr and Angier of Britain to monitor the theatre planning and technical installations for the theatre and the conference hall designed by a team led by Gregotti Associati Int Risco. Theatre installations were simplified and the planning of technical systems improved.

QUATAR
National Theatre, Doha
1980

This 520 seat proscenium arch auditorium was designed by Triad, Cico architects and Theatre Projects Consultants both of Britain. Lavishly finished for His Highness the Ruler, it is used as a touring theatre for both Arab and western companies.

SAUDI ARABIA
Riyadh University Auditorium
1978

As part of the design joint venture HOK+4, British architects Gollins, Melvin, Ward and Theatre Projects Consultants also of Britain devised 1800 seat and 600 seat auditoria within a new University Campus.

Below: Olavshallen, Trondheim

SOUTH AFRICA
**Natal Performing Arts Centre, Durban, Natal
1986**

This project included the remodelling of the Playhouse, a new drama theatre, studios and rehearsal rooms. Theatre Projects Consultants of Britain specified the stage lighting and sound systems. Architects: Small, Petit and Robson.

SOUTH AFRICA
**Wits Theatre, University of Witwatersrand, Transvaal
1984**

This liberal University achieved its long awaited performing arts theatre ten years after the first plan was announced. John Bury, then Director of Design at Britain's National Theatre advised the School of Dramatic Art and architects Irvine-Smith, Joubert, and Lennard of Johannesburg on the overall concept and on the stage and auditorium of the main theatre in particular. 367 seats are arranged in three facets around a five sided thrust stage. This can be removed to provide 92 additional seats. There is a full flytower behind a 10.5m proscenium opening. The whole space is timber clad. There is also a 100 seat studio theatre and full production facilities.

SPAIN
**Catalan National Theatre, Barcelona
1994**

Theatre Projects Consultants of Britain provided schematic design advice to Architect Ricardo Bofill for this lyric theatre also equipped for conferences.

SYRIA
**National Theatre, Damascus
from 1995**

Roderick Ham, the British architect, wrote the brief and acted as technical adviser for an international architectural competition held in 1979. The winners were Renton Howard Wood Levin Partnership with a British design team including Theatre Projects Consultants and building engineers Ove Arup and Partners. Rod Ham continued to advise the Syrian government and local architects Milihouse. The project includes a 1500 seat lyric theatre, 750 seat drama theatre, multi purpose hall, drama studio and adjoining School of Music and Drama. The latter opened in 1990 while the remainder is scheduled to open when completed in 1995 and 1996.

Cerritos Center: concert format

TAIWAN
**National Theatre, Chang Kai Shek Memorial Hall, Taipei
1987**

Architects C C Yang and Associates of Taiwan achieved a remarkable double, a National Theatre for 1526 and, alongside, a similar size Concert Hall. Both are contained within palatial pavilions in unabashed classical Chinese style. Inside are remarkably intimate auditoria with three balconies and stepped side boxes. The stage of the National Theatre is similar to a German opera house with side and rear stage wagons. The entire technical installation was co-ordinated by a joint venture of N.V. Philips Gloeilampen Fabriek and G + H Montage Gmbh who engaged Theatre Projects Consultants of Britain to commission the equipment, train staff and supervise technical aspects of the opening season. To this season the New York City Ballet, the Netherlands Danstheater, the Cleveland Orchestra and the National Dance Troupe of Korea were invited as well as all the major Taiwanese Western and Chinese companies.

TAIWAN
**Kaohsiung Cultural Centre
1981**

Theatre Projects Consultants of Britain were commissioned as project managers and technical consultants for the fit-out of this 1500 seat multi-purpose theatre.

USA
**Ahmanson Theater, Music Center of Los Angeles County, California
1994**

The Ahmanson forms part of the Music Center which also includes the Dorothy Chandler for opera and concerts and the Mark Taper for thrust stage drama. In 1990 Theatre Projects Consultants of Britain conducted a study to transform the Ahmanson from a 60s cinema-like auditorium into a more intimate theatre with a more intense actor audience relationship. In 1994, working with architects Ellerbe Becket, they added side boxes, moving walls to reduce the size of the auditorium for smaller shows and the detailed infrastructure for the most sophisticated lighting and sound systems. The Ahmanson is home to the Center Theater Group which produces large scale drama and also invites in the bigger musicals.

USA
**California Center for the Arts, Escondido
1994**

Escondido's Center includes a 1,524 seat lyric theatre, 408 seat community theatre, museum, art gallery, and reference library and was designed by the late Charles Moore and architects Moore, Ruble and Yudell advised by Theatre Projects Consultants of Britain. The large theatre has three balconies and can be transformed into a concert hall.

USA
**Cerritos Center for Performing Arts, California
1992**

The design for this versatile performance space was developed by Theatre Projects Consultants of Britain from their concept for Derngate, Northampton. The auditorium and stage are transformed by using omni-directional air casters to move three-level seating towers and also blocks of stepped seating which fit five large elevators. The management regularly permutate the 1818 seat concert hall into an 1894 seat arena, 1450 seat lyric theatre, 972 drama theatre or event space with 690m² of flat floor. In only their second year of operation the management achieved the third highest gross box office for theatres seating under 2,000 in the USA. The architect was Barton Myers of Los Angeles and the engineers Ove Arup and Partners of Britain. (See also p. 56)

USA
**Addison Center Theatre, Texas
1992**

Theatre Projects Consultants of Britain (American office) provided the concept design for this 2800m² performance space which offers almost infinite staging possibilities to Addison's innovative theatre company. Architects Gary Cunningham Associates described the building envelope as 'built found space'.

USA
Blumenthal Performing Arts Center, Charlotte, North Carolina
1992

The Center comprises the 2,100 seat lyric Belk Theater and the 440 seat Booth Playhouse. Both were designed by Cesar Pelli and Associates in conjunction with Theatre Projects Consultants of Britain. The lyric theatre features three balconies above the main floor linked to the stage by sixteen stepped boxes to increase the feeling of intimacy. A proscenium arch which opens up to 20m allows an orchestra to play within an acoustical enclosure which stores upstage when not required. The Center is home to the North Carolina Opera Company and the Charlotte Symphony as well as staging seasons of Broadway musicals on tour and other popular entertainment.

USA
The Head Theatre, Center Stage, Baltimore, Maryland
1991

Baltimore's major drama company invited Theatre Projects Consultants of Britain (American office) and architects Ziger, Hoopes and Snead to develop a flexible second performance space within the 'found space' of an old Jesuit Seminary. Towers for audience on two levels can create different configurations or be rolled away.

Above: Belk Theater, Blumenthal Center

Right: The Dunfermline Opera House in Scotland
Below: The Dunfermline Opera House rebuilt in Sarasota

USA
Steppenwolf Theatre, Chicago, Illinois
1991

This is the main stage for the Steppenwolf Theatre Company and is designed to reflect this ensemble's gritty, urban origins. The company and its designer, Kevin Rigdon, worked closely with architect James Morris Kutyla and Theatre Projects Consultants of Britain (American office). The intimacy of the company's smaller capacity previous theatre had to be retained : here none of the 500 audience is more than 11m from the stage. The form is classic American : wide proscenium, raked orchestra stalls, single gallery and triple stepped boxes.

USA
Whittier College, Los Angeles County, California
1990

A 463 seat theatre with flexible flooring system and flytower providing technical theatre training facilities for the college. The Architects were A.C. Martin, with Theatre Projects Consultants of Britain being responsible for the concept of the room and technical design.

Below: The 456 seat main theatre at Cornell University

USA
**Fairfield Center for Creative Arts,
Solano County, California
1990**

This new flexible 400 seat community theatre was designed by California architects ELS, Elbasani and Logan working with Theatre Projects Consultants of Britain. It can be arranged either with a thrust stage or with a proscenium arch stage with or without orchestra pit.

USA
**Asolo Center for Performing Arts,
Sarasota, Florida
1990**

The interior of the Dunfermline Opera House, Scotland, designed by architect J W Swanston and opened in 1920, was dismantled in 1982. Four years later Theatre Projects Consultants of Britain, who had been engaged to advise the well established Asolo Theatre company for their new theatre, suggested the incorporation of the Dunfermline Opera House in the Center, which also includes a second theatre and accommodation for the University of Florida. The Scottish Arts Council, owners of the plasterwork and plans, required supervision of the reinstatement by British experts Professor James Dunbar-Nasmith and Iain Mackintosh. Theatre Projects Consultants of Britain designed the technical installation and advised on seating and sightlines. The proscenium arch was widened and lighting positions achieved without otherwise altering the lovingly recreated interior. Architect for the whole scheme, Stuart Barger of Sarasota, devised a colour scheme which re-presented the Scottish classical plasterwork in the context of a very different climate.

USA
**Ruth King Theatre, Milton Academy,
Boston, Massachusetts,
1990**

Architects Kallmann, McKinnell and Wood of Boston and Theatre Projects Consultants of Britain were engaged simultaneously to create a Performing Arts Centre for one of America's most liberal schools. The theatre at the heart is a square galleried space holding 400 and offering either a square thrust or a fully equipped proscenium arch stage.

USA
**Westminster School Centennial Theatre,
Connecticut
1990**

Architect Graham Gund of Boston joined with Theatre Projects Consultants of Britain to create a triple tiered semicircular auditorium of 400 in a neo-classical style. The

Intermediate Theatre, Portland

Theatre Royal, Bury St Edmunds, together with the Martha Cohen Theatre, Calgary, were its inspiration. The building also includes a workshop, music rehearsal spaces, a dedicated dance studio and a rehearsal room.

USA
**Centre for Performing Arts,
Cornell University, New York State
1989**

James Stirling, Michael Wilford and Associates of Britain and Wank, Adams Slavin Associates of New York were the architects for this Centre which is both a teaching facility and a performance centre for the university. The main theatre is a 456 seat semi-circular proscenium arch theatre with two concentric galleries. The proscenium zone offers either a forestage or orchestra pit. In addition there is a flexible theatre holding between 140 and 175 on adjustable seating platforms, a dance studio which can hold up to 132 on retractable seating, a small black box studio, a cinema for 103 plus classrooms, workshops and other support areas. The whole cluster of theatrical spaces is app-roached via a loggia leading off a road linking town and gown.

USA
**Portland Center for Performing Arts,
Oregon
1987**

The Center consists of three auditoria: the refurbishment of the 1927 Paramount Theatre as the Arlene Schnitzer Concert Hall seating 2,780; the Intermediate Theatre seating 916 with orchestra, stalls and two embracing tiers terminating in stage boxes and the Winningstad Showcase Theatre, a versatile courtyard theatre for up to 370. An architectural joint venture was created for the project by BOOR/A of Portland, the ELS Design Group of Berkeley, California, and Barton Myers of Los Angeles. They worked closely with Theatre Projects Consultants of Britain who originated the auditorium and stage design for the two new and smaller theatres. The Intermediate Theatre itself is the product of a particularly close collaboration between Barton Myers and Theatre Projects Consultants

USA
**State Theatre, Easton,
Pennsylvania
1985**

This 1927 1700-seat Vaudeville theatre and movie palace was renovated as a civic theatre. Theatre Projects Consultants of Britain (American office) worked closely with architect Craig Morrison through the stages of study, master plan and design of stage rigging, stage lighting and sound.

CRUISE SHIP ON THE HIGH SEAS
**S S Oriana, P & O Cruises Ltd
1995**

This is the largest cruise ship in the world afloat in 1995. John Wyckham Associates of Britain advised naval architects Arkitektkontoret Robert Tilbery AB, Viken, Sweden on the incorporation of a 650-seat theatre into a ship already in the third year of design.

CRUISE SHIPS ON THE HIGH SEAS
**Nieuw Amsterdam, Caribbean Cruise Liners
1989**

Architect De Vlaming Fennis Dingemans of Utrecht collaborated with Theatre Projects Consultants of Britain on the theatre and entertainment spaces on this and other Holland America cruise ships.

THE LEARNING CENTRE
HAMMERSMITH AND WEST
LONDON COLLEGE
GLIDDON ROAD
LONDON W14 9BL

Appendix
INDEX OF THEATRE BUILDING COSTS 1958–1985

This takes into account construction costs and, to some extent, both enhanced expectations of audience and performers and increased standards of technical equipment.

The vertical scale indicates the factor by which 1958 costs are multiplied to give comparative costs at the years measured on the horizontal scale. Example: to convert the 1971 costs of the Crucible to those of 1995 take quoted cost of Crucible in 1991, £0.88m, divide by 4.8 and multiply by 8.8 to give comparative cost in 1995. The answer is £1.6m. However a further adjustment would have to made if the quoted cost is as is the case so often, not the completed cost

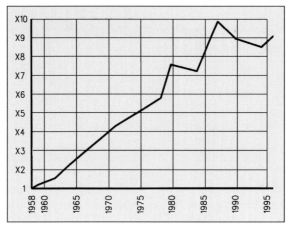

but the contract cost from the beginning of the construction contract. In that case a further adjustment would have to be made for the increases due to inflation and for other variations between the contract date, i.e. the start of construction, and the completion date shortly before the theatre opened.

The index applies to building costs not project costs. To establish project costs take the building costs, add 25–30% to allow for professional fees and other costs and finally add site acquisition costs if any.

It must also be remembered that in many instances the published building costs are kept artificially low for political reasons.

Information kindly supplied by John Clarke of Bucknall Austin, Quantity Surveyor

Photographic Acknowledgements
The Catalogue

The publishers have made every effort to identify and acknowledge copyright holders of original photographic material. If any copyright holder has been overlooked, we apologise and shall be glad to include proper acknowledgment in a future reprint, if the omission is brought to our attention.

p. 119 Clive Barda (*top and bottom*)

p. 121 Richard Einzig (*top and bottom*)

p. 123 Clive Barda (*bottom*)

p. 125 Martin Charles (*top and bottom*)

p. 127 Martin Charles (*left and right*)

p. 129 Richard Davies (*top and bottom*)

p. 131 Allan Hurst (*top left*)
Courtesy of Nottingham Playhouse (*bottom left*)
Allan Hurst (*right*)

p. 133 Clive Barda (*left, centre, right*)

p. 135 Richard Einzig (*top and bottom*)

p. 137 Courtesy of Eden Court Theatre

p. 139 Martin Charles (*top left, right top and bottom*)

p. 141 Courtesy of Pitlochry Festival Theatre (*left and right*)

p. 143 Clive Barda (*top and bottom*)

p. 145 Glasgow Picture Library (*left*)
Courtesy of Arup Associates (*right*)

p. 147 Christopher Hill (*top and bottom*)

p. 149 Courtesy of RHWL Partnership (*top*)
John Walsom, Courtesy of RGWL Partnership (*bottom*)

p. 151 *Architecture and Building News, 4 April 1930 (bottom left)*
John Walsom, Courtesy of RHWL Partnership (*right*)

p. 153 Clive Barda (*top left and bottom*)
Courtesy of Edinburgh Festival Theatre (*top right*)

p. 157 Courtesy of Powell and Moya Partnership (*left and right*)

p. 159 Gerry Murray (*left and right*)

p. 161 Carlton Studios, Courtesy of Levitt Bernstein Associates (*top right*)

p. 163 Steve Stephens (*top*)
Annette Steele (*bottom*)

p. 165 Bruno de Hamel (*top and bottom*)

p. 167 Michael Mayhew (*right*)

p. 169 Martin Charles (*top left, centre, and bottom centre*)

p. 171 Peter Rourke (*all photos*)

p. 173 Courtesy of Howell, Killick, Partridge and Amis (*top*)
Martin Charles (*bottom*)

p. 175 Steve Stephens (*top and bottom*)

p. 177 Clive Barda (*left and right*)

p. 179 Dennis Gilbert (*top*)
Mark Foley (*bottom*)

p. 181 Courtesy of Strand Lighting Archive

p. 184 [Sydney] *Courtesy of Ove Arup Associates*
[Calgary] *Courtesy of Alberta Theatre Project*

p. 185 [St Lawrence Centre] *Robert C Ragsdale*
[Albert] *Courtesy of Ian Ritchie Architects*

p. 186 [Hong Kong] *Courtesy of Simon Kwan Associates*
[Tel Aviv] *Courtesy of John Wyckham Associates*

p. 187 [De Maagd] *S. Voeten*

p. 188 [Enschede, small theatre] *Barend Gerritsen*
[Enschede, large theatre] *Courtesy of Onno Greiner Martien van Goor*
[Trondheim] *Courtesy of Technical Planning International*

p. 189 [Cerritos] *Tim Street-Porter*

p. 191 [Sarasota] *Courtesy of Theatre Projects Consultants*
[Cornell] *Richard Bryant*
[Portland] *Courtesy of Theatre Projects Consultants*